Congregational Polity

Congregational Polity

A Historical Survey of Unitarian and Universalist Practice

Conrad Wright

Skinner House Books
Boston

ISBN 1-55896-361-8

Printed in Canada.

10 9 8 7 6 5 4 3 2 1
00 99 98 97

Cover design: Bruce Jones
Text design: Suzanne Morgan

Contents

Preface

This is a specialized study, originally undertaken by request for a specific purpose. It was Eugene Navias who suggested that I prepare, especially for those just entering the Unitarian Universalist ministry, a historical account of congregational polity, as practiced by the denomination and adapted to changing times and circumstances.

Polity represents but one strand in the history of the denomination and so, while that larger story is repeatedly relevant, much of it receives scant attention or is passed over completely here. A specialized treatment of polity may stray from time to time into matters of administration, but that could be a subject for investigation in its own right. So while the outer boundaries of this study are fuzzy, and its usefulness may extend beyond the special purpose that initiated it, the central focus is polity.

Friends have reassured me from time to time that this project is a useful one, and have prodded me to get on with it. I am particularly indebted to the following who have reviewed parts or all of the text: Wayne Arneson, Philip Giles, Charles Howe, Elizabeth Parish, Eugene Pickett, Peter Raible, William Schulz, Alan Seaburg, Carl Seaburg, Corelyn Senn, Robert N. West, and Conrad Edick Wright.

Conrad Wright

Introduction

Congregational polity is so much taken for granted by Unitarian Universalists that they tend to overlook its importance, particularly its importance as one of the key elements in the consensus that holds the denomination together. When Unitarian Universalists identify the set of values they hold in common, they resort to high-level abstractions like freedom, reason, and tolerance. Yet the meaning of freedom and tolerance is revealed more clearly by the way people behave than by the generalizations they utter. So it is a fact of no small consequence that Unitarian Universalists stand in a tradition of congregational polity that is almost four centuries old; that they are much more conservative with respect to the practice of that polity than they are with respect to doctrine; that they have been congregationalist in polity much longer than they have been liberal in theology; that, indeed, their congregationalism has proved to be more durable and adaptable to changing times than any of the doctrinal formulations—whether of God, or human nature, or human destiny—that dominate accounts of the history of liberal religion.

There are doubtless a number of reasons why Unitarian Universalists pay little attention to polity, either in their historical accounts or in their contemporary discussion. One of them may be that when the Unitarian controversy developed in the early nineteenth century, leading to a split between orthodox and liberal congregationalists, the focal points of debate were the Trinity and the doctrine of human nature. Both Trinitarians and Unitarians were congregationalists, so polity was not central in the matters of dispute between them. Hence the liberals readily understood their self-identity in terms of their divergent doctrinal position, rather than in terms of the shared polity. In recent times, questions of ecclesiastical organization within the denomination have tended to be dismissed as matters of "mere administration"— and so not half as interesting as such topics as religion in an age of science, or programs of social action, or getting in touch with one's feelings.

Yet congregational polity remains deeply embedded in the half-conscious awareness of the denomination, so that appeal to its norms is made repeatedly in times of controversy. Because such appeals are evoked by crisis, rather than being derived from ongoing disciplined understanding and study, some curious distortions of congregationalism have resulted. In 1963, for example, in the course of a discussion in the annual General Assembly of a proposed amendment to the bylaws of the Unitarian Universalist Association, one delegate declared: "Congregational polity permits the Association to set theological, liturgical, educational, and financial conditions upon membership, voting, and fellowshipping."

Our polity is important because it defines the way in which we believe human beings should be related to one another for ecclesiastical purposes, and it may be a guide or model for human relationships of other kinds. There are real differences between democratic, hierarchical, oligarchical, and authoritarian patterns of social organization. Behind these social forms lie understandings of the nature of human beings. When conceptualized and phrased in theological language, this means both a doctrine of human nature, and a doctrine of the Church. So polity is not a matter of casual social arrangements, but goes very directly to the heart of basic issues of theology.

Introduction

These chapters will attempt to sketch the historical development of the doctrine of the Church as revealed in ecclesiastical organization and practice among American Unitarians and Universalists. The purpose is not, as some might suppose, to define the tradition as normative in such a way as to make it restrictive. It is rather to increase self-understanding, so that we can know more clearly some of the things that make us what we are, and can understand more clearly why we do some of the things we do and why our organizational problems take the shape they do. It may even help us to adapt our ways so as to meet the demands of new situations without jeopardizing freedoms we have cherished through the generations.

The historical development with which we are concerned may be divided into six periods. The first of these is the period of the "Standing Order" of the churches of New England down to the period of controversy, which soon led to the final separation of Church and State in the early nineteenth century. In this period, the liberals who became Unitarians were part of the Standing Order; the Universalists were in opposition to it but necessarily shaped by its domination.

The second period, from the early nineteenth century to the Civil War, is the time of the organization in American Protestantism generally of voluntary associations for ecclesiastical and charitable purposes. Historians refer to the proliferation among the evangelical denominations of societies for the promotion of good causes as the "Benevolent Empire." Unitarians adopted the identical pattern of organization of voluntary associations. Universalists did not; the differences between the denominations in this period are especially instructive.

The third period, from the close of the Civil War to the end of the century, was a time of increased denominational awareness in both denominations. The Unitarians organized their National Conference as their main ecclesiastical body, while the American Unitarian Association (AUA) remained the chief administrative body; the Universalists consolidated their structure of state conventions, while independent organizations such as the Universalist Publishing House and the Women's Centenary Association carried on the administration of affairs.

The period from the beginning of the new century to the Great Depression was a time of increasing bureaucratic organization among the Unitarians. The weakness of Universalist structure was apparent in this period, and the denomination lost ground.

In the fifth period, from the 1930s to merger in 1961, the Unitarians found a fresh sense of direction under Frederick May Eliot, elected president of the AUA in 1937, and undertook new ventures—in missionary activity (the "fellowships"), social service (the Service Committee), and religious education—that had implications for polity. The Universalists copied many of these initiatives.

The consolidation of the the American Unitarian Association and the Universalist Church of America in 1961 required significant restructuring of denominational organization. In crucial matters, Unitarian precedents were accepted. The ensuing decades were times of stress in American life generally, and increasing fragmentation in the new denomination reflected the turbulence in the society. A consequence was a failure of institutional memory with respect to congregational practices well understood by earlier generations.

In a historical survey of this kind, there will be a number of persistent themes, and certain questions that must be repeatedly addressed. It is well to identify them at the outset, since they define the scope of the investigation.[1]

1. What is the authority to be appealed to in matters of ecclesiastical organization? Scripture? Tradition? Reason? Practical experience?
2. What constitutes a church? That is to say, what is the

difference between a collection of religiously concerned individuals and a church?

3. How is the boundary of the church established? How is membership in it defined? What are the qualifications for membership? How are the qualifications of would-be members tested, and by whom?

4. What leaders, or officers, are essential to the well-being of the church? And what is their relationship to the body of the members?

5. Granted that ministers have an obvious responsibility to the churches they serve, what responsibility do they have toward their fellow ministers? Is the ministry a calling or a profession? Or both?

6. Is some kind of community of churches essential to their well-being, if not to their being? How are particular churches related to one another? What is the area of responsibility properly to be entrusted to denominational organization, and what kind of authority should be granted it?

7. How are churches related to the larger society in general, and to civil government in particular?

8. What are the central purposes of the church? Why do people bother to organize themselves into such bodies and struggle to keep them going? What functions does the church fulfill that could not just as well be fulfilled by other organizations?

Taken together, the answers to questions such as these will amount to a doctrine of the Church; and a historical perspective may make possible a richer understanding of what a doctrine of the Church means than we have had for a long time.

Congregationalism Prior to the Unitarian Controversy

"A DUE FORME OF GOVERNMENT"

Governor John Winthrop preached a lay sermon aboard the *Arbella* in 1630, in which he declared the purpose of the great migration to New England to be "to seeke out a place of Cohabitation and Consorteshippe vnder a due forme of Government both ciuill and ecclesiasticall."[1] So far as church polity was concerned, the due form of government was to be congregationalism; there is no difficulty in tracing a continuous tradition from Massachusetts Bay in the 1630s to the present-day Unitarian Universalist denomination. We may take as a starting point, therefore, the polity of the New England Puritans, and in particular the normative statement of it set forth in the Cambridge Platform of Church Discipline (1648).[2]

The Platform begins with the assertion that church government is not a matter of simple human improvisation, but rather of God's command as revealed in Scripture: "The partes of Church-Government are all of them exactly described in the word of God . . . & therefore to continue one & the same vnto the apearing of our Lord Jesus Christ."[3] Church polity is based on the New Testament, where there is no mention of popes, or archbishops, or bishops as officers with jurisdiction over other clergy, or presbyteries with authority over particular churches.

Each particular church is a "gathered" church—that is to say, it is made up of a select body of those who may be presumed to be of the elect. Behind this definition is the Calvinistic doctrine of predestination and God's eternal decrees, by which some souls will be saved while the rest are passed over and condemned to eternal misery. The concept of the gathered church contrasted with that of a church in which membership was coextensive with the realm of England, as in Anglicanism and Presbyterianism both. For the New Englanders, "cohabitation" makes not a church, because "*Atheists* or *Infidels* may dwell together with beleivers."[4]

A number of the elect in a particular locality are not yet a church until they establish a continuing relationship with one another. It is the covenant that creates that relationship: "*Saints by Calling,* must have a Visible-Political-Union amongst themselves, or else they are not yet a particular church. . . . This *Form* is the *Visible Covenant,* Agreement, or consent wherby they give up themselves unto the Lord, to the observing of the ordinances of Christ together in the same society, which is usually called the *Church-Covenant.*"[5] The original covenants were ordinarily quite brief statements of a willingness to walk together in Christian fellowship, and were not creedal in character.

But how can one know in this life who is of the elect, since that determination lies in the secret counsel of God, to be made clear only at the Day of Judgment? The Puritans knew that human attempts at such discriminations are at best matters of probability only; but they still thought that most of the time the difference between the regenerate and the unregenerate was clear enough to include most of the former and keep out most of the latter. In determining who were "Saints by Calling," one would of course exclude notorious evil-doers and all who showed no repentance for their sins; one would expect to find in the saints a basic understanding of the principles of the gospel and faith in Jesus Christ as the mediator through whom salvation is wrought. Beyond these basic essentials, one would look for some evidence of an experience of regeneration, a visitation of the spirit of God by which the inward bias of the soul is turned from attachment to worldly things to love of holiness. "A personall & publick *confession*, & declaring of God's manner of working upon the soul, is both lawfull, expedient, & usefull."[6]

The church, then, is a community of the Saints, distinct from the world, united for worship and for "the mutuall edification of one another, in the Fellowship of the Lord Iesus."[7] Fellowship with the Lord Jesus meant above all the ordinance of communion: admission to the Lord's table was the cherished privilege of the church member, and excommunication was the severest form of discipline. The absence of structures for discipline, for the mutual strengthening one of another in holiness and good works, was one of the persistent Puritan criticisms of the Church of England.

Such a covenanted body of the Saints is a complete church, under the Lordship of Jesus Christ, with no need for any hierarchy to mediate his authority to it. Indeed, it is the members who constitute the church; and officers, such as ministers, ruling elders, and deacons, are not essential to its *being*, however much they may be necessary to its *well-being*. No priestly officer is necessary to administer the sacraments as the indispensable channel of God's grace in the redemption of sinners. Still, the Lord Jesus "out of his tender compassion hath appointed, and ordained officers which he would not have done, if they had not been usefull & need full for the church."[8]

Of the several officers described in the Cambridge Platform, only the ministers, the ruling elders, and the deacons need mention. According to the Puritan scheme of logical classification,[9] the officers exercising authority in the church are termed *elders*, of which there are two kinds: the ordained ministers and the lay ruling elders. The ministers in turn are divided into two kinds: the pastors and the teachers. The pastors are "to attend to exhortation: & therein to Administer a word of *Wisdom"*; the teachers "to attend to *Doctrine,* & therein to Administer a word of *Knowledg.*"[10] Either pastor or teacher might administer the two sacraments of baptism and communion. Actually, the distinction between pastor and teacher was hard to maintain in practice and did not outlast the seventeenth century. But it is interesting to note that some of the great leaders of the first generation—John Cotton in Boston and John Eliot in Roxbury—were the teachers and not the pastors of their churches.[11]

The ruling elder, in the Cambridge Platform, is a lay officer. His work is "to joyn with the *Pastor & Teacher* in those acts of spiritual *Rule* which are distinct from the ministry of the word & Sacraments committed to them." Specifically, the ministers and ruling elders give leadership to the church by calling it together in meeting, by preparing business in advance for effective decision, by executing the judgment of the meeting in such matters as admission to membership, or excommunication, or ordination. In short, they are *"Guides & Leaders* to the church, in all matters what-soever, pertaining to church administrations & actions."[12] In actual fact, the lay office of ruling elder did not last, any more than the distinction between pastor and teacher did, and by the eighteenth century, leadership was concentrated in the ordained ministry.

The deacon was the fiscal officer of the church, entrusted with receiving the contributions of the faithful; with spending what was needful for the proper celebration of the Lord's Supper, the support of the ministry, and relief of the poor; and with investing any surplus as profitably as possible, usually in land. The notion of the deacon as a person of exemplary piety, concerned with the spiritual well-being of the communicants, is a later development of the role.[13]

Since the church was a community of the Saints, all of them equal in spiritual standing, the result has all the appearance of a little democracy, and congregationalism has often been eulogized as one of the sources of liberal democratic theory and institutions. This is, at best, only a partial truth. The forms of democracy were surely present; but the rule of the elders in the life of the church was authoritarian rather than democratic, as the Platform itself suggests. Samuel Stone, teacher of the church in Hartford, stated it epigrammatically: "A speaking aristocracy in the face of a silent democracy." Yet if it is anachronistic to represent the Puritans as incipient democrats, it may be said that they adopted institutional forms into which later generations could breathe a democratic spirit.

One further point needs to be made with respect to the minister: he was called and ordained by the covenanted body to which he was to minister. One could no more have a minister without a church than one can have a husband without a wife. On the one hand, this is a reminder that a man did not become the minister of a congregation by appointment of civil authority, or a diocesan bishop, or the patron of a living. But it also meant that there was no such thing as a minister at large. "*Church Officers, are officers to one church, even that particular, over which the Holy Ghost hath made them overseers. Insomuch as Elders are commanded to feed, not all flocks, but that flock which is committed to their faith & trust, & dependeth upon them.*" There was no indelible imprint from ordination; a man dismissed from his ministerial office by his church was no longer a minister unless called in orderly fashion to some new post of duty, when "*wee know nothing to hinder, but Imposition of hands also in his Ordination ought to be used towards him again.*"[14]

Every particular church is the equal of every other such church in authority; none may have dominion over another. Yet all are united to Christ as their common head, and so ought to preserve friendly communion with one another. Chapter Fifteen of the Platform defines six different ways by which the communion of the churches is to be exercised, such as concern for one another's welfare, or recommendation when a church dismisses a member to reside elsewhere, or relief and succor when poor churches stand in need of assistance. Most crucial, however, is the definition of the second way of communion between churches, by way of *consultation* when a question arises on which a church may benefit by disinterested advice from without. In such cases, the Platform allows for the assembly of elders and other messengers from the several churches to give advice. The term "synod" is used in this connection; later that term was restricted to meetings in which the churches considered general problems of concern to all the churches, while a meeting to deal with a problem confronting a particular church—as, for example, the dismissal of a minister—was termed a "council." But the Platform acknowledges no extraparochial structures with permanent authority over the particular churches; and on more than one occasion, a church refused to send messengers to a council or synod on the grounds that a form of hierarchical control might result. The "autonomy" of the local church was carefully protected. Yet it is not a proper understanding of congregationalism to leave it at that. Congregationalism meant, not the autonomy of the particular church, but the communion of autonomous churches—a significantly different thing.[15]

Finally, the Puritans believed in a careful and rigorous separation of church and state. On this matter they have more often than not been misunderstood. It is all too common to find, even in the writings of scholars who should know better, statements such as this: "When the Puritans settled Massachusetts they had no intention of separating church and state."[16] But the Cambridge Platform refers to the "distinct & due administrations" of each, and declares: "As it is unlawfull for church-officers to meddle with the sword of the Magistrate, so it is unlawful for the Magistrate to meddle with the work proper to church-officers."[17]

The problem in understanding the Puritan position on this matter arises from the fact that they drew the line between church and state in a different way than we do, and so they included within the jurisdiction of the state certain matters that we would not. But that there should be a line, and that it should be clearly drawn and carefully adhered to, was a principle on which they agreed. The judgment of one recent historian is that Massachusetts Bay, "so far from presenting an identification of church and state, had made a long step toward that separation which was to become the American way." At any rate, the step was "long enough to differentiate Massachusetts sharply from most of the rest of the world at the time."[18]

DEPARTURES FROM THE CAMBRIDGE PLATFORM

Even before the second generation had come and gone, departures from the norms of the Cambridge Platform were evident. The dual concept of the ministry was simplified by conflation of the roles of pastor and teacher, and the lay ruling elder disappeared altogether. Other changes of even greater consequence were under way, affecting (a) the definition of membership; (b) the mode of intercommunion among the particular churches; and (c) the relationship between the churches and the civil government, particularly with respect to taxation for the support of public worship.

The definition of membership. In simplest terms, a congregational church was a community of the elect, of Saints. But the Cambridge Platform was ambiguous on this basic question. "The matter *of* a visible church are *Saints* by calling," the Platform declares. It then elaborates further the definition of Saints:

> By Saints, wee understand, 1 Such, as haue not only attained the knowledge of the principles of Religion, & are free from gros & open scandals, but also do together with the profession of their faith & Repentance, walk in blamles obedience to the word . . . .
> 2 The children of such, who are also Holy.[19]

The first category, adult believers, seems straightforward enough. But why should their children also be Saints by definition? Does an individual inherit his or her spiritual estate? Are God's eternal decrees limited by lines of genealogical descent? And as a practical matter, how does this definition square with the presence of rebellious children of pious parents who become notorious blasphemers and evil livers? The Anabaptists were more consistent: they refused to baptize children in infancy and waited for evidence of regeneration before considering one to be within the covenant.

The concept of a gathered church implies a rejection of the corrupt world without, and sectarian withdrawal so that purity within may be maintained. Restriction of communion to the faithful, and the baptism of adults, is congruent with that concept. But the Massachusetts Bay Puritans, even though they adopted a sectarian polity, were proposing to dominate and reform society, not withdraw from it. Hence they were pulled in two directions, and the Cambridge Platform reflected the tension. They were compelled in one direction by the example of the New Testament churches and by the logic of their Reformed theology. Yet they also cherished the hope and expectation of creating a Bible commonwealth, which their children would inherit and carry forward after them; therefore, they kept the practice of infant baptism, which is customary in churches that claim a spiritual authority coextensive with the whole society. To buttress their position they referred to God's covenant with Abraham, which extended to his descendants: "And I will establish my covenant between me and thee and thy seed after thee in their generations for an everlasting covenant, to be a God unto thee, and to thy seed after thee."

The original assumption was that children baptized in infancy, and so included in the covenant, would experience regeneration in due course and be admitted as full church members to the Lord's Table. It did not work out that way. Before long there appeared on the scene a body of people for whom the theory could not account, made up of persons baptized in infancy, but now grown to adult estate, who could not testify to an experience of conversion. They were not in rebellion against the ecclesiastical order; they might be hopeful that some day they, too, would be converted; and meanwhile they might well be the most solid and most useful of citizens. But as conscientious and scrupulous persons, they dared not claim to have experienced the visitation of the Holy Spirit that would give them assurance as to their eternal estate. If they were church members by virtue of baptism, why were they not entitled to all its privileges, including admission to communion? If they were not now church members, how and when had their membership been forfeited?

The problem was compounded when these baptized but unconverted church members married and begat children. Were their children proper subjects of baptism when the parents, for aught one could tell, were unregenerate and perhaps lost eternally? But unless the children were kept within the covenant and within church watch and care, how could the church be renewed through the generations? Was it fated to shrink to a small remnant? The way out of this dilemma was the Half-Way Covenant, recommended to the churches by a synod meeting in 1662. It permitted the baptism of the children of unregenerate but baptized members, provided the parents were not scandalous in life and were prepared solemnly and publicly to acknowledge their covenant obligations. The Half-Way Covenant produced controversy, and not all the churches accepted the recommendations of the synod. But where they did, the minister began to keep two distinct lists of church members: those admitted to full communion, and the "half-way" members who had "owned the covenant" for the sake of baptism for their children.[20]

The architects of congregationalism had originally supposed that it would be possible with reasonable accuracy to distinguish between the regenerate and the unregenerate.

The experience of conversion was relied on as the essential clue. The Half-Way Covenant resulted from the failure of conversions to replenish sufficiently the membership of the churches. A falling off in the frequency of conversions jeopardized the church order and brought into question the concept of a Bible commonwealth. But the adoption of the Half-Way Covenant did not end the matter. The problem of conversions persisted and other modifications in polity followed. In Northampton, Solomon Stoddard decided that it no longer made sense to try to distinguish the Saints from the sinners, and he threw the Lord's Table open to all, in the hope that the heightened solemnity of that ceremony would precipitate conversions. In Boston, the founders of the Brattle Street Church in 1699 discarded the requirement of a public profession of faith from those seeking admission to communion and declared that baptism should not be refused "to *any* child offered to us by *any* professed Christian."[21]

Intercommunion among the churches. With respect to the mode of intercommunion among the churches, not only was the polity in process of development, but differences in practice were emerging between Massachusetts and Connecticut.

The Cambridge Platform made no mention of ministerial associations or of ecclesiastical councils, though it did provide for the "second way of communion," by consultation. At an early date, in 1633, the ministers began to meet fortnightly, "where some question of moment was debated."[22] This practice drew immediate criticism as possibly leading in the direction of presbyterianism, with the result that the purely advisory character of such meetings had to be affirmed. An unbroken history of ministerial associations from that date on would be hard to establish, but by the end of the century, such associations had come into being on a regular basis. Some time in the 1690s, the congregational ministers throughout the Province of Massachusetts Bay began to meet annually at election time as a General Convention. The Convention assumed "no *Decisive* Power," according to

Cotton Mather, "yet the Advice which they give to the People of GOD, has proved of great Use unto the Country."[23] By the eighteenth century, the calling of ecclesiastical councils was the regular procedure for the second way of communion. When a church proposed to ordain or install or dismiss a minister, or when an aggrieved person sought to appeal to disinterested outsiders, letters missive would go to the nearby churches, begging their assistance by the presence of the minister and one or more lay messengers. In the course of the century, the manner of calling such councils, their organization, their procedures, and the form of their recommendation, or "Result," became very much standardized, and by the force of custom their authority, though advisory only, was considerable.

One difficulty with ecclesiastical councils was that, as transportation improved, it became possible to reach beyond the neighboring churches to handpick a council whose favorable judgment could be anticipated. In Connecticut, this problem was avoided by the adoption by law in 1708 of a system of regular ministerial associations and consociations of churches on a countywide basis. The associations of ministers were given "power of examining & Recomending the Candidates of the Ministry to the work thereof,"[24] and they were to be consulted by "bereaved churches" when vacancies were to be filled. The consociations were, in effect, standing ecclesiastical councils, whose makeup was fixed and not subject to manipulation in a given dispute. These arrangements, known as the Saybrook Platform, moved Connecticut congregationalism a considerable distance toward presbyterianism. The Massachusetts churches, despite urging by Increase and Cotton Mather, refused to go that way and clung to the Cambridge Platform, with its greater degree of local autonomy.[25]

The churches and the civil authorities. In the third place, Massachusetts congregationalism moved away from the principles of the first settlers with respect to the relationship between the churches and the civil authorities, especially regarding tax support of public worship.

The original assumption had been that public worship would be supported by the voluntary contributions of "all that are taught in the Word." Human nature being what it is, the system of voluntary support did not distribute the burden equitably, so in 1638, the General Court provided that "every inhabitant who shall not voluntarily contribute, p'portionately to his ability, wth other freemen of the same towne . . . shalbee compelled thereto by assessment."[26]

On this basis, taxation for the support of public worship became almost universal in the country towns. (Boston, lacking territorial parishes, never resorted to ecclesiastical assessments.) The intent was to make certain that no one would evade the common responsibility to provide for a common benefit, just as today everyone is liable to taxation for the support of schools or other activities from which society at large derives benefit. This meant that the towns played an important role in ecclesiastical affairs. The church would ordain the minister, of course, but the town meeting would provide the costs of initial settlement and would fix the salary. The town also was responsible for the construction and repair of the meeting house. With the growth of population it sometimes happened that a town was divided for ecclesiastical purposes but not for other civic purposes; in such cases the part set off was called a *precinct*, while the original area of settlement was designated the *First Parish*.[27] This kind of relationship between towns (parishes, precincts) and churches is what is meant by the term "Standing Order" as applied to the ecclesiastical arrangements of Massachusetts, Connecticut, and New Hampshire.[28]

One consequence was an erosion of the concept of the ministry as essentially related to a covenanted body of Christians. The Cambridge Platform acknowledges that there may be churches without ministers, but there cannot be a minister without a flock to whom one ministers. It made no provision for an itinerant minister or a ministry-at-large. But the principle underlying the Standing Order, as it developed in the eighteenth century, was that since the preaching of the Word conduces to civic order, it is a matter of common concern to all the inhabitants of a town. The minister was settled by the town in recognition of the fact that he performed a civic as well as an ecclesiastical function.

But what of a new town in which a church has not yet been gathered? Or a town that neglected or refused to support public worship by settling a minister? In the first case, by an act of the General Court in Massachusetts in 1693, the town itself was authorized "to choose and call an orthodox, learned and pious person to dispense the word of God unto them." In the second case, as when the Quakers of Dartmouth and Tiverton rejected altogether the concept of a hireling ministry, the court of general sessions for the county sent a minister to the recalcitrant towns. Thus the concept of ministry as related to a covenanted body of Christians was undercut by the notion of the minister as also a public teacher of piety, religion, and morality for regenerate and unregenerate Christians alike.[29]

THE GREAT AWAKENING

The revivalism of the Great Awakening, which swept through the colonies in the late 1730s and early 1740s, affected all three of the tendencies just discussed. At last New England experienced the conversions that had been taken to be a qualification for church membership. For some ministers and churches, the Awakening resulted in a repristination of the original notion of a gathered church of the Saints. Jonathan Edwards, for example, threw over the Half-Way Covenant and Solomon Stoddard's practice of opening communion to all, and admitted only the regenerate to the Lord's Table. But others, appalled by the emotionalism of evangelical religion, insisted even more explicitly than before that heightened emotions are no indication of true religion and that a sincere attempt to lead a righteous life is a better test for admission to communion. This was the position of Charles Chauncy, who pointed the way to the liberalism that later became Unitarianism. Thus the churches were clearly moving in divergent directions with respect to the definition of membership.

The Awakening also disrupted the relations among the churches of the Standing Order. Previously each town had had its own meetinghouse, its own covenanted church, and its own minister. But now evangelists like George Whitefield, Gilbert Tennent, and James Davenport itinerated throughout the country, sometimes invited, but more often intruding into the parish of a settled minister without his consent and over his strong objections. The early insistence of the Puritans that a minister is a minister to his own flock and not to the world at large was further eroded.

The tie between a minister and a particular church was also weakened by a growing tendency for ministers to be called from the churches where they had been ordained and installed, presumably for life as had been the practice, to others with larger prospects for salary, service, and distinction. This tendency, along with the development of ministerial associations, meant that ministers increasingly identified with their profession and thought in terms of a professional career, instead of emphasizing the ministry as a call to service wherever the Lord might direct.[30]

The reliance on revivalism in the Great Awakening as a way of renewing church membership had further consequences for polity. Churches now became divided over the propriety of revivalistic methods, and each faction in a church would reach out to find support among the like-minded in other communities. In some places, the revivalists were convinced that the settled minister himself was unconverted. They might then withdraw to form a "Separate" congregational church, only to be confronted with the question whether a schismatic congregational church was entitled to the same kind of exemption from local taxation already accorded Baptists, Quakers, and Anglicans.[31] In many cases, Separate congregational churches eventually became Baptist. Hence one result of the Great Awakening was to weaken the Standing Order, partly because of defections to the Baptists and partly because of internal conflict between evangelicals and liberals. Congregationalism could not help but be affected by the changes that were increasing the religious pluralism of New England and diminishing the proportionate influence of the churches of the Standing Order.

UNIVERSALIST POLITY PRIOR TO 1803

Universalist churches in New England, with but few exceptions,[32] do not trace their lineage to the Standing Order but arose in opposition to it. There, as elsewhere, many new Universalists had previously been Baptists. This means that while both Unitarian and Universalist churches were congregational from the beginning, there were significant differences in practice between the two groups. On the Unitarian side, while congregational polity was not rigidified or impervious to change, there were nevertheless accustomed ways of doing things and familiar procedures to follow. Universalists, building churches anew, could not rely on established models and certainly had no fondness for the congregationalism of the Standing Order. The influence of Baptist congregationalism appears especially in the formation of associations. But the early Universalists formed local groups in a rather casual way, with much improvisation and untidiness, and with a good deal of the primitivism that sectarian groups are likely to manifest in their earliest phase.[33]

Churches and societies. The experience of Gloucester church under John Murray may not be wholly typical, but it is suggestive of some of the informal ways of doing things the Universalists adopted in the beginning.[34] Murray preached in Gloucester in 1774 from the pulpit of the First Parish during the final illness of the minister. His views on universal salvation were not generally well received by the parish. A small number of members, however, were attracted to them and opposed the settlement of the next minister, who was firmly orthodox in doctrine. The minority drifted away and began to meet with Murray in a private house. Since they were members of the Gloucester church and bound by covenant to share in its discipline, the church sent to inquire why they were neglecting the ordinances, and to request them to state their grievances, if any, so that satisfaction might be given. There being no formal response, the church suspended the erring members in September 1778.

In January 1779, the Universalists prepared what amounted to a covenant, which they called the "Articles of Association" of the Independent Church in Gloucester.[35] In it they resolved "to walk together in christian fellowship" and agreed to receive Murray as "our Minister, that is our Servant, sent to labour among us in the work of the gospel." The result was doubtless a congregational church of a primitive sort: it had a covenant to bind its members together, and it had designated one of its number to be its minister. From the point of view of the First Church, to be sure, the proceedings were irregular; but beyond excommunicating the persons involved, there was nothing it could do.

The question of the relationship of the Universalists to the parish was a different matter.[36] The Massachusetts Constitution of 1780, continuing earlier practice, required that "towns, parishes, precincts, and other bodies politic, or religious societies" should provide at their own expense for public worship, but that the assessment on any taxpayer might go to the support of the public teacher of his own sect or denomination. The Universalists in Gloucester took this to mean that they were exempt from parish taxes. But the parish assessors responded that they had no basis on which to adjudge an informal gathering of persons interested in universal salvation to be a religious society entitled to exemption. There had been no notice of withdrawal from the parish; there had been no incorporation of a society to receive money and pay the salary of a minister; there had been no public ceremony of ordination or installation, by which Murray's relationship had been formalized; and, indeed, Murray was receiving no salary. The assessors' position was that the unpaid leader of a small voluntary religious group meeting in a private house hardly qualified as a "public" teacher of piety, religion, and morality. Besides, given the prevailing ethical theory, which took it for granted that the threat of punishment in the next world is the chief incentive for righteous behavior in this, they argued that an advocate of universal salvation could hardly be described as a teacher of morality.

In Gloucester, in short, a primitive congregationalism of a sectarian kind confronted a structured congregationalism that articulated fully with the larger society. The final outcome was that while the dominant ecclesiastical practices had to be modified to accommodate increasing pluralism, the sectarian group had to accept the requirements of the larger society. The question whether a believer in universal salvation could be a teacher of morality was eventually settled in Murray's favor when the courts declined to become involved in the business of refining philosophical and theological distinctions. The question whether a religious society had to be incorporated to secure tax exemption was one on which both courts and legislature wavered; but to avoid further legal problems, the Gloucester Universalists secured a charter from the legislature anyway. And while they had no apology for the way they had designated Murray as their minister, which they regarded as ordination enough, they reordained him in a ceremony to which ample publicity was given, so that henceforth there could be no misunderstanding on that score.

Thus the Universalists in Gloucester were forced, willy nilly, to adhere to more formal congregational practices than came naturally to them. By 1806, the process of formalization had gone so far that the communicants within the society adopted a covenant and articles of faith, and they elected "wardens," or deacons. Thus they duplicated the dual organization of the Standing Order. This practice became sufficiently widespread in the denomination that in 1840, in the reporting of statistics, churches were listed as distinct from societies. But there was no unanimity among Universalists as to whether the trend should be encouraged or condemned.

As compared with the Liberal Christians, or Unitarians, within the Standing Order, the Universalists developed a less formal mode of ministerial leadership. Many Universalists had been accustomed to Baptist farmer-preachers, and so were not inclined to make as much of the distinction between minister and laity. Besides, the Universalists had more groups—most of them short-lived, to be sure—that had sprung up without much ministerial guidance. But for the Unitarians, a church simply of the faithful, without a minister, or supply preaching at least, was not enough. When the liberals and the orthodox in the Standing Order came to the parting of the ways, the Unitarians ended up with their full share of struggling churches without settled ministers, but the notion of anything comparable to the modern lay-led "fellowship" was wholly foreign to them. If supply preaching could be had, they arranged for it; otherwise they closed the meetinghouse and stayed home or went elsewhere on Sunday morning, even if they found themselves squirming uncomfortably during an evangelical minister's orthodox sermon.

Associations and conventions. When the Universalists gathered at Oxford, Massachusetts, in 1785, one of their purposes was to unite "in our common defence." As a model for organization, they had close at hand the Baptist development of associations of churches. The Baptist Philadelphia Association dated from 1707, the Warren Association (Rhode Island and Massachusetts) from 1767. Under the leadership of Isaac Backus, the Warren Association was the chief instrument for mobilizing Baptist opposition to the Standing Order. As with the Baptists, and in contrast with the strictly ministerial associations of the Standing Order, the Oxford meeting included laity as well as clergy.

Actually, the litigation in which the Gloucester Universalists were then involved was more important in securing minority rights for the Universalists than anything the Oxford assembly accomplished. Indeed the history of the Oxford Association in the following years is so obscure that there is no assurance that it lasted more than a year or two. The association approved a "Charter of Compact," or plan for the organization of local societies, but it seems to have done nothing for its own permanent organization.[37]

Other similar meetings of Universalists were held in the course of the next two decades. At first both the terms "association" and "convention" were used without careful discrimination; but in time, "convention" came to be used for the more permanent organizations of larger territorial scope. The most important of these were the Philadelphia Convention, dating from 1790, and a "General Convention" of New York and New England Universalists meeting in 1793. Since the Philadelphia body lasted only about twenty years, it was the New England organization that eventually developed into the Universalist General Convention.

The Philadelphia Convention proposed an inclusive organization of all Universalists on the continent and adopted a Plan of Government both for local societies and for the "General Church." The communion of the churches was to be sustained by an annual convention in which they would be represented by "deputies or messengers." The convention would receive reports on the condition of each church and its prospects, and it would send ministers out to spread the gospel and establish new churches. But all acts of the convention "which relate to the interests of particular churches, shall be issued only by way of advice or recommendation."[38]

The Philadelphia plan was endorsed by the New England group as well, but in neither case was it translated into bylaws or other specifics. That had to wait until 1803, when the New Englanders, meeting at Winchester, New Hampshire, adopted provisions for annual meetings, the regular representation of local societies, the standing of ministers in the convention, convention officers, the order of business, sanctions that might be imposed on societies, and amendments of the plan of government itself.

Thus in their search for order the Universalists eventually adopted a more connectional style of church government than the Unitarians. This is not to say that they were then better organized, or more structured in their polity, for they were not. But they had a general organization in which the churches were represented—by laity as well as by ministers—at a time when the Liberal Christians still related churches to each other more through the lateral connections of ecclesiastical councils than in any other way. Furthermore, the Universalists gave their Convention powers of fellowshiping and disciplining ministers, and even ordaining them, that have something of a presbyterian flavor to them.

CHURCHES OF THE STANDING ORDER IN 1805

By the end of the eighteenth century, the practice of congregational polity in the churches of the Standing Order that were liberal in sentiment and moving towards Unitarianism may be summarized as follows:

Membership. Some of these churches still adhered to the Half-Way Covenant; others encouraged all who have faith in Christ and sincerely strive to lead righteous lives to seek admission to the Lord's Table. The Half-Way Covenant was obsolescent, however, and soon would disappear entirely. In any event, a public testimony of religious experience was not required, nor was a creedal test imposed, as was increasingly common in the more orthodox churches of the Standing Order.

The ministry. The minister was the only ordained officer of the church. It was still the case that he ordinarily served in the same church for his whole professional career, but moves from one parish to another were not so uncommon as to occasion comment. Ministers served for life, and there was no provision for retirement on pension; but a minister no longer able to perform his duties would request a younger colleague and often would yield to him all or part of his salary. A colleague was not an "assistant minister." He was called by the church and settled by the parish in his own right and not by sufferance of the senior colleague. Sometimes the two established a harmonious relationship; sometimes the gap between generations was too great. Doubtless in many cases a parish sought deliberately to move in a new direction when it settled a younger colleague of a conservative older minister.

The liberals still conceived of the ministry as limited to a particular town or parish. They had earlier opposed the excesses of the Great Awakening, and had seen nothing but disorder coming from itinerant revivalists like George Whitefield, who regarded the whole world as his parish. At the same time, their definition of the religious community the minister was to serve emphasized the whole town or parish, not just the covenanted community of the church within it. They had discarded the Calvinistic doctrine of election, and for the liberals the distinction between regenerate Christians within the church and unregenerate Christians outside it was increasingly obscure.

Yet the liberals acknowledged one extraparochial role for the minister. The professor of divinity and the president of Harvard continued to be accepted as ordained ministers, even though by strict definition they were so no longer, since they did not administer the sacraments within a covenanted community, and the discipline in which they participated was the paternal discipline of a college, not the ecclesiastical discipline of erring church members.

Lay officers. Of the church, the only lay officer remaining of those mentioned in the Cambridge Platform was the deacon. The deacons still were responsible for setting forth the

Lord's Table, but the support of the ministry was now wholly a concern of the parish or society, and what the deacons might do for relief of the poor was minimal, as the chief responsibility shifted elsewhere in the community. By a law of 1754, deacons in Massachusetts were a body corporate to hold title to church funds and other property, such as the communion silver, and so they were central participants in disputes of the ownership of church property as churches split in the Unitarian controversy.[39] But the important lay officers were not officers of the church, but of the parish or society. Members of the Parish Committee, or Standing Committee, and the Treasurer and Collector of the Parish had important duties with respect to financial matters, and they were likely to be substantial persons in the community.[40]

Church and parish. In many towns by the end of the eighteenth century the gathered church of the like-minded was no longer representative of the whole community. The social structure was too complex and the subgroups more differentiated. The result was that the minister of a church of the Standing Order found that he had two constituencies, and two roles to play. On the one hand, he was the pastor of a particular body of Christian believers, instructing it in religious truths according to its doctrinal preferences, administering the sacraments, and participating in the discipline of erring members. But as the settled minister of the town or parish, his public function was to clarify and transmit, not the doctrinal peculiarities of a particular sect, but the moral precepts that made civilized living possible for the community at large. This function found recognition in the Constitution of the Commonwealth of Massachusetts (1780), where the clergy are referred to, not as ministers or pastors, but as "public Protestant teachers of piety, religion, and morality." It was the importance of this public function to the temporal well-being of society that was the standard justification for the tax support of public worship. In present-day terms, the inhabitants of a town or parish were taxed, not for the support of the sectarian worship of the churches, but for the civil religion of the whole community.[41] Eventually it proved impossible for ministers to combine these two distinct roles. It was altogether too easy for them to suppose that their sectarian doctrine, whether orthodox or liberal, was the same thing as the value system on which civilization depended. Minority groups, such as the Baptists and the Universalists, knew better; but the illusion was broken only when the unity of the Standing Order churches itself dissolved. As of 1804, however, at the outbreak of the Unitarian controversy, the standard defense of "public teachers" of morality and tax support of public worship was advanced by liberals and orthodox alike.

Associations, conventions, and councils. By the end of the eighteenth century, the fear that meetings of ministers would be a kind of crypto-presbyterianism had been dispelled, and ministerial associations were taken for granted. These were relatively informal organizations, made up of ministers from adjacent communities, the territorial scope usually being smaller than a county. The meetings were as much for fraternal social intercourse as anything; but from time to time they would take a stand on an issue of general concern, such as the evils of itinerancy or the threat of infidelity. There were also instances of associations publishing catechisms. And it became common for associations to give licenses to preach to young students for the ministry who were seeking their first settlement.

In Connecticut, a General Association of all the congregational clergy was formed in 1709, but in Massachusetts, the only statewide body continued to be the century-old Massachusetts Convention of Ministers, which gathered once a year to hear a sermon and take up a collection, but which exercised no authority over its members. Jedidiah Morse, a leader of the orthodox wing of the churches, was eager to organize a General Association in Massachusetts, on a firmly orthodox basis, but all the liberals and a great many of the orthodox would have none of it, and his proposal came to naught. When the liberals were forced into separate denominational existence, the Massachusetts Convention, almost structureless, was the only such organization with which they were familiar.

Recourse was still had to ecclesiastical councils to advise on the settlement or dismissal of ministers, or to settle disputes. When both parties to a controversy agreed to refer the matter to a council, it was termed a *mutual* council. When one party refused but the other sought outside advice anyway, it was an *ex parte* council. The determination of a mutual council carried especial weight, and when property rights were involved—as might be the case in the dismissal of a settled minister—the civil courts ordinarily accepted the judgment of the council. In certain cases, where much was at stake, each party secured highly skilled legal counsel. In Dorchester in 1811, for example, counsel for the parish included the Honorable Samuel Dexter, perhaps the most widely respected advocate among Boston lawyers, while the church was represented by Daniel Davis, solicitor general of the Commonwealth. This particular council was no trivial affair: its deliberations began on a Tuesday, continued until Saturday, resumed on Monday, and finally terminated on Thursday with the issuance of the decision, or "Result."[42]

In short, the Liberal Christians, soon to be pushed into separate denominational existence, inherited a very decentralized version of congregational polity. There was no ongoing central authority to serve as a vehicle for common action, let alone to maintain any common discipline. The Liberal Christians were united, not by ecclesiastical structures, but by patterns of social interaction, family relationships, a common culture, the influence of Harvard College, and the latent power of the Commonwealth over the territorial parishes. Perhaps under these circumstances no more formal extraparochial structures seemed necessary. Too often, however, Unitarians took it for granted that no such structures would ever be needed, even when times changed and the old linkages became frayed. That was what Henry W. Bellows had to contend with in 1865 at the time of the New York convention. "Is not the notion of *the Church* as distinct from the Churches, pretty much lost out of the New England consciousness?" he complained, "especially out of the Unitarian consciousness?"[43]

Denominationalism:
Associations and Conventions, 1805-1865

A series of developments in the early decades of the nineteenth century had important consequences for congregational polity. They include the renewed vigor of evangelical orthodoxy, as manifested in the revivalism of the Second Great Awakening; the beginnings of industrial society, and specifically the appearance of the New England mill village; population increase in urban centers such as Boston; foreign immigration, especially in New England with the arrival of thousands of Irish Catholics; and the expansion of population into the trans-Allegheny west. These developments contributed to greater diversity of population, increased complexity of social structure, and growing religious pluralism. Confronted by social changes of such magnitude, institutions appropriate for an earlier day had to be reshaped if they were to continue to be functional.

Social change may well come about gradually over a period of time, only to encounter a situation of crisis when inner tensions become too great for familiar institutions to accommodate. The Great Awakening of 1740–43 was one such period, which introduced to congregational polity such novelties as itinerant preaching, "Separate" congregational churches not part of the Standing Order, and creedal language in church covenants. The Unitarian controversy of 1805–35 was another period of crisis for the congregational churches of New England. One immediate consequence was the fragmentation and final demise of the Standing Order.

THE DISSOLUTION OF THE STANDING ORDER

The Standing Order in New England was predicated on an essentially homogeneous population sharing a common theological heritage. So long as almost all the inhabitants of a town possessed a common religious outlook, even though not all were visible Saints, assessments on all for the support of public worship made sense. But what was acceptable in a relatively homogeneous society would not work in a pluralistic one. Already by the end of the seventeenth century, small groups of Baptists, Quakers, and Anglicans were permanently established in Massachusetts. After considerable agitation and some defiance of the law, they were able in the late 1720s to secure exemption from taxation for the support of the public worship of the town or parish, provided they attended their own worship and (excepting Quakers, of course) supported a minister of their own persuasion. After the Great Awakening, numerical growth of the Baptist churches greatly enlarged the dissenting interest; by the end of the century, the Methodists and the Universalists were growing in numbers also.

The growth of dissent diminished the Standing Order; but it was internal conflict that finally brought about its abandonment. Ever since the Great Awakening, there had been a tendency for the Puritan tradition to divide into two streams, one evangelical and Calvinistic, the other liberal or Arminian. Throughout the eighteenth century, the two remained parts of one unbroken religious community. In the 1790s, when loud outcry was heard about Tom Paine's *Age of Reason* and the threat of the spread of deism, evangelicals and liberals stood together in opposition to the rising tide of infidelity. The ministers as "public Protestant teachers of piety, religion, and morality" felt a common responsibility for shaping and advancing the values regarded as essential to the well-being of society at large. But when the threat of infidelity abated, the two wings of the Standing Order moved quickly to the time of crisis.[1]

In many of these parishes, liberals and orthodox were found in the same congregation. How was a minister to avoid a divisive situation? He would offend half his congregation if he preached evangelical doctrine pungently and persistently, or offend the other half if he programmatically refused to discuss the peculiar doctrines of Calvinistic theology. The liberals chose to omit preaching on disputed theological issues and to stress truths held in common by both parties. This was to emphasize the role of the minister as a "public teacher" of morality, rather than his role as the pastor of a church gathered on the basis of a particular and now disputed understanding of Christian doctrine. The orthodox ministers would have none of this. The omission of the "peculiar doctrines of the Gospel," they insisted, was as fatal to true religion as the preaching of Arminianism. A line would have to be drawn.

In the decentralized congregationalism of eighteenth-century Massachusetts, what tied together the churches of the Standing Order was not some formal structure of district organizations or other delegate bodies representing the churches. It was rather an intricate network of interpersonal relationships, especially among the clergy, of which the practice of pulpit exchanges was a most important expression. It was the gradual destruction of that network by the refusal of orthodox ministers to exchange with any fellow ministers whose doctrines were not in accord with their own, rather than any act of the churches as a whole, that excluded the liberals and forced them to be a community by themselves.

Soon familiar congregational practices were distorted or abandoned. Ecclesiastical councils were no longer able to give disinterested advice to troubled churches, but repeatedly divided according to party—if, indeed, they had not been deliberately stacked in advance.[2] Litigation in a dispute over church property between liberal and orthodox factions in Dedham in 1818 resulted in a decision that advanced a seriously distorted interpretation of basic principles and historic practices of New England congregationalism. Bad law, bad history, and bad congregationalism, it embittered relationships between liberals and orthodox.[3]

It had once been possible for the same person to be both the public teacher of a town or parish and the minister of the gathered church within it. In deeply divided communities, that combination of roles could no longer be maintained.[4] Voluntary support of public worship was the inescapable outcome. Tax support was abolished in Connecticut in 1818 and in New Hampshire the following year. In Massachusetts, a constitutional convention considered the matter in 1820 but did no more than recommend a clarification of familiar provisions; and even that modest revision was rejected by the voters. In the decade that followed, there were a number of applications to the General Court for the incorporation of poll parishes, made up of those who wished to withdraw from the local territorial parish and support their own worship; such applications were symptomatic of the disintegration of the old order. By 1833, the Standing Order was clearly no longer functional, so only a few voices protested when an amendment to the Massachusetts Constitution ending it was submitted to the voters. The amendment prevailed by a margin of about ten to one.[5]

CHURCH AND PARISH

The abandonment of the Standing Order did not mean the dissolution of the parishes. In effect, they too became poll parishes, membership in which was wholly voluntary. Those discontented with the preaching of the local minister and reluctant to contribute to his support had only to "sign off" with the parish clerk. They were free to join a religious body more to their liking or to join the ranks of the religiously

indifferent. The congregations that remained became identified either as liberal or orthodox, and the parish shrank corre-
spondingly. The parishes were then no different, legally or
functionally, from the "religious societies" in Boston, where
there never had been territorial parishes, or from religious
societies newly organized. In each case there was a body
corporate under Massachusetts law, existing to hold title to
the meetinghouse and to provide financial support for the
ministry, but now serving a particular congregation rather
than the whole community.

How to raise money to meet the expenses of parishes or
religious societies was a problem for which several solutions
were devised. Parishes that had been accustomed to assess
the polls and estates of their inhabitants continued, at least
for a time, to assess their members on the same basis. Often
when a new meetinghouse was built, the cost was met by
auctioning the pews, which were then held as real property
by the individual owners, and assessments were made on the
basis of a valuation of the pews. The pew owners, or proprietors, collectively held title to the property. The disadvan-
tage of this arrangement was that title to pews might descend
to persons with no active interest in the life of the congregation, who nevertheless retained voting rights as proprietors.
To meet this objection, in a number of parishes the owners
deeded their pews to the parish, so that sittings in the meetinghouse might be rented to active participants. In some
cases, there were modest endowments held either by the
deacons of the church or by separate trustees of a ministerial
fund for the support of the ministry. In any event, there was
nothing like an every-member canvass, and voluntary dona-
tions were commonly for charitable purposes rather than for
ministerial support.

Just as the parish or religious society in New England
continued as the ecclesiastical structure charged with temporal or prudential affairs, so too the church continued as a
covenanted body of those who participated in the Lord's

Supper. Even the Universalists, who had no reason to accept the patterns of the old Standing Order, sometimes made a distinction between the members of the society and a covenanted body of believers within it, though there was considerable criticism in the denomination of this tendency.[6] For evangelicals, the distinction between church members and the rest of the congregation was an important one; for liberals, it became increasingly problematic. It could not be defended on the basis of a required conversion experience, so it came to be essentially a special commitment to an explicitly Christian type of piety.

While the claim of Christian commitment was strong, even in Transcendental times, Christian commitment is a matter of degree, and the boundaries of church membership became increasingly obscure. Cyrus A. Bartol and Sylvester Judd both argued against any distinction between church and congregation, and urged that all members of the whole church community should be encouraged to participate in the communion service.[7] As a way of restoring the service to a central place in the life of congregations, their arguments had questionable success. Where churches continued as distinct bodies, they did little more than celebrate communion every other month.[8] The locus of significant decision-making moved inexorably to the proprietors of pews or other body corporate recognized as the society.

Outside of New England, where Unitarian and Universalist churches started as small sectarian movements, there was no tradition of a church-parish symbiosis, and ordinarily none resulted. Even where a "church" existed, in the sense of a body of communicants united by a covenant, it exercised no significant authority distinct from the society.[9]

UNITARIAN ASSOCIATIONS AND CONVENTIONS

The Unitarians became a community by themselves in the course of one generation, from 1805 to 1835. Their churches and parishes, however, continued to be separate, particular congregations, with no formal or structural relationship uniting them. There was no representative or delegate body to give coherence or to shape common action. An aversion to any such body had been part of the congregational tradition in Massachusetts from the beginning. This parochialism was reinforced by the assumption of many of the liberals that their cause was triumphing by the silent, gradual liberalization of orthodoxy, and that separate organization would be counter-productive.

Not all the liberals shared this view. A group of younger ministers—notably Ezra Stiles Gannett, Henry Ware, Jr., and James Walker—urged that organized support of missionary activity was needed if liberal Christianity was to meet the challenge of reinvigorated evangelical orthodoxy. The result was the formation in 1825 of the American Unitarian Association (AUA), not as a delegate body of the churches, but as an association of individuals. Its purpose was to spread liberal religion by the publication of tracts, and by the sponsorship of missionaries, or "agents," to encourage the formation of churches in the remoter parts of New England and the trans-Allegheny west.[10]

At this very time, the evangelicals were organizing to spread their message, using the device of such voluntary associations as the American Board of Commissioners for Foreign Missions (1810), the American Education Society (1816), and the American Home Mission Society (1826). These new bureaucratic organizations differed from the familiar ecclesiastical structures in their purposes, their membership, their form of organization, and their method of operation. Extraparochial ecclesiastical structures—whether congregational councils, or presbyterian synods, or episcopal dioceses—existed for the orderly government of the church and the discipline of clergy and laity, but not for the publication of tracts or the financial support of missionaries. The new voluntary associations were *bureaucratic* and not *ecclesiastical* organizations, and their appearance greatly altered the polity of all denominations.

The evangelical voluntary associations were modeled on the British and Foreign Bible Society (1804), whose very successful plan of operation was spelled out in detail in a book entitled *An Analysis of the System of the Bible Society* (1821). Membership in one of these societies was open to individual subscribers. The members elected a Board of Managers, who in turn chose the officers: a president, who would be a prominent layman to give visibility to the society; perhaps a dozen vice presidents, likewise persons of distinction, chosen from various parts of the country to give a national coloration to the enterprise; a secretary; and a treasurer. The treasurer was almost always a layman, but the secretary was usually a clergyman, who ran the show, together with a small group drawn from the Board of Managers. Auxiliary societies were formed by individual members within the churches, but they were not structurally a part of the local church or society. Their role was to collect money and forward it to national headquarters in New York or Boston; in return they were entitled to the services of the parent organization, as when the American Tract Society supplied tracts for local sale, or the American Education Society allowed local auxiliaries to nominate hopeful youths preparing for the ministry to receive its bounty.[11]

In somewhat simplified form, the same plan of organization was adopted by the AUA. Begun as a voluntary association, it was not legally incorporated until 1847. The first president was the aged and widely respected Dr. Aaron Bancroft of Worcester. The vice presidents included such well-known men as Joseph Story, associate justice of the Supreme Court, and Stephen Longfellow, member of Congress, 1823–25. Ezra Stiles Gannett, the youthful colleague of William Ellery Channing at the Federal Street Church, served as secretary from 1825 to 1831. One of his special concerns was to develop local auxiliaries, and at one time there were more than one hundred of them.[12] The members of the AUA met in Boston each year in May to elect officers and hear reports. Since other philanthropic and educational societies were accustomed to meet at the same time, the occasion was commonly referred to as the May Meetings.

The main activities of the AUA in the period before the Civil War were the publication of tracts and financial support of new and struggling churches. It did not presume to exercise ecclesiastical functions, such as control over the ordination or credentialing of ministers. Ordination remained the prerogative of the local congregation, advised by an *ad hoc* ecclesiastical council; students completing theological studies and seeking settlement often sought the approval of a local ministerial association.

Yet a certain influence of an ecclesiastical kind, even if not recognized authority, inevitably accrued to the secretary of the Association. He was in a position to know what churches were destitute of preaching and what men were seeking settlement, and he sometimes served as intermediary in the process. (Certain of the leading parish ministers played the same role, as when Henry W. Bellows handpicked the successor to Thomas Starr King in San Francisco in 1864.)

Sometimes the secretary of the Association was in a position to help solve local problems, as when a minister came into conflict with his parish; that may be one reason why ecclesiastical councils for the mediation of controversies fell into disuse.[13] In 1853, when the Board of Directors of the AUA approved a conservative theological statement defining the basis for its operations, they acknowledged that they could speak only for the Association and not for the churches at large, yet their declaration was inevitably taken as a rejection by the denomination of its more radical or Transcendentalist wing. Thus the AUA, though by initial definition a bureaucratic agency created by individuals rather than an ecclesiastical structure responsible to the churches, gradually acquired certain limited ecclesiastical functions.[14]

Here, then, were institutions of two different kinds. On the one hand there were ecclesiastical institutions—churches, ministerial associations, councils—exercising ecclesiastical authority in a very decentralized way. On the other hand, there was the AUA, a bureaucracy in the making, dependent for effectiveness on a concentration of resources and centralization of authority over those engaged in carrying out its mission.

Side by side with these two contrasting kinds of organizations, there appeared a third. It was the public convention, called to discuss issues of common concern to all the churches. Many reform movements in the generation before the Civil War resorted to public conventions as a way to clarify issues and influence public opinion. The sponsors would present for debate a series of resolutions carefully prepared by a business committee, dealing with a particular issue. Each convention was separately organized to deal *ad hoc* with a particular matter of concern; but together they may be regarded as a distinct social institution, structured according to well-understood principles and following generally accepted procedures.

From 1842 to 1863, the Unitarians met in "Autumnal Conventions," each year in a different location, as far south as Philadelphia, and as far north as Montreal. They were admittedly rather informal gatherings of laity and clergy, and could not claim the mandate from the churches that a representative body might have done, even though the participants were often referred to as "delegates" from the churches. But in the absence of a hierarchical structure like that of the Presbyterians or the Episcopalians, the Autumnal Conventions were the most significant extraparochial structure of a quasi-ecclesiastical kind of more than local scope, as contrasted with the administrative or bureaucratic structure of the AUA.[15]

Neither the Autumnal Conventions nor the AUA was fully representative of the denomination. Of the two, the AUA came closer to being a focus of denominational identity, but it had no organic relationship to the churches and was regarded with indifference by parochial-minded Unitarians, of whom there were many. By the 1850s, the denomination as a whole was stagnant, even though many local churches were thriving. There was, as Henry W. Bellows put it, "an undeniable apathy in the denominational life of the body; with general prosperity, in short, there is despondency, self-questioning, and anxiety." Part of the explanation, he suggested, might be that the drift of theological change in the American churches generally was toward increased tolerance and the softening of dogmatic orthodoxy, so Unitarianism was losing some of its earlier urgency and point. But more basically, he argued, Unitarianism revealed the ultimate tendency of Protestantism to an individualism which was "the self-sufficiency of man" and "an absolute independence of Bible or Church." That tendency had gone as far as it could, he thought, and a reassertion of the importance of the corporate nature of human life, in family, state, and church, was indicated. "Nor is there any complete and satisfactory, perhaps no real way, to come into this corporate capacity, except through a publicly recognized and legitimate organization, whether domestic, political, or religious."[16]

The opportunity for Bellows to implement his belief in the importance of the church as an institution came at the close of the Civil War; and his position found vindication in the surge of Unitarian energy and growth that followed. His leadership in creating the National Conference in 1865 made possible the revitalization of the denomination at a time when it seemed fated to shrink to insignificance, just as a brilliant nova in the sky gradually dies down to become a fifth-magnitude star. Bellows was convinced that the AUA was sadly limited by Boston provincialism and was too much a clerical operation. But instead of trying to reform it (which would have stirred defenders of vested interests), he set out to construct a complementary organization to supply what the AUA lacked while leaving it to carry on the special work it had been organized to do.

The National Conference was established as a representative body of the churches, not an assemblage of individuals, and its delegates were predominantly laypersons, including some women. Its role was to provide an opportunity for discussion of problems concerning the denomination's immediate work and future prospects, to define policy and set directions, working in close relationship with the AUA, which would continue to be "the instruments of its power." Though not proposed explicitly as a replacement for the Autumnal Conventions, it carried forward their functions by means of a permanent organization with an established and defined relationship to the churches. By 1865, therefore, the Unitarians had in the AUA an *administrative* and *bureaucratic* organization to carry on the work of missionary expansion, aid to ministers seeking settlement, and publications; while in the National Conference it had for the first time a national *ecclesiastical* organization by which denominational purposes, identity, and sense of unity might be fostered and shaped.[17]

UNIVERSALIST ASSOCIATIONS AND CONVENTIONS

The Universalist story differs from that of the Unitarians in significant ways.[18] On the one hand, the Universalists developed what appears on paper to be a somewhat more connectional polity than that of the Unitarians. But they were slower to construct bureaucratic organizations for the publication of tracts, the promotion of missions, and the formation of new churches. Unitarian leaders like Henry W. Bellows complained often enough of the parochialism of Unitarians, who were apathetic in support of the AUA. Despite the theoretical connectionalism of Universalist polity, localism was at least as pervasive among them; their denominational activities received inadequate support, their enterprises were chronically underfunded, and their resources were repeatedly spread so thin as to be wasted.

Universalist polity in its earliest phase involved a multiplicity of associations and conventions, conforming to no overall plan. These were ecclesiastical bodies, existing for fellowship and the exercise of ecclesiastical control. While they sometimes passed resolutions encouraging the organization of educational institutions or the publication of denominational newspapers, they had no machinery for administering such enterprises themselves. Except as particular committees might be authorized, there was no continuing activity between annual sessions.

Ecclesiastical authority was asserted almost from the beginning. Thus in 1803, the New England Convention assumed the right to promulgate a normative statement of Universalist principles to be used as the basis for the admission of churches to fellowship. Delegates from thirty-eight societies met at Winchester, New Hampshire, where they adopted a Profession of Faith, and a Plan of General Association. The Winchester Profession was a very simple three-point statement; but it is significant that it was adopted by an extraparochial body representative of the churches, and was intended to define the status of churches that thought of themselves as Universalist.[19]

The Plan of General Association was essentially a formalization of practices with respect to the fellowshiping of churches, and the fellowshiping, ordination, and discipline of ministers, already being followed by the Convention. In 1800, the Convention had set up a Committee on Ordination, had licensed four individuals to preach, and had admitted three preachers to fellowship. The following year, two men were ordained by the Convention itself, and a committee appointed "to examine all applicants for ordination, and to ordain, if need be, in the recess of the Convention."[20] In 1800, a disciplinary committee was appointed to inquire into complaints about a minister in New Marlboro, Massachusetts; and in 1801, one minister, whose fellowship had previously been suspended, was excommunicated for "various irregularities of life and conversation."[21] The exercise of such authority by the Convention represented a departure from earlier, more strictly congregational practice,[22] and it stood in contrast with the Unitarian procedure of ordination by the local church on the advice of an ecclesiastical council. Since ministers were admitted to fellowship with the Convention by that body itself, their standing did not depend on status as the minister of a particular church; and in this respect the polity was more presbyterian than congregational. The local government of churches, however, was wholly congregational.

The New England Convention was only one of several regional associations or conventions in the early years. Attempts were made to maintain correspondence among them, but the situation was so untidy and confused that by the late 1820s the need for some sort of reorganization was widely recognized. The New England Convention, as the most influential, considered a series of proposals at successive annual meetings, culminating in its transformation in 1833 into the General Convention of Universalists in the United States. Its purposes were "to concentrate the interests of the denomination in the United States; communicate useful information on all subjects connected with such interests; to promote ministerial intercourse and fellowship among the brethren; and to subserve the great interests of the cause of gospel truth at large."[23]

The General Convention was established as a delegate body of clergy and laity, chosen by state conventions. The first state convention had been organized in 1825, and others were created in the years following, so as to fill out a coherent structure. The state conventions themselves were made up of delegates from local associations formed by the particular churches. This looks very much like a presbyterian structure, but formal centralization was belied in actual operation. The role of the General Convention was defined as advisory only, while the real locus of ecclesiastical authority rested with state conventions, which handled most cases involving ministerial discipline. Ordinations were performed both by associations and by state conventions, though on at least one occasion, a state convention declared an ordination by one of its constituent associations to be "null and void," as a usurpation of power reserved to the state conventions.[24]

The establishment of the General Convention in 1833 meant presbyterian structure but not presbyterian authority, and problems persisted. Associations and state conventions might ordain and discipline, but there was no assurance that they would adhere to common standards, or even that one state convention would respect the determinations of another. There was no common listing of ordained ministers. The state conventions differed greatly in size and strength, yet all were entitled to equal representation in the General Convention. Year after year attendance at its annual sessions by the duly appointed delegates was poor—in itself an indication of the failure of the Convention to develop as a significant forum for denominational discussion and policy decision.

Over the next thirty years, there were repeated calls for further reform, usually in the direction of more effective centralization. The question of jurisdiction in matters of ordination and discipline of the clergy was again and again the focus of discussion.[25] A report to the Convention in 1844 argued for resting full power over ordinations in the Convention, though the actual exercise of authority might be delegated to the state conventions; in disciplinary matters, appeals should be taken to the General Convention as the "ultimate tribunal." Vigorous opposition to such "anti-democratic" proposals was expressed, not least in the Indiana Convention, where a prominent minister condemned them as a conspiracy to create a "religious aristocracy." No real reform resulted, only continued piecemeal tinkering with the structure.[26]

Complaints about the ineffectualness of the General Convention were persistent. In 1853, the corresponding secretary of the Maine Convention remarked: "having represented this

Convention in that body one or two years, I have . . . little interest or patience with its proceedings. . . . As it now is, its influence is hardly equal to that of the smallest subordinate association among us."[27] In 1858, the "Report on the State of the Church" to the General Convention stated baldly: "our organization is sadly defective, approaching far more nearly to no organization at all, than to an official denominational unity."[28] In 1859, the Report began: "We want a more efficient operation."[29]

There were some who argued that the denomination might as well give up the pretense of centralized authority and revert to a purely congregational polity. But the 1860 Report responded: "Whatever be the wishes and predilections of individuals among us, our general policy is not Congregational. The fathers . . . voluntarily departed from Congregational usages many years ago, and adopted the general principles which everywhere mark our polity. A return to Congregationalism, even if desirable is doubtless impracticable."[30] This is not quite as anticongregational as it may seem, however, since what is understood here by congregationalism is the isolated autonomy of the local church.[31] New England congregationalism stood rather for the communion of autonomous churches, a significantly different thing. Nevertheless, such language is a reminder that the traditional language and symbols of New England congregationalism, such as the Cambridge Platform, had no resonance among the Universalists, and certain traditional practices expressive of the communion of the churches, such as ecclesiastical councils, had never taken root.

In response to such concerns, the General Convention appointed a series of committees on organization in 1858 and the years following. These committees addressed various aspects of the problem. One drew up a recommended set of bylaws for local churches, which explicitly rejected the distinction between "church" and "society."[32] Another was instructed to prepare a plan for the organization of missions; a third was to devise a plan of operations for a publishing house.[33] Incorporation was advocated both for state conventions and for the General Convention, so that they would be able to raise and spend money for denominational projects and to establish a permanent administrative structure.[34] Yet implementation of such proposals lagged. In 1860, the General Convention approved a scheme to set up a publishing house "which shall be under its control," and chose nine trustees to begin the work; but the following year the trustees reported that in view of the national crisis it was "inexpedient . . . to launch such an enterprise."[35]

In 1863, the Convention received an elaborate report with proposed sets of bylaws for local churches, associations, state conventions, and the General Convention.[36] Referred to the state conventions for comment, the proposals aroused so many objections that the following year only a revised and simplified constitution for the General Convention remained for consideration. It asserted jurisdiction over state conventions in matters of discipline and fellowship; but its most important innovations were the establishment of a permanent secretary and a permanent treasurer, and provision for the larger state conventions to be represented by additional delegates. With minor amendments, this constitution was adopted in 1865.[37] The Convention then received incorporation by action of the New York state legislature.[38]

The establishment of an incorporated General Convention with a salaried executive did not end the process of tinkering with constitution and bylaws and of proposing ideal blueprints for local parishes; but 1865 did mean significant advance toward a sense of national denominational identity. That sense was reinforced by the centennial celebration in Gloucester in 1870. Yet so tenacious was the tradition of decentralization that the stronger state conventions were at least as strong as the General Convention, regardless of the assertion on paper that the latter "shall have jurisdiction over the State Conventions in its fellowship."[39]

The General Convention was an ecclesiastical body, concerned with matters of ordination, fellowshiping, and discipline. It was not an administrative body, prepared to engage in missionary work, the publication of tracts, and the raising of money directly for the support of such activity. At the state level, however, something was accomplished. The New York Missionary Society was created in 1839, the Boston Home Missionary Society in 1847. In Maine, three societies were sponsored by the state convention in 1849 and held their first annual meetings in 1850: a missionary society, an education society, and a tract society. These societies cooperated in employing a paid agent—a recognition at last that while committees may set policy, they are poor administrators of programs.

The Maine societies met regularly for their annual meetings at the same time as the state convention, and for several years in the 1850s the annual reports were printed jointly with the Proceedings of the convention.[40] A close relationship between the societies and the convention also developed in Massachusetts, where the convention secured incorporation in 1859 and absorbed the separate tract, missionary, and Sabbath school enterprises.[41] In 1862, the Massachusetts Convention took steps toward the establishment of the Universalist Publishing House. But most state conventions were too small and weak even to think of developing a bureaucratic organization with paid agents.

Universalists also sponsored some extraparochial enterprises, specifically a considerable number of educational institutions. But they were subject to no official denominational control, the financial base was local, and the resources consistently inadequate, even at a time when a "college" might have a faculty of no more than half-a-dozen teachers.

In short, while other Protestant denominations saw the need for administrative structures with a national scope, and created the evangelical "benevolent empire" of voluntary associations for the promotion of a variety of good causes, the

Universalists continued to be even more parochial than the Unitarians—of whose provincialism Bellows so often despaired.

THE LOCAL CHURCH

Industrialization, urbanization, foreign immigration, and the movement of population westward forced denominations generally to develop organized and systematized programs of home missions and the publication of tracts. In a somewhat different way, these same social forces began to transform local church life and structure.

As long as New England was primarily rural and agricultural, and with few major commercial centers and no mill villages, the functions of churches and parishes were relatively simple and their structure uncomplicated. The town or parish was required to support public worship by maintaining the meetinghouse and paying the salary of the public teacher of piety, religion, and morality. Town officers, or the standing committee of a parish, were directly responsible. The inhabitants were involved in decision-making only in the annual election of parish officers or the occasional settlement of a new minister. The church as a select body of communicants met infrequently, perhaps to pass judgment in a disciplinary case, or to call a new minister, or to select delegates to an ecclesiastical council in some nearby church. The church had few prudential concerns, and they were entrusted to the deacons. The minister's role was to preach twice on the Sabbath; to administer the sacraments; to keep a record of baptisms, deaths, and admissions to full communion; to catechize the children; and to make pastoral calls on the sick and dying of the congregation.

In short, the ecclesiastical institutions were not designed to promote participatory interaction among individuals. Even the Sunday services of worship provided a rather passive sort of participation, dominated as they were by the minister as he read the Scriptures, prayed at length, and preached the sermon. There were no subgroups within the congregation, such as men's clubs, volunteer choirs, or social action committees. Those who assembled for worship were the same people who interacted with one another throughout the week in the civic, economic, and social life of the community, hence the church was not needed as a significant locus of interaction. The religious culture no doubt played a more important part in the lives of the people than it does today. But ecclesiastical institutions performed a narrower and more specialized function.

As urban centers grew in size, their populations became less homogeneous and their social structures more differentiated. In a town like Boston, there were now more people and more different kinds of people. An urban merchant, for example, might well find his life segmented, encountering one group of associates in business, dealing with another on political matters, and enjoying the company of a different set in informal social relationships.[42] While these circles would overlap to some extent, a particular church could not assume the existence of a ready-made community for which it performed a specialized function. It would have to create its own community. This would require the development within the congregation of an associative life of participatory activity.

The response to the changing social situation is exemplified in the history of the Twelfth Congregational Society in Boston. A new church, it had no established structure inherited from earlier times to slow or impede its adjustment to the urban environment. It was located in the West End, where the growth of population had produced overcrowding in Dr. Charles Lowell's West Church. In 1823, therefore, a subscription paper was circulated to members of the several liberal churches of the town, and 102 persons subscribed $23,300 to make possible the erection of a new meeting-house.[43] In December 1824, the sponsors of the enterprise invited Samuel Barrett to take charge of a church and society that were yet to be organized, and he accepted. The pews were sold at auction in January 1825, and the pewholders, as the new proprietors, bought out the original subscribers. A church was gathered within the religious society before the month was out. When Barrett was ordained in February, the initial organization was complete, with a religious society comprising the proprietors of pews, a church of communicants, a minister, and a place of worship.[44]

Specialized groupings within the congregation soon appeared. The first was a choir of four or five singers. Next a parish library was formed under the supervision of eight "trustees." At an early date, Barrett gathered a Bible class of young ladies, and he assembled the younger children for instruction on Sunday after the morning service. The historian of the church comments: "As Sunday schools and Bible classes, at that time, had only begun to be adopted by the Unitarian churches, these were regarded as novelties by many, indicating a creditable advance in liberal and progressive ideas."[45]

In 1826, an Association of Gentlemen for Benevolent Purposes was organized in the parish. It sought to focus the concerns of the congregation for charitable and philanthropic work, and one of its projects was the series of "Franklin Lectures" addressed to the mechanic and laboring classes of the town. In 1827, a parish Sunday school was formally organized, the deacons of the church serving as superintendents. Next, in 1828, was the formation of a Female Benevolent Association to visit the poor and to distribute garments and groceries to the deserving. After 1826, when several of the churches developed such work on a cooperative basis under the leadership of Joseph Tuckerman, a branch of the Benevolent Fraternity was established within the Twelfth Congregational Society.[46]

Other Boston congregations likewise began to develop a more differentiated inner life and structure. In 1824, Ezra Stiles Gannett started to hold what he called "vestry meetings" at the Federal Street Church. These became essentially adult education courses, dealing with such topics as Mosaic history, the parables, or practical religion. "I valued those meetings even more than the Sunday services," recalled one participant. "All were very social, the conversation free; and for a time at least, it was quite a parish meeting."[47] About the same time, a number of churches, Universalist and Unitarian both, began to sponsor Sunday schools, at first as philanthropic undertakings to give moral instruction to poor and neglected children in the city, but increasingly as time went on concentrating on the children of members of the congregation. Support of missionary and charitable activities in the larger society often meant local support groups, as when the American Unitarian Association promoted the formation of auxiliaries in local congregations. Quite apart from the specific objectives for which these groups were organized, they provided opportunities for participative interaction and the promotion of a sense of community.

As evidenced by a report to the Second Church in Boston in 1824, Henry Ware, Jr. was one minister who saw very clearly why such associative action was needed:

> The great principle, on which the prosperity and edification of the church must depend, appears to your committee to have been entirely overlooked in the general habits of all the churches with which we are connected. This is the *principle of association, union, sympathy, cooperation.* The church is, in its very essence, an association. . . . If this be forgotten, and, instead of a constant union in worship and action, Christians only meet infrequently at the table of the Lord, this primary purpose is lost sight of, and it cannot, therefore, be expected that the greatest religious prosperity should be attained. . . . Let us, then, henceforth resolve to regard this church as an association, actually and actively united for the accomplishment of religious and benevolent purposes.

Ware therefore held a Bible class every Monday, and every Tuesday evening "his house was open to the parish, who met there in an unceremonious manner for religious intercourse and conversation." The result, according to his biographer, was not only "an increased activity, zeal, and religious interest in the church," but also increased voluntary financial support, which in due time made possible the erection of "a spacious and commodious vestry."[48]

The fullest embodiment of these new tendencies was the Church of the Disciples, gathered in 1841; the most thoughtful and coherent rationale was given by its minister, James Freeman Clark. Three principles, he explained, shaped the methods and arrangements of the church: the social principle, the voluntary principle, and the principle of congregational worship. The *social principle* recognized the need for the people to meet and know each other if the church was to foster the highest culture of which human nature is capable. "To come together and sit side by side in pews, is surely not the meeting here alluded to." As human nature has three elements—Intellect, Affections, and Will—meetings of three different kinds were organized. To stimulate intellectual culture, discussion meetings in private homes considered questions of morals, theology, and personal religion. For "the expression of devout thought and religious affection," there were prayer and conference meetings. And to engage in the practical application of religion, some of the ladies of the church met regularly "to cut out and give out work to poor women, who are thus assisted to clothe their children."[49]

The *voluntary principle* meant "that the expenses of the church shall be defrayed by a voluntary subscription, and pews shall not be sold, rented, or taxed." Clarke repeated the usual arguments against pew ownership: that those who cannot afford to buy a pew will feel left out; that men of property may buy a pew as a contribution toward the cost of building a meetinghouse without ever intending to attend with any frequency; that the pew owners "are not necessarily the friends of Christian and humane movements," but are in a position to put pressure on a minister whose preaching offends them. He acknowledged that rental instead of ownership of pews avoided such problems, but considered that to be a halfway reform only. By abolishing pew taxes and rentals, the Church of the Disciples could also reject the conventional distinction of church and parish. There was but one organization, the church, made up of all who expressed a desire to unite for religious purposes. "Everything which relates to our action as a religious society is done by our church, at its meetings, or through its various committees. The church has its Pastoral Committee, its Finance Committee, its Committee on Music, its Committee on the Young, which has charge of the Sunday school, and its Committee for Benevolent Operations."[50]

Clarke's third method of operation was *congregational worship*. This was an attempt to break away from customary patterns in which congregations were almost entirely passive during the service. In many churches, he complained, the "minister and the choir conduct the worship; the people take no active part in it, they are only listeners." At the Church of the Disciples there was no choir, and the people had to learn to sing the hymns themselves. Of deeper significance was Clarke's insistence that members of the congregation should take part in the service, and conduct it themselves if the minister was absent. In most of our churches, he noted, "it is thought that if the minister be absent, another must be procured, or the service cannot be carried on." There is no reason, he went on to argue, why, on Protestant principles, "the members of a church should not administer the ordinances when necessary." More than that, "Why, indeed, should not churches be frequently organized without a regular ministry?" Did not the Cambridge Platform declare that "there may be the essence and being of a church without any officers"?[51]

Older urban churches moved more slowly than the Church of the Disciples to develop inner associative structures;

churches in country towns were under less immediate pressure to change. But this was the inescapable direction of evolving church life, and institutional survival was at stake. Churches that did not, perhaps could not, develop as communities of active participants disappeared—and the casualties were many. A conspicuous instance was Theodore Parker's Twenty-Eighth Congregational Society in Boston. In his first years in Boston, Parker attempted to institute Sunday afternoon meetings for free consideration of religious issues, but he abandoned them when a few outsiders monopolized the discussion. Lectures on the Bible brought little response. He eventually gave up. In his farewell letter to his people he acknowledged failure: "Together we have tried some things, which did not prosper, and so came to an end."[52]

In rural West Roxbury, Parker's ministry had consisted simply of preaching and parish calling; in Boston the pastoral side of ministry got squeezed and preaching was what remained. He had been invited to Boston by a group of men who were resolved that he should "have a chance to be heard" there. He went to Boston to preach, and preach was what he did. But his success was never translated into institutional strength. His large congregations were not a church, but a kind of mass meeting. The Music Hall where he preached was crowded while he lived, but the Society experienced prompt decline and lingering death when he was gone.

Large numbers attracted by Parker's preaching gave the Twenty-Eighth Congregational Society the outward appearance of success. But a personal following is not a church unless it is transformed into one; and Parker's goals for the Society, as revealed in "The True Idea of a Christian Church," show no awareness of a problem, let alone an indication of how it might be addressed. The deficiencies in his ecclesiology were transmitted to younger men who took their cue from him, like Octavius Brooks Frothingham, with similar results. When deteriorating health forced Frothingham to withdraw from the active ministry in 1879, his Independent Liberal

Church in New York promptly disbanded, because there was nothing left.

Parker's ministry to the Twenty-Eighth Congregational Society at least was based on the congregation, even if at times it seemed to owe as much to the lyceum platform as to the Cambridge Platform. Elsewhere, however, the concept of the ordained ministry bit by bit expanded beyond its original parish boundaries. Ministers appointed to the faculties of Harvard Divinity School and Meadville Theological School, in Pennsylvania, were regularly identified in print with the adjective "Reverend" before their names; this was a plausible extension of long-standing usage. A more significant departure was the development of ministers-at-large. When Joseph Tuckerman undertook the work of ministering to the poor of Boston, after twenty-five years in the parish ministry, he was as fully involved in "ministry" as ever, and no one questioned his ordained status.

The next step was the ordination in 1834 of Charles F. Barnard and Frederick T. Gray as his associates. In his ordination sermon, Tuckerman stated: "We are about to engage in the solemn act of separating two ministers of Christ to a department of service to which no others have in this manner been separated."[53] True enough, the proceedings were unusual. The ordination was not in accordance of a call by a church, but rather on behalf of the Benevolent Fraternity of Churches, constituted by delegates from the Boston churches. The delegates elected a Central Board, which chose an Executive Committee, which in turn assembled the ecclesiastical council to ordain the two men.[54] In his charge, William Ellery Channing declared: "You have now been set apart to the Christian ministry according to the rites of the congregational church."[55] The familiar rites of ordination were indeed respected: sermon, prayer, charge, right hand of fellowship.

But no one seems to have questioned the right of the executive committee of an administrative body to authorize an ordination.

Nor was anyone prepared to provide a reinterpretation of congregational polity to give a plausible rationale for the departure. Indeed, in the same year that Barnard and Gray were ordained, the Dudleian Lecturer at Harvard, addressing the topic of the validity of congregational ordination, insisted that the power of ordination belongs to the people. "And by the people, I mean the congregation or Parish."[56] To this day, practical necessity has not been accompanied by theoretical justification or validation.

CONSENSUS

For social groups to coalesce, their members must share a binding consensus, explicit or implicit, at some level of generality. Religious groups are no exception. "Can two walk together except they be agreed?" asked the prophet Amos. The answer is: No, they cannot, unless they are agreed on some things of importance to them. Their consensus need not be all-inclusive, so as to preclude all disagreement, nor is it necessary that their unifying consensus be primarily doctrinal. It may well be that historical or sociological factors will be more important than theological factors in defining it. But a common value system, a common way of defining and addressing significant problems, is needed if religious groups are to cohere; and churches spend a lot of time and energy trying to articulate and strengthen the consensus that keeps them together.

Such a consensus cannot develop and be sustained without a communications network by which views may be shared widely and differences of opinion reconciled. We do not ordinarily think of the communications network as an aspect of congregational polity, since much of it is informal and extra-ecclesiastical. But the effectiveness of communication within

59

the denomination is crucial to its well-being; it can matter greatly, so far as polity is concerned, whether the communication is inclusive or segmented, lateral or hierarchical, formal or informal.

In the period before the Civil War, the most effective channels of communication for the ministers were ministerial associations; private correspondence; and anniversary occasions such as Harvard Commencement, Divinity School Visitation Day, the Berry St. Conference meeting annually at the time of May Meetings, and the Autumnal Conventions. The laity also attended May Meetings and the Autumnal Conventions, but they had to rely even more on such publications as the weekly *Christian Register*. In any event, except insofar as AUA tracts circulated within the churches, there was no central denominational authority with a hierarchically structured communications network by which an authorized position might be stated and control exercised.

The content of the consensus of a religious group, which may differ from time to time, is largely irrelevant to questions of ecclesiastical polity. But the process by which the consensus is defined and stated, and the sanctions used to maintain it, are central issues. The most common procedure, taken for granted in most denominations, is for some recognized ecclesiastical authority to prepare a normative statement of doctrine, to which all are expected to assent if they are to be recognized as in good standing.

Someone seeking admission to a church may be examined as to soundness of doctrine as well as moral character, and a member accused of doctrinal irregularity may be subject to discipline. A candidate seeking ordination must likewise assent to the established orthodoxy, and a minister who departs significantly from it risks being charged with heresy. It is the group that defines consensus, and the group, through recognized procedures, that applies sanctions to deviants. Creeds and confessions of faith, then, are devices to make clear the standards by which those seeking acceptance may be judged. In a relatively homogeneous and stable group, the binding consensus may not be spelled out in detail, but will be expressed piecemeal and indirectly in patterns of worship, conventional behavior, and individual expressions of opinion. When some divisive issue arises, it becomes imperative to define the limits of consensus by some authoritative determination, so that a boundary line that was previously fuzzy may be made plain.

Creeds therefore are products of particular disagreements, arising at particular moments, under particular circumstances. The problem is that their compilers customarily are confident that they are stating eternal and universal truths, while later generations may find themselves burdened by doctrinal statements that are no longer useful and to which conscientious assent is no longer possible. In New England history, the obvious example is the Andover Creed (1808), born of an attempt to unite two factions of Calvinists in opposition to the Liberal Christians.[57] Professors at the Andover Theological Seminary were required to assent to it on assuming office and at five-year intervals thereafter. By the time two generations had passed, there was no one on the faculty who could conscientiously subscribe to it. Eventually, after a heresy trial and prolonged litigation, the creed was set aside and it became a historical curiosity. Even the most conservative of religious groups may discover that the boundaries of its consensus refuse to stay fixed, and the creeds that once defined it no longer seem to be eternal and unchangeable truth.

It is easy for congregational churches to make doctrinal orthodoxy the basis for local church membership, if they choose to do so. Covenants may be written so as to include creedal tests, and the threat of excommunication may curb deviance. It is more of a problem to assure conformity in the larger community of congregational churches. The Cambridge Platform does provide that a church guilty of a "public offense" may be "admonished" by other churches; and if it remains obstinate, the other churches "may forbear communion with them."[58] A minister accused of preaching unsound doctrine might be condemned by a council, as were Lemuel Briant in 1752 and John Rogers in 1757.[59] But such procedures were so loose-jointed that they proved weak barriers against unorthodox views. Arminianism, which rejected the Calvinist doctrines of election and original sin, was able to make its way in eastern Massachusetts in part because there was no hierarchical structure in a position to exercise discipline.

In the eighteenth century, the Arminians who later became Unitarians inveighed against the adoption of creedal statements in church covenants, and protested their use in disciplinary procedures. Anticreedalism thereby became a fixed dogma for the liberals. But condemnation of the use of creeds for the definition of boundaries does not mean a rejection of boundaries themselves. When the liberals insisted that one should turn to the Bible for a revelation of God's plan of salvation, not to human systems of doctrine phrased in nonscriptural language, they were marking out a boundary line that excluded deists and freethinkers, such as Tom Paine.

When the Universalists adopted the Winchester Profession in 1803, they sought to define boundaries that would be generous enough to include all believers in universal salvation but would exclude "partialists" of all kinds. When William Ellery Channing protested the "system of exclusion" adopted by the orthodox, and pleaded that Christian character should be the basis for Christian fellowship, it was still Christian fellowship that he sought to enlarge, and that is a limiting concept. When he preached at the ordination of Jared Sparks in Baltimore in 1819, he was stating "the distinguishing opinions" of the Liberal Christians—that is, clarifying the boundary line between them and the orthodox. Some ways of drawing the line may be more generous-spirited than others; but to disagree with an adversary as to where the line is to be drawn, or the basis on which it is to be drawn, is not to abolish boundaries altogether.

Instead of adopting creedal statements, the liberals articulated their consensus through controversial preaching and writing. In the period of the Unitarian controversy, they wrote tracts for publication by the AUA and critical reviews in the *Christian Examiner* and other journals. Henry Ware argued their concept of human nature in *Letters to Trinitarians and Calvinists* (1820), while Andrews Norton dealt with the doctrine of the Trinity in his *Statement of Reasons for Not Believing the Doctrines of Trinitarians* (1819, 1833). In the 1830s when Transcendental stirrings began to agitate the denomination, Norton turned his attention to a defense of its Christian identity in his *Latest Form of Infidelity* (1838). For this address he was much criticized, then and by later generations. His rhetoric was indeed open to criticism; his air of superior intellectual authority was obnoxious to many; and his principles of Christian apologetics were soon to be outmoded; but this method—an appeal to informed opinion—was unexceptionable.

Instead of resorting to formal disciplinary procedures, the liberals defined the boundaries of their consensus by individual acts of agreement or disagreement. Taken together, these acts were a form of social pressure, as Theodore Parker discovered. Most of the Boston clergy regarded his views as unscriptural, unsound, and mischievous, since they seemed to deny the claim of Christianity to be a revealed religion. How should an advocate of such opinions be treated? Ezra Stiles Gannett asked. Not silenced, "unless open argument and fraternal persuasion may reduce him to silence." But on the other hand, there is no obligation to assist in the diffusion of opinions with which one disagrees. "No principle of liberality or charity can require any one to aid in the diffusion of what he accounts error, especially if he thinks it pernicious error." For a minister to decline to exchange pulpits with Parker, Gannett argued, is a matter of individual decision. To go beyond that to some formal denominational censure would be "contrary to the spirit and practice of our denomination.

. . . It is not our way, to pass ecclesiastical censure. We are willing—at least we have said we were—to take the principle of free inquiry with all its consequences."[60]

UNITARIANS AND UNIVERSALISTS IN 1865

Both the Unitarians and the Universalists made major advances in 1865 toward a more coherent and effective denominational organization. For the Unitarians, the result was the National Conference, engineered by Henry W. Bellows with the indispensable assistance of men like Edward Everett Hale and James Freeman Clarke. For the Universalists, the outcome was the adoption of a new constitution for the General Convention, the culmination of several years of complaints, discussion, committee reports, and preliminary drafts.

The Universalists now had a national structure, with its General Convention made up of delegates from state conventions, these in turn consisting of delegates from the churches. It was a question, however, whether the formal symmetry on paper took realistic account of the disparity among the state conventions in size and resources; in any event, the Universalists had at best inadequate administrative or bureaucratic machinery. The Unitarians, on the other hand, had a working bureaucracy in the AUA, though hardly an impressive one in terms of staff or resources; but their formal cooperative structure had just been constructed, and only the future would reveal whether it would actually succeed in focusing the common concerns of the churches and bring them into closer relationship.

At the local level, congregational self-government prevailed. Certain organizational arrangements surviving from earlier times, such as the church-parish or church-society distinction, still persisted; but the tendency toward unified responsibility for both religious and prudential concerns was strong. Parochial localism and individualism still marked both denominations. Sometimes it took the form of an aversion to all kinds of organization as in some way an infringement on the human spirit, as in Octavius Brooks Frothingham's attack on Bellows's enterprise; this attitude was in part the imprint of Transcendentalism. More often it was an expression of the limited horizons of those who found the problem of keeping local churches alive and moving forward to be more than enough to consume all their energies. But in both denominations, important voices were protesting excessive individualism, seeking more effective common action, and rejecting "pure" congregationalism.

Associational Proliferation and Bureaucratic Development, 1865–1898

DENOMINATIONAL, PAROCHIAL, AND INDIVIDUALISTIC UNITARIANISM

The organization of the National Conference of Unitarian Churches in 1865 at a convention held in New York was a major commitment by the Unitarians to a broader, more national vision of their mission and was a recognition of the need for strengthened organization if that mission was to be accomplished. But not everyone agreed with Henry W. Bellows, the leading spirit of the New York convention, that denominational organization was the way to promote the spread of liberal religion. Some, like Rufus Ellis and Chandler Robbins, ministers of the oldest Boston churches, stayed away from the convention because they were satisfied that the silent spread of liberalism was already gradually transforming the orthodox churches. No intervention was needed, they felt, and aggressive denominationalism might well isolate the Unitarians further. Their churches were prospering well enough, so they could afford to be very passive and parochial.

More articulate were the Radicals, especially Octavius Brooks Frothingham, who stayed away also, and bitterly attacked Bellows's leadership of the convention. Frothingham's concern was to defend the complete intellectual and spiritual freedom of the individual, which institutions invariably compromise. To the extent that he had a concept of religious fellowship, it was a purely spiritual relationship of individual seekers after religious truth, with no necessary embodiment in a covenanted community.

All three of these attitudes—the institutionalism of Bellows, the parochialism of Ellis, and the individualism of Frothingham—had deep roots in Unitarian history. The resulting tensions continued for a full generation or more. To this day, they remain imperfectly reconciled, often within the minds and hearts of individual Unitarian Universalists.

Bellows serves as the type figure of the institutionalist. He believed that the religious impulse, common to all, needs religious fellowship if it is to mature and bear fruit. It is therefore our obligation to assure the health and well-being of the churches. The isolated individual, he insisted, "has not, and cannot have, the affections, internal experiences and dispositions, or the power and blessings, which he can and may, and will receive in his corporate capacity." No doubt, he acknowledged, there is an invisible church, a church of the spirit, as well as a visible one. But "the invisible church takes due care of itself"; it is the visible church that has been committed to our hands. The Family, the State, and the Church are the three "great departments" of our common humanity. "Nor is there any complete and satisfactory, perhaps no real way, to come into this corporate capacity, except through a publicly recognized and legitimate organization, whether domestic, political, or religious." Hence the need for "the organic, instituted, ritualized, impersonal, steady, patient work of the Church," through which the individual soul may find its religious wants supplied.[1]

Frothingham represents the individualistic rejection of ecclesiasticism in general and Unitarian denominationalism in particular characteristic of the so-called Radicals. Of the New York convention he wrote: "There has never been a Convention so narrow and blind and stubborn as it was. . . . Instead of the pure fraternity of noble minds and hearts, we have a close corporation of secretaries." It was doomed to failure in the face of the much stronger ecclesiasticism of the orthodox churches: "What can their inconsistent, illogical, and irresolute sectarianism, do against a sectarianism . . . whose glory is in its absolute intolerance?"[2]

What Frothingham offered in his own church was a place where absolute freedom of conscience was assured both in pulpit and pew. There was no covenant or any equivalent, and no distinction made between church and congregation. Frothingham had been deeply influenced by Ralph Waldo Emerson, and even more directly by Theodore Parker. From Emerson he learned that "nothing is at last sacred but the integrity of your own mind," and that "society everywhere is in a conspiracy against the manhood of every one of its members."[3] For Emerson, the practical result was "churches of two, churches of one," and solitary Sunday walks in grove and glen. Parker had not gone that far, but he continued to preach to a congregation only to discover that restless, unsatisfied individuals were not easily made into a church. He finally ended with a largely transient audience attracted by vigorous preaching.

Frothingham likewise found that it was the sermon rather than the preliminaries that drew the crowds; many of his hearers arrived only just in time for it. On Sunday afternoons, no attempt was made to conduct a second service, and the time was devoted to "pastoral lectures and instructions." We are told that "social reunions" were sometimes held on "secular evenings," and that "among the groups of his select acquaintances," Frothingham was "the flower of courtesy and companionship—a gentleman of the most refined and genuine school."[4] But nowhere in the life of the society was there either cultivation of the devotional spirit through sacrament or ritual, or organization to promote cooperation for human betterment. Frothingham's preaching was what mattered. He was an effective public speaker with a personal following, enlarged by many curious casual listeners. In 1879, when ill health made it necessary for him to give up his preaching, the church disbanded because nothing remained.[5]

Despite the accusations of the Radicals, there was no disposition on the part of the leaders of the National Conference to impose hierarchical control over the churches or to establish creedal boundaries around the denomination. Bellows did think it necessary to identify the actual doctrinal stance of the denomination in Christian terms, since that clearly represented the position of the overwhelming majority of Unitarians. But he was insistent that a normative statement of belief was not to be used as a standard of inclusion and exclusion. Even Francis Ellingwood Abbot, one of the Radicals, acknowledged that the New York convention was "unmistakably opposed to creeds in any form."[6]

The Preamble to the Constitution of the National Conference, however, defined its basis as discipleship to the Lord Jesus Christ. To the Radicals this was, if not a creed, at least a creedlet. Failing to secure modification at the meeting in Syracuse in 1866, some of them resolved to come together in a new fellowship that would avoid the limitations of denominationalism and sectarianism and would respect the complete intellectual freedom of every participant. The result was the Free Religious Association (FRA), of which Frothingham served as president for a dozen years. Like the National Conference, it provided a forum for wide discussion of religious ideas and issues. Unlike the National Conference, which was directly related to the churches and relied on the AUA as "the instruments of its power," the FRA was made up of individuals. It served as a vehicle for the discussion and dissemination, by public meetings and publications, of a particular point of view. But, as William Channing Gannett once said, it was "a voice without a hand." It depended on the devotion of a few committed persons, such as William J. Potter, who served as secretary for twenty-five years. When their energies flagged or their interest changed, there was no reservoir of institutional strength to carry the enterprise over low points of leadership. While the FRA lasted in a formal sense for more than half a century, its vitality and influence fell off after the first decade.[7]

UNITARIAN DEVELOPMENTS, 1865-1898

In the decades following the Civil War, the Unitarians felt impelled to construct new machinery to deal with enlarged denominational responsibilities.[8] These included the following: the organization of local conferences of churches; more formal procedures for ministerial supply and settlement; the development of a fellowship committee to pass on qualifications of applicants for the ministry; both new and reinvigorated denominational organizations in addition to the AUA and the National Conference; and the beginning of the process of making the AUA responsible to the churches.

Local conferences. In 1866, when Bellows presented the report of the Council of the National Conference to its first regular session, he urged that "it needs to be supplemented by more general and more efficient local organization." This was not the first time that such a suggestion had been made, but it was characteristic of Bellows to seize on and provide the initiative for a development that others had tentatively and inconclusively advanced. Noting that other denominations had found it essential to have regional structure of limited geographical extent—such as Presbyterian synods and presbyteries—he argued that the "Unitarian domain should be territorially divided," and that "every church should belong to *some* Association or Conference." Such local conferences should be entitled to send delegates to the National Conference; indeed the time might come when, by growth of the denomination, direct representation of the churches would no longer be possible, and the National Conference would be made up of representatives of the local conferences.[9]

The meeting endorsed the proposal, and by the time the Conference next met, in 1868, fourteen such local conferences had been organized. They had as a common purpose to invigorate church life, to afford opportunities for fellowship among the churches, and to be channels of communication between the churches and the national leadership. Yet they inevitably varied as to size, territorial extent, organization, and activities. In 1870, the smallest were the Lake Erie Conference and the Western Illinois and Iowa Conference, both comprising only four churches, geographically dispersed. Small wonder that the secretary of the Lake Erie Conference stated that it existed chiefly on paper. By way of contrast, the South Middlesex Conference was made up of thirty churches, meeting four times a year for discussions "of a practical character."[10]

Bellows had hoped that the local conferences would take responsibility for missionary activity, the encouragement of local churches, the filling of vacant pulpits, and similar works. For a time, the conferences did serve as the mechanism for soliciting funds from the churches for support of the AUA, but they did not develop very far as bodies with administrative responsibilities. The New York and Hudson River Conference began a program of missionary work, but it soon decided to leave it to the AUA and became "a body seeking mainly the fellowship of the churches associated."[11] While the Reverend A. D. Wheeler was alive, the Maine Conference was actively committed to missionary labor and he traveled many miles in its service, but on his death in 1876 the work languished. While secretary of the Western Conference from 1875 to 1884, Jenkin Lloyd Jones was a tireless promoter of the cause throughout the western states, but he was a one-man missionary society and only secondarily the secretary of the conference.[12] The Suffolk Conference sponsored theater meetings for a few years as outreach to the unchurched.[13]

But for the most part, the conferences settled back into a pattern of meeting twice, or at most four times a year, to listen to addresses on current issues—perhaps doctrinal, perhaps of social concern—and to engage in friendly social intercourse. Though these meetings never came up to Bellows's intention, they were not without value, and many of the local conferences organized in 1866 and 1867 survived until merger with the Universalists in 1961 produced a somewhat different district organization.[14]

Ministerial supply and settlement. Down to the time of the Civil War, procedures for candidating and settlement in Unitarian churches were primitive and inefficient. The secretary of the AUA might be consulted about vacant pulpits, and from time to time, Unitarian publications listed the names of men seeking settlement. Certain ministers knowledgeable about denominational affairs, such as Bellows, might be able to advise a candidate or advance his prospects.[15] But for the most part, candidates and churches were left to find each other. All too often a church would hear a succession of candidates over many weeks and finally decide on the basis of superficial impressions and sketchy information. Some candidates in desperation resorted to the employment of agents, or "middlemen," to engage in searches on their behalf.[16]

In 1863, the executive committee of the AUA sought to end "the scandal attaching to the present system" and adopted a report clearly fixing responsibility on the secretary of the Association for maintaining lists of candidates and vacant pulpits. The secretary was even authorized to supply churches with select lists of men who, in his best judgment, would be appropriate for their consideration.[17] Among the ministers themselves, a movement was afoot for the organization of a professional society, to be concerned with standards of conduct, the exercise of discipline, and control over admission to professional status. There had been cases when ministers who had been failures in orthodox churches had secured Unitarian pulpits, only to continue a record of disruption and damage. Some mechanism was thought necessary by which the qualifications of such men could be assessed and parishes, if need be, put on their guard.

Local ministerial associations often had taken responsibility for the "approbation" of candidates to preach, but they were inadequate for this task. They were essentially fraternal gatherings of settled ministers, and outside of New England the pulpits were so widely scattered that there was no structure of associations at all. The need for an inclusive body was a topic of discussion among the brethren at the Autumnal Convention at Springfield, Massachusetts, in October 1863. An informal committee was assembled, headed by Edward Everett Hale, which summoned an organizing meeting for January 12, 1864.[18]

The preamble of the constitution of the resulting Ministerial Union emphasized the desire for closer fellowship, for assistance to those just entering the ministry, for protection of the ministerial office "from incompetent and unworthy men," for mutual edification, and for cooperation "for the diffusion of the Gospel." It was agreed that graduates of the two theological schools, Harvard and Meadville, should be admitted without question, but the applications of all others would be referred to a Committee on Membership and voted on by the members at large. Early records indicate that approval was not automatic and that applications were occasionally rejected. The membership committee was also given jurisdiction over charges of immoral conduct against a member, and on the basis of its investigation, "by a concurring vote of two-thirds of the members present," the Union might strike the name of the offender from its list.[19]

Before long, there were about 200 members enrolled, widely representative of the whole body of the Unitarian clergy. At the monthly meetings, papers were read, mostly dealing with professional matters, such as "Ministerial Efficiency," "Laymen's Views of Preachers," "Preaching Without Paper," and "The True Aim of Ministry of Today."[20] The character of the Ministerial Union as a professional society was reinforced in 1870, when an amendment to the constitution provided for "the relief of any in poverty or sickness," and an assessment was made on the members to make that possible.[21] But as time went on, the more distant ministers failed to pay the annual assessment, and the number of those active was more in the range of fifty or sixty, mostly from the Boston area. With changes of name and focus, it survived to become at last the Unitarian Universalist Ministers Association.[22] The problem of unemployed ministers at a time when many pulpits were vacant recurred many times in meetings of the Union. Although the secretary of the AUA had been given the responsibility for facilitating settlements, the ministers felt he was not as active as he should have been. In 1876, therefore, the Union approved the appointment from its membership of three settled ministers to work with the assistant secretary of the AUA as a "Bureau of Supply."[23] A circular went out to the churches recommending the good offices of the Bureau, outlining preferred procedures for settlement and in particular suggesting the consideration of no more than three candidates in place of an interminable procession of them. The organization and work of the Bureau were explained in detail in a report to the National Conference in September 1876, and the Conference endorsed the Bureau without dissent.[24] In practice, however, the Bureau served New England churches only; and even there, the old patterns of independent negotiation persisted, to the dismay of those who hoped for reform.[25] Under various names, the Bureau lasted until the early 1930s.[26]

Admission to fellowship. Related to problems of pulpit supply were questions of qualifications for and admission to the ministry. In a simpler day, local ministerial associations had given approbation to preach to young candidates; but now the Boston Association insisted on referring applicants to the Ministerial Union as "the proper body to give admission to our ministry." The Union's response was that it was prepared to control admission to its own number, but that it had "no function to admit men to the Unitarian ministry." In the absence of an accepted and authorized body to admit fit men to the ministry, it was evident there was no way to keep unfit men out.[27]

As early as 1870, at the urging of Bellows, the question of the authority to grant fellowship came before the National Conference. Meeting in New York that year, the Conference voted to ask each local conference to create a "Committee on Fellowship" to examine candidates, testing "their natural competency, acquirements, and moral and religious character, and only when satisfied of these, grant letters of admission into the Christian ministry and the Unitarian pulpit, it being understood that no dogmatic test shall be applied."[28] The New York and Hudson River Conference already had such a committee, doubtless because Bellows was active there, but most of the other conferences ignored the suggestion. The Essex Conference rejected it outright, declaring that any such "tribunal" was "foreign to the purposes of its organization."[29]

The problem would not go away. In 1878, the directors of the AUA recommended that the National Conference itself establish a Committee on Fellowship. The proposal was sharply debated at the meeting in Saratoga, New York, in 1878. The Wisconsin Conference entered a protest, arguing that "any attempt to curtail the individual responsibility of Societies seeking for ministers, to inquire into qualifications and character, is hurtful to the independent policy of our churches." The Conference nevertheless authorized a Committee on Fellowship, which was promptly established with twelve members, three for each of four geographical areas, each of which constituted a subcommittee: Eastern, Middle, Western, and Pacific. It soon issued a simple set of rules. Applicants not graduates of Harvard or Meadville should apply to the chairman of the Committee on Fellowship, or to the chairman of the subcommittee closest to his residence, supplying testimonials and, if coming from another denomination, a certificate of dismissal. Within this limited sphere of operation, the Committee admitted 97 men and 2 women to fellowship in the period 1878 to 1891. The process involved many personal interviews, much correspondence, and often counseling of those rejected.[30]

The creation of a Committee on Fellowship provided a method of admission, but no way of withdrawal. The members of the Committee thought it anomalous that it could grant letters of fellowship but had no power to recall them, either for cause or because of a departure to a wholly secular occupation. An accurate list of Unitarian ministers could not be compiled; the one in the Year Book of the AUA was admittedly unofficial and incorrect. A significant report to the National Conference in 1891 discussed the problem forthrightly. In 1897, the Fellowship Committee was instructed to consult annually with officers of the AUA in regard to the list in the Year Book "and recommend the addition or dropping of names, so as to make as nearly as possible a list of those who are entitled to such recognition." A revised set of rules adopted in 1899 allowed for dropping any person when the Committee "is satisfied that in conduct and character such person has become unworthy to continue to hold the office of a Christian minister in the Unitarian Fellowship." But no action would be taken "till a minister has had full opportunity to be heard in the matter."[31]

The task of the Fellowship Committee was to help the churches avoid inadvertently installing a "moral adventurer." It was not intended to diminish the responsibility of the church to choose its own leadership, and the committee did not assert that only those on its own lists should be considered. The accepted position was stated by the editor of the *Christian Register:* "It is, of course, entirely optional with the minister whether he will seek the recommendation of the Committee on Fellowship or not, and entirely optional with the churches whether they will heed its recommendations. The duties of the committee are simply hospitable and advisory."[32]

The fellowshiping and possible discipline of a minister is distinctively an ecclesiastical matter. It was proper, therefore, that it should have been undertaken by the National Conference, which was an ecclesiastical body, rather than by the AUA, which was a bureaucratic agency of the denomination, not an ecclesiastical body. In a sense, the Committee on Fellowship was to take the place of the ecclesiastical councils that in an earlier day had provided a way for the larger community of faith to validate entrance to the ministry and, if need be, to exercise discipline. As usual, it was Bellows who saw it most clearly in the perspective of a development of polity over the years. Once, he noted, the ecclesiastical council was the "necessary and essential representation" of the principle of fellowship among independent churches. But we have "gradually, in our ever-increasing passion for liberty and our ever-diminishing sense of the only uses for which liberty is valuable, weakened the only bond that made possible an effectual fellowship in the Congregational order; *i.e.*, this ecclesiastical COUNCIL." The Committee on Fellowship was a substitute for the abandoned ecclesiastical council, which might be expected to do the work with less time and trouble. More than just an administrative device, Bellows saw the committee as expressive of basic principles of congregational polity:

> it seems, to at least the writer of this report, that the only possible escape from an utter dispersion and complete disintegration of our fellowship is the putting again into use the old ecclesiastical Council which makes and saves Congregationalism, but which absolute Independency (which historically, we do not represent) repudiates and destroys, and with it all possibility of an organic existence as a denomination.[33]

The AUA and the churches. When the National Conference was formed in 1865, it was composed of delegates from the churches. The AUA, on the other hand, had always been an organization of individual members. For a time early in its history, there had been an attempt to form auxiliary societies in the churches, but these were not part of the church or parish structure, and indeed did not long survive.

There were those who thought the AUA, like the National Conference, should have a formal relationship with the churches on whose behalf it acted and from which it solicited funds. To that end, a consolidation of the two bodies was suggested in some quarters as early as 1880. A committee of the Conference was appointed to assess the matter, but rather than recommend consolidation, it suggested that the AUA admit voting delegates from the churches to its meetings.[34] Prompted by the report of this committee, the Directors of the AUA proposed appropriate amendments to its bylaws at the annual meeting in 1883. "We are persuaded," they argued, "that all feelings of hostility toward the Association have their root in this: that our Secretary is not the elected representative of the churches, and the votes of our Directors do not come before the denomination for approval or correction."[35] As finally adopted in 1884, the bylaws provided for representation by the minister or president of "any church or missionary association" that had sent a contribution for two successive years. The already established practice of allowing individual life memberships was not abolished, however, so for the next forty years there were two categories of members entitled to vote.[36]

The decision of the AUA to admit voting delegates from the churches was soon followed by similar action by the Unitarian Sunday School Society. The origins of that society may be discerned in an association of Sunday school teachers in Boston as far back as 1827, but as a general denominational body it dated from 1854. In 1866, when it was virtually inactive, a merger with the AUA was considered, but fresh leadership gave it renewed life and an enlarged publication program developed. At the annual meeting in 1884, a revision of its constitution provided "for giving a representative character to this meeting (as is now done in the American Unitarian Association) by permitting two delegates from each 'contributing' Sunday-school to vote, whether they are already members of the society or not."[37] When the Society was incorporated the following year, a comparable provision, allowing for three delegates, was included in its bylaws.[38]

Other national organizations: women and young adults. Although women regularly attended meetings of the National Conference as delegates, and on occasions made formal reports to its sessions, their numbers were small and their role limited. Desiring "to act more fully in its work," a number of those present at the 1878 meeting resolved to form a women's auxiliary. A committee prepared the way, and at the 1880 meeting, the Women's Auxiliary Conference was formally established "to stimulate the interest of women in the work of the National Conference, and to assist in raising money for such measures as it recommends." Branches were soon organized in many local churches, and the Auxiliary began to raise funds, which it paid over to the AUA. The strength of the Auxiliary was in the Eastern churches, while in the area of the Western Conference, the Women's Western Unitarian Conference was formed in 1881. A Women's Unitarian Conference, Pacific Coast, was organized in 1890.[39]

As the work gathered momentum, the Auxiliary outgrew its original constitution, which assumed a subordinate relationship to the National Conference. A revision was adopted in 1890, establishing the National Alliance of Unitarian and Other Liberal Christian Women. Instead of turning the funds it collected over to the AUA, the Alliance retained control over them. They were, however, to be used "only for such work as shall be in harmony with the existing National Unitarian organizations." Branch alliances in the local churches were entitled to send delegates to the annual meeting, "one delegate for every thirty members." In due course, the Women's Western Conference and the Pacific Coast Conference were dissolved, and the Women's Alliance became the inclusive national women's organization.[40]

A comparable organization of young adults soon followed, in keeping with the tendencies of the times. Christian Endeavor societies, chiefly but not always Congregational, spread widely in the 1880s; the Methodists organized the Epworth League in 1889 and the Universalists the Young People's Christian Union (YPCU) that same year. Jabez T. Sunderland thereupon criticized his fellow Unitarians for "a singular lack of anything in the organization or activities of the churches calculated to call out the young, and train them to independent thinking and speaking on religious topics." His specific concern was ministerial supply; little wonder, he felt, that Unitarian churches and families produced few home-grown recruits for their pulpits.[41]

The scene was not quite as barren as Sunderland represented it. In the Western Conference, Jenkin Lloyd Jones was promoting Unity Clubs, devoted to discussions of literature and philosophy; a National Bureau of Unity Clubs was formed in 1887. But the Unity Clubs came under criticism for their emphasis on the intellectual side of religion to the neglect of the spiritual side. The corrective was the organization of young people's Guilds, with the goal of "teaching the young people those habits of devotion, those earliest impulses of divine affection toward God and each other that shall make a church within a church, that shall be more sacred and more wholesome in affection as being made up of the church's youngest life." A National Guild Alliance was organized in 1889.[42]

The Unity Clubs were strongest in the West and the Guilds in the East, but the two organizations competed for the same constituency. Inevitably there was pressure for the two to combine. Discussion began in earnest at May Meetings in 1895. A joint committee prepared a plan for an organization "neutral in character and denominational in its aims."[43] The resulting Young People's Religious Union (YPRU) was formally established on May 28, 1896, as a delegate body of clubs and societies. Its Executive Board was made up of six directors, "either officers or past officers of some local young people's society," together with the usual four officers.[44]

It is important to keep in mind that the YPRU was not a

college-age group, let alone a high school group. The upper age limit was understood to be thirty-five. The early promoters and first officers included several young ministers, and the Reverend Thomas Van Ness, the first president, was thirty-seven years old in 1896. The purposes of the organization were to promote local societies, to support them with the service of a paid agent, and to prepare materials, such as a hymnbook and liturgy, geared to the requirements of the local constituency. It was essentially a missionary society, focused on younger—but not very young—Unitarians.

MINISTER AND CONGREGATION

The reconstitution of congregational life advocated by James Freeman Clarke of the Church of the Disciples in Boston before the Civil War became a matter of urgency following it. If a congregation was to do more than assemble once or twice on Sunday to listen to a sermon, if it was to become in some sense a living community, it would have to develop a range of social, intellectual, and charitable activities in which its members would participate. That would call for the development of internal organization: committees and people to lead them.

The development of participating subgroups within the local congregation was a phenomenon characteristic of Protestant churches generally in the later decades of the century.[45] In New England it created problems for the familiar structure of church and parish. The parish had been responsible simply for providing for public worship by maintaining a meetinghouse and paying the salary of the minister. The church had been the body of communicants united by a covenant, which met no more often than half-a-dozen times a year to celebrate the Lord's Supper and on rare occasions to administer discipline. Neither church nor parish had much reason to meet as a body to transact business; neither considered it part of its responsibility to promote sociability, or to organize discussion groups, or to engage in charitable work. Such activities, when they did develop, were carried on outside the formal structure of church and parish, on the initiative of individual persons in the congregation, women perhaps most often, who might or might not be covenanted members of the church or legal members of the parish or society.

Thus significant activity was to be found neither in the atrophied church of the communicants, nor in the incorporated parish of men responsible for temporalities. The congregation of worshipers and adherents, a community with fuzzy boundaries and no formal membership requirements, was now the real religious body. In some instances, though not routinely, the congregation itself developed a structure, with an elected committee and an annual meeting. Local branches of national organizations like the Women's Alliance, with their Cheerful Letter and Post Office Mission committees, were structurally independent.[46]

The dual organization of church and parish had problems enough without introducing a third element. A familiar complaint was that the business affairs of the parish or society were not "vested in the highest religious souls, but rests largely with those who will most freely contribute to its secular prosperity." Decisions by the parish committee might well be taken without regard for the larger religious concerns of the congregation. Ought the business affairs "be regulated by, and conducted within the 'inner circle'"? There was a growing sense that the dual organization should be abandoned and the role of the church enlarged to encompass the entire congregation. The organization of "free religious societies" by the Radicals of the denomination, wiping out old distinctions, was one response.[47]

The need to adapt traditional organization to the new situation was addressed very pointedly in at least one local conference. In 1868, the South Middlesex Conference scheduled a session on "Church Organization" and commissioned a special committee to prepare a report for general discussion. The committee, headed by Edmund H. Sears, sent a questionnaire to all the churches in the Conference, asking whether they had a church as distinct from the congregation as a whole, and what their practices were with respect to the communion service. Twenty-two ministers replied. In four congregations there was no covenanted church; in three more, the distinction between church and congregation had effectively disappeared and anyone could participate in communion; in nine congregations a covenanted body existed but showed no signs of growth; and only in six was there a church with any evidence of vitality. "You must see from this brief recital," wrote Sears, "that our system of church organization, as it now operates, is not giving us generally any results with which we ought to be satisfied."[48] Some of his respondents suggested simply merging the church into the congregation; others demurred but expressed various degrees of perplexity as to what the role of the church might be.

Like James Freeman Clarke, Sears and his committee saw the need for local congregations to assume enlarged functions. One of these was to create "a warm sphere of Christian sympathy and love" in order to meet the emotional needs of people living in lonely isolation. A second was Christian education—why should it be "an adjunct to the society, and not an interest involved in its most vital and central organism?" The third was Christian charity, "for it is true of a church as an individual, that it receives only as it gives." Sears's committee would have the church form a committee on pastoral aid, one on Christian nurture, and one on charities. The church would still be an organization with a covenant and terms of membership, so as to include "the permanent and reliable members," not the floating part of the congregation "having no personal interest in the society, bound to it by no personal tie and never intending to be." But it would be "not only a religious but social institution" and "the home centre for common sympathies and a common fellowship."[49]

Sears belonged to the Christian wing of the denomination, and thought that "the church should be kept in living relations with Jesus Christ." He had no interest in the church as a mere aggregation of curious listeners—which is how some would have characterized Theodore Parker's Twenty-Eighth Congregational Society. Just as Bellows at the national level sought to achieve some sense of organic unity among parochial congregations and opposed the individualism of the day, so at the congregational level, Clarke, Sears, and doubtless others sought to create genuine community as an antidote to "this terrible isolation of our extreme individualism."[50]

The altered shape of congregational life had consequences for the ministry. The preparation and preaching of sermons, and the conduct of Sunday worship, were still the minister's primary obligations and what the laity expected of him. When a prominent member of Bellows's church in New York presented a paper to the National Conference in 1881, entitled "The Layman's Demand on the Ministry," it was almost entirely devoted to the role of the minister as preacher, with only brief reference to "duties of active benevolence and sympathy."[51] But the multiplication of subgroups within the congregation must have affected the pastoral role. The minister was offered new opportunities to reach members of the congregation in a personal way, even though he was himself not the organizer of such groups, except possibly the Sunday school.

Unfortunately, what the minister was gaining in terms of increased contact with members of his flock, he was losing to some degree in terms of intimacy, at a time when lifetime pastorates were less and less common. A paper read in 1868 to the Ministerial Union by one of the older ministers described "A Changing Ministry, or the Brevity of the Pastoral Relation in These Days." It acknowledged advantages to the new order; a church may "find a new impulse, and awaken to new life," while the minister may find new vitality in a change of scene. But to be regretted was the loss of intimate relationships built up over the decades that make it possible for the people "to come to him with freedom for advice in doubt, or for comfort in sorrow."[52]

The concept of the minister as parish administrator was far in the future. A parish might have a part-time sexton, and a very part-time choir director and organist, but it operated without a church office staffed from nine to five. A very active and well-known minister like Edward Everett Hale might eventually have to have the assistance of a personal secretary, but ministers generally wrote their own letters, in longhand—as did Bellows, mostly before breakfast. The finances of the parish were entrusted to a treasurer, very likely a businessman or lawyer in the congregation, who handled them himself as an adjunct to his business affairs. There was no church secretary to produce weekly newsletters, send out notices of meetings of the Standing Committee or Board, prepare the bills for pew rents, run errands for the minister, and respond to miscellaneous inquiries.

The pace of the minister's life was less pressured than in one of the larger churches today, and in important ways more was accomplished. A minister still had time available for thoughtful study and careful writing. The literary quality and intellectual content of the essays, reports, and sermons published in the *Christian Register,* and the *Monthly Religious Magazine,* in the reports of the National Conference, and in book form, command respect. That a high standard of literary achievement was expected of the minister is very clear. Yet even so some saw dangers lying ahead. Speaking to the Unitarian Festival in 1897, Dr. W. H. Lyon feared that the energies of the minister were being diverted in so many directions that the Unitarians were in process of losing their intellectual leadership. One thing threatens no good, he asserted, "the decline of scholarship and literary ability, and an increasing indifference to the learning and knowledge of this wide-awake and abundant time." We pride ourselves on the list of scholars and literary men the denomination has produced, he noted. "Where are their successors?"[53]

UNITARIAN CONSENSUS

From 1865 to 1894, the denomination was engaged in a search for consensus, an attempt to identify the boundaries of the denomination. The tensions between conservative Unitarians and Transcendentalist Unitarians before the War continued after it as a dispute between those who insisted on a Christian identity for the denomination and those who stood for "free religion." There was a genuine concern in some quarters that the denomination would come apart as a result. It did not, and at Saratoga in 1894 an understanding was achieved that assured a united denomination for the next generation.[54]

A consensus necessarily involves limits. Some Unitarians wanted to draw the line so as to include only those who considered Christianity to be a divinely ordained religion, and Jesus Christ in some sense a unique messenger of the way of salvation. The Radicals of the denomination protested that such a boundary would exclude them, and they often argued against any limitation whatsoever. Actually, their objection was to the way the boundary would be drawn, not to the idea of boundaries. None of them would have included within the consensus Trinitarians, believers in double predestination, or those who accepted the infallibility of the pope.

The temptation was resisted to define the boundary with a creedal statement, supported by a mechanism by which a maverick minister might be tried for heresy and disfellowshiped, or an erring church excluded. The Radicals, to be sure, complained that the attempts of Bellows and others to make a descriptive or even normative statement of the position of the denomination was to propose a creed in disguise in an attempt to exclude them. But Bellows's position was that "no excision, denial of Christian standing, or refusal of fellowship, is to be encouraged in either direction, whether towards those leaning towards the old creeds, or those leaning towards Rationalism."⁵⁵ If anyone should be found outside the boundary, it would be by his or her own choice, not by any official act of exclusion. That was how George H. Hepworth took himself out of the denomination at the conservative end of the spectrum and Francis Elling-wood Abbot at the other, while Jabez T. Sunderland and William J. Potter chose to remain within. In this subtle and delicate way, the boundary was established.

The story of the search for consensus from 1865 to 1894 is usually told in terms of various efforts to revise the preamble of the constitution of the National Conference. But what made the final happy outcome possible was not so much debate in formal sessions of the Conference, or similar discussions in meetings of the Western Conference, as it was the existence of a common forum for discussion in the various publications of the denomination. The *Christian Register* appeared weekly; if a divisive issue arose or a controversial report was issued, its columns were open for immediate response and comment. The Year Book controversy in 1873, for example, when the name of William J. Potter was dropped by the AUA from the list of ministers because he did not identify himself as Christian, was disputed over many weeks.

More scholarly discussions of philosophical and theological questions in response to new currents of thought were possible in the *Monthly Religious Magazine* and its successor, the *Unitarian Review and Religious Magazine.* The more radical position within the denomination found an outlet for ongoing commentary in *Unity,* first a fortnightly and then a weekly publication. For ten years, from 1886 to 1897, *The Unitarian* was the monthly journal of the more traditionally Christian group of the Western Conference. These publications made possible the shaping of opinion that was given formal ratification in the decisions of the AUA and National Conference.

All of the publications, it is important to note, were independent of the AUA. They were not the product of a bureaucracy with an official line to promote. Their independence and frequency of publication made possible wide lateral communication within the denomination. Not every minister, let alone every layperson, kept up with what was going on in the denomination by assiduous reading of these publications. But many did, and the possibility existed for all. A common forum was provided, whereby a Rufus Ellis in Boston could learn what was bothering Jenkin Lloyd Jones in Chicago, or William G. Eliot in St. Louis could measure the extent of his disagreement with Octavius Brooks Frothingham. When sharp differences of opinion on matters of policy arose, civility in dispute was no doubt promoted by the awareness that debate was being carried on in public view. It is fair to argue that the resolution of differences that was finally achieved in 1894 had been made possible by the slow growth of consensus through widespread, ongoing exchange of views.

UNIVERSALIST POLITY, 1870–1898

In 1870, a Centennial Session of the General Convention of Universalists was held at Gloucester to commemorate the arrival of John Murray in 1770 and the beginnings of organized Universalism in America. It was a high point of enthusiasm for the 12,000 Universalists attending the celebration. The main accomplishment of the official sessions of the convention, made up of 111 delegates from state conventions, was the adoption of a series of "Laws, Rules, Constitutions and By-Laws." These arrangements, a culmination of the discussions that had gone on for a generation, fixed the formal structure of the denomination for decades thereafter—indeed in important respects until the merger with the Unitarians in 1961.[56]

The Constitution of 1870. The plan provided for three levels of organization: parishes, state conventions, and the General Convention. The parish was recognized as a self-governing congregation, but it was specifically required as terms of fellowship to acknowledge the authority of the General Convention and to adhere doctrinally to the Winchester Confession of Faith (1803). A recommended set of bylaws for local parishes spelled out these limitations. The dual organization of church and parish was recognized as preferred by most Universalists, and recommended bylaws for each were drafted. Individual memberships and the right to hold office at the local level should be terminated in case of refusal to conform to the established conditions of fellowship; no one should serve as minister who was not in fellowship with the General Convention; and in case of the dissolution of a parish, all property should vest in the state convention.

State conventions were recognized as having "jurisdiction" over the parishes. They were to be organized in each state or territory in which there were at least four parishes close enough to cooperate effectively. Their membership should include the following: (1) all ordained clergy in fellowship who were actively engaged in ministry unless "disabled by years or sickness"; (2) the officers of the convention; and (3) lay delegates from the parishes. The previous practice of constituting state conventions by delegates from local associations was deliberately discarded. Such smaller groupings of churches might still be useful and could continue and, indeed, did so. But their purpose was to stimulate fellowship among the churches, and they were not part of the ecclesiastical structure.

The General Convention was envisaged as the ultimate tribunal "by which shall be adjudicated all cases of dispute and difficulty between state conventions, and a Court of Final Appeal before which may be brought cases of discipline and questions of government not provided for and settled by subordinate bodies." It was to be made up of the presidents and secretaries of the state conventions, together with one clerical and two lay delegates from each state or territory. Provision was made for additional delegates from the larger state conventions. "Expressed assent" to the Winchester Confession was a requirement for fellowship with the Convention. The officers were to be a president and a vice president, elected annually, a Board of Trustees elected for four-year terms, and a secretary and a treasurer to hold office at the pleasure of the convention but removable for cause by the Board. The secretary would be an *ex officio* member of the Board. While the Convention was empowered to hold trust funds and raise money, and was authorized to require reports and statistics from organizations and clergy "subject to its jurisdiction," its role was essentially ecclesiastical, not administrative.

This hierarchical structure was presbyterian rather than congregational, and there were distinctly uncongregational features in the structure of state conventions. Ministers were members of state conventions by definition, not because they were sent there by their churches. A basic congregational principle is that each local church has full power over the choice of its leadership, but the Universalists restricted that choice to ministers in fellowship with the state convention. A church would lose its standing in the state convention if it settled a minister not in fellowship, or one who had been refused fellowship, or one disfellowshiped. Fellowship was likewise to be withdrawn from any minister who accepted settlement in a church that had been disfellowshiped, or who entered "upon ministerial labor under the auspices of, or into fellowship with, any other denomination." While ordinations should be by advice of councils, the councils would be authorized by the state convention, not summoned by the ordaining church, as was the traditional congregational practice. The use of ordaining councils soon disappeared, and later versions of the "Laws of Fellowship, Government and Discipline" made the state conventions themselves the ordaining authority.

As a blueprint for ecclesiastical organization, these provisions were clear, consistent, and architectonically nicely balanced. As a plan for a large denomination of Presbyterians, widely distributed geographically and accustomed to hierarchical authority, they would have been most appropriate. But they were wholly unsuited for a small denomination, unevenly distributed throughout the country, whose members had never been eager to support centralized organization. For Universalists, they perpetuated rather than solved the problem of the ineffectualness of the General Convention.

The emphasis on state conventions was especially damaging since the times called for the development of administrative structures to deal with a variety of denominational concerns, and disciplinary structures are not well suited for administration. The conventions operated through part-time officers and *ad hoc* committees. Committees can formulate policy, but they are never effective for the administration of policy.

A suggested model constitution for state conventions asserted an obligation to devote attention to such matters as "the history and statistics of Universalism within its borders; educational interests including Sunday Schools and the best methods for their management, missionary works, and the care of infirm or indigent ministers and their families." Characteristically this obligation was met by the passing of resolutions: that more churches should be organized; that the members should contribute more money; that a higher sense of obligation to the cause should be aroused. Sometimes the secretary of one of the larger conventions or one of the settled ministers did some missionary work in addition to regular duties. But the usual response was that funds were lacking to do more. That was indeed a persistent problem. But equally crucial was a pervasive acceptance of the notion that administration needs no more than part-time attention. The state conventions were too small to justify professional administration, while the General Convention was too weak to undertake it.

CONSENSUS: THE BOUNDARIES
OF THE UNIVERSALIST DENOMINATION

Within two years of the 1870 convention, two cases of discipline had been appealed to the General Convention. One of them occasioned widespread discussion. It was the disfellowshiping of Herman Bisbee by the Minnesota State Convention on grounds of "preaching heretical doctrines" and "unbrotherly conduct."[57] Bisbee was the minister of the Universalist church in St. Anthony, near St. Paul. While serving briefly in Quincy, Massachusetts, in 1869, he had developed a sympathy for the transcendentalism of men like Emerson and an interest in the "radicalism" then agitating the Unitarians. On his return to St. Anthony he became an advocate of "natural religion," which led to a controversy with the minister of the Minneapolis Universalist church. His views were denounced in Universalist journals, and charges brought against him in the Minnesota State Convention were sustained by a vote of 47 to 23.

He appealed to the General Convention, where the Board of Trustees established a special six-man Board of Appeal. It is a curious fact that no mention whatsoever appears in the official minutes of the Convention. The report of the Board of Appeal, which sustained the action of the State Convention, was printed without comment in the record of the annual session of the General Convention of 1873.[58] Bisbee himself eventually joined the Unitarians.

The importance of the Bisbee heresy trial was that it raised the question whether the denomination really wanted the Presbyterian-style discipline it had adopted in 1870. The Convention that year had established "explicit consent" to the Winchester Confession as a requirement for fellowship with the denomination, and it had provided disciplinary procedures so that ecclesiastical authority could maintain the boundaries of the denomination. But some promptly argued that the Winchester Confession had never been intended, and for almost seventy years had never been used, as a creedal test of good standing. It had stated in simple terms three basic principles identifying the Universalists among the several sects and denominations, but it had added a so-called "liberty clause," providing that churches and associations were free to formulate their own confessions so long as "they do not disagree with our general profession and plan." The Winchester Confession is best understood as a consensus statement, identifying a normative understanding of the Universalist position as of 1803, not as a creedal test to be used for disciplinary purposes.

How the boundaries of a denomination are established, and who makes the decision whether a minister or a church belongs outside rather than inside the boundary, are basic questions of church polity. It was soon obvious that the decision of 1870 could not stand. For twenty-five years, the denomination's response was to try to revise the Winchester Confession so as to accommodate the developing views of Christian Universalists—though not to include free-religionists like Bisbee. The attempt was fruitless. Finally, in 1899, a new article was added to the Constitution of the Convention, which in effect restored the old "liberty clause" that had been omitted in 1870. It repeated the words of the Winchester Confession as a document of historic significance embodying essential principles of the Universalist faith, but added: "neither this, nor any other precise form of words is required as a condition of fellowship, provided always that the principles above stated be professed." The denomination had once again affirmed a consensus statement, leaving it to individuals and churches to decide if they could properly and conscientiously assent.[59]

UNIVERSALIST ADMINISTRATION

In the absence of any central administrative machinery to act for the denomination as a whole, such activities as missionary extension, publications, and support of struggling churches were carried on piecemeal by a patchwork of organizations of limited scope. The most important program of missionary activity was undertaken by the women of the denomination, sometimes in cooperation but often in tension with the General Convention. This work had its inception at the time of the 1870 celebration, when the "Murray Centenary Fund" was projected for the education of the clergy, for publications, and for church extension. The drive never reached its goal, since a number of states never met their quotas, but a very substantial contribution was made by the women, organized as the Woman's Centenary Aid Association. The women did not disband after the celebration, but continued under a succession of names: Woman's Centenary Association (1871–1905), Woman's National Missionary Association (1905–39), and the Association of Universalist Women (1939–63).[60]

The Woman's Centenary Association (WCA) was a dues-paying organization of individuals, headed by a president and an executive board. The funds raised through dues and special collections were divided, part to be spent in the state where they were raised and part going to the treasurer of the General Convention for national work. Women organized some state missionary societies as well, either auxiliary to the WCA or independent of it. The WCA sponsored a missionary in Scotland beginning in 1878 and later made contributions to the Japan Mission. The independent status of the WCA created tension at times between it and the General Convention. In 1874, the report of the Board of Trustees to the General Convention noted that the purposes of the WCA were substantially the same as those of the Convention, but complained that the Association was a body which is the rival, not to say the antagonist, of the Convention, alienating sympathy from it; and which, assuming to make appeals and to exercise functions that, by the whole genius of our organization, belong exclusively to the Convention, is challenging the attention and loyalty of our people, and asking for their money, as if there were no Convention, or as if its right to make such appeals and to exercise such functions were as legitimate and unquestionable as that of the Convention itself.[61]

The officers of the Association and those of the Convention reached an understanding, by which the Association was recognized as an arm of the Convention, reporting to it. But in practice, the Association continued as a virtually independent enterprise. No doubt an ingredient in the situation was that the General Convention was predominantly male and its Board of Trustees entirely male for most of the time between 1870 and the end of the century. In addition, the leading spirit and first president of the Association was Caroline A. Soule, a woman of great drive and energy despite ill health.[62]

The most flourishing Universalist enterprise was surely the Universalist Publishing House, likewise independent of the General Convention. It had its beginnings in 1862, sponsored by the Massachusetts State Convention. In 1872, the suggestion was made that it become a "truly denominational interest" by placing it under the control of the General Convention.[63] Instead, the shareholders transferred their stock to a board of trustees, elected by the state conventions of the six New England states, dominated by Massachusetts. The Publishing House acquired property in downtown Boston, and for many Universalists the building was a more tangible focus of denominational identity than the address of the secretary of the Convention. It was the Publishing House that independently compiled and published the annual *Universalist Register* with its listing of churches, ministers, state conventions, colleges and academies, and necrology. The *Register* duly listed the officers of the Convention, but it gave no post office addresses for them; the only such address included was that of the Publishing House itself.

By 1882, the Publishing House was able to produce a descriptive catalogue of books, tracts, and periodicals, running to eighty-five pages.[64] The periodicals included such important Universalist journals as the weekly *Christian Leader*, the *Universalist Quarterly*, and a weekly Sunday school magazine entitled *The Myrtle*. These magazines represented the merger of a number of earlier journals, at least one of them dating from 1819. As was the usual practice in American Protestantism, they had been founded by enterprising individual ministers, but were taken over by the Publishing House, one by one, in the 1860s and 1870s.

Thus the state conventions were responsible for fellowshiping; the Publishing House produced the books, tracts, and journals of the denomination; and much of the missionary work was carried on by the Woman's Centenary Association. The administrative responsibilities left to the General Convention consisted of the investment of certain permanent funds and the distribution of the income to needy churches, together with such additional funds as could be extracted from reluctant local churches. The minimal administrative duties were carried out most of the time by the permanent secretary whose primary task was to publish the annual *Minutes* of the Convention and to keep in touch with all the state conventions. A separate office, that of General Secretary, was established in 1867, continuing briefly under the new constitution of 1870. The general secretary was intended to be the administrative officer of the Convention. He was to "aid in the more complete organization of Universalists"; as opportunity afforded he was to visit conventions and churches to appeal for funds; he was to "attempt the rehabilitation of suspended Societies, and suggest the help of weak ones" and "in all ways, by counsel or otherwise, aid the

Churches toward greater prosperity."[65] After a decade of indifferent success and difficulty in finding the right person to fill the office, it was allowed to lapse in 1876.[66] The need continued and led, two decades later, to the establishment of the office of General Superintendent.

UNITARIANS AND UNIVERSALISTS IN 1899

By the close of the century, the two denominations had developed significantly different polities. Both were congregational so far as local churches were concerned. But the Universalists had constructed, at least on paper, a hierarchical disciplinary polity, while the Unitarians had emphasized associational organization in support of missionary activity.

The two denominations were alike in their rejection of the Reformed theology, and beginning with Bellows in 1865, occasional voices urged closer relationships. In 1899, a resolution was introduced at the annual meeting of the AUA, inviting the Universalist General Convention to join in appointing a conference committee "which shall consider plans of closer co-operation, devise ways and means for more efficient usefulness."[67]

The committee was established, though it accomplished little. The differences between the two denominations were still too great. Some of the differences were social, going back to the time when the Unitarians were part of the Standing Order while the Universalists were opposed, and antagonisms remained. The Universalists had never passed through a Transcendentalist phase, nor did they have a free-religionist or radical wing, and they cherished a warmer style of piety than the Unitarians. Certain Universalists, Edwin G. Sweetser the most prominently, opposed anything but token cooperation, on the ground that the Unitarians were no longer a Christian denomination.

The consequence was that any leader from either side who advocated cooperation had to protest that no organic union was intended.[68] Hence the questions of adjustments in polity that a merger would entail never entered the discussion, though differences in polity would doubtless have precluded union at that time.[69]

Professionalized Administration, 1898–1937/41

For similar reasons, 1898 was an important year for both the Unitarians and the Universalists. In that year, Samuel A. Eliot became the chief administrative officer of the AUA. His title at first was Secretary, but two years later, a revision of the bylaws gave him the title of President. Likewise in 1898, the Universalists finally established the office of General Superintendent and chose Isaac M. Atwood for the position. Eliot saw it as his task to professionalize a bureaucratic organization already existing but run by amateurs.[1] The Universalists had to begin much farther back; they really never caught up.

THE AUA—ADMINISTRATIVE REFORMS

In 1894, when Samuel A. Eliot was elected for a three-year term on the Board of Directors of the AUA, the paid administrative staff consisted of the secretary and the assistant secretary—the Reverend Grindall Reynolds and George W. Fox—and one clerk. The treasurer received a small stipend for very part-time services. The Association also contributed to the salaries of "superintendents" engaged in missionary activity in five designated sections of the country. While money was used for certain special causes—the Montana Indian School, for example—the resources of the Association were almost entirely devoted to missionary work and aid to struggling churches. General supervision was entrusted to standing committees of the Board of Directors.[2] In cooperation with the Committee on Supply of Pulpits of the Ministerial Union, the assistant secretary of the AUA was involved in ministerial settlement. In short, denominational administration was carried on by a group of committees made up of devoted volunteers, with minimal paid staff support.

Much that later became a part of headquarters administration was outside its sphere. The Church Building Loan Fund was formally under the jurisdiction of the AUA, but it had a separate set of trustees and operated with virtually entire autonomy. Retirement allowances were left to the Society for the Relief of Aged and Destitute Clergy.[3] The Committee on Fellowship was established by the National Conference. The Unitarian Sunday School Society, engaged in the preparation of curricular materials, was an independent organization related directly to the churches. Like the AUA, its membership was made up both of individual members and of delegates from the churches. It had its own annual meeting, addressed by ministers concerned with problems of education; it printed an annual report including a listing of member churches; it had its own invested funds and sources of income; it had its own program for the publication of books and tracts.

When Eliot became a member of the board, he already had a clear idea of the reforms he hoped to advance. He laid out some of them in December 1894, in an address to the Unitarian Club of Boston—an organization of prominent Unitarian laymen from the several Boston churches.[4] His first concern was the organizational setup, by which the secretary's task was merely to implement the decisions of the Board. "Our work has far outgrown our organization," Eliot declared. "The administrative methods of fifty or twenty-five years ago are utterly inadequate for the present emergency." It is absolutely necessary, he continued, "that the secretary should have larger discretion and more responsible authority." To give him "a dignity and an authority and a force," the chief executive officer should be given the title of President. It looks very much as though Eliot was drawing on a role model close at hand, the president of Harvard University, who was his own father.

Eliot's second concern was the policy of providing continued small subsidies to churches that never made the effort to become self-supporting. "We pauperize too many churches," he complained. "Our methods of continued aid plug the springs of local effort." He would have such subsidies reduced year by year, to stimulate aided churches to financial independence.

His third recommendation addressed the prevailing practice of using bequests for current expenditures. It is a well-established principle in the administration of trust funds, he argued, "that it is wise to invest all bequests and legacies as permanent endowment." He recognized the many temptations to use such funds immediately and was well aware of the arguments used to justify the practice. But this system encourages a short-range view of the Association's mission, he insisted, with the result that "expenditure is too often improvident and the unwelcome retrenchments difficult to make." He would encourage the building of a permanent endowment sufficient to meet the salaries and fixed charges of the Association, so that contributions from the churches could go directly into field work. Let the "diffusion of pure Christianity" be "a perpetual, and not a temporary beneficence, by making our funds permanent, our institutions secure, our expenditure wise, just and economical."

Eliot's influence was quickly felt on the Board. In March 1896, he served on a committee that recommended the adoption of the second and third of his proposed reforms.[5] In addition, a system of budgeting annual income and expenditures was introduced, structured by four "departments": maintenance, publications, foreign missions, and home missions.[6] Eliot's first proposal, to give the executive larger authority and discretion, was to all intents and purposes achieved when the secretary of the Association resigned at the end of 1898, and the Board chose him to fill the vacancy. William Wallace Fenn of Chicago, who had opposed certain of Eliot's reforms, was one of four members of the Board to vote against his election, because he feared that as a strong executive he would increase the power of the central organization at the expense of the churches.[7] It was obvious that Eliot intended to be a much more energetic and forceful administrator than his predecessors, and the title was soon changed, as he desired, to President.

The designation of Eliot as President was more than a simple change in nomenclature, since in that capacity he now presided both over annual meetings of the Association and over meetings of the Board, and he frequently chaired special committees to deal with topics that particularly interested him. Small but indicative changes came quickly: the *Year Book* and the published annual reports were redesigned with new format, larger type, and half-tone pictures. More significant changes came as well. "If the work of the Association is to be extended," Eliot wrote, "an adequate and experienced office staff is necessary, and the appointment of such a staff is a real economy."[8] A publication agent was appointed in 1901 to give attention "to the improvement and enlargement of the tract list, to the securing of manuscripts, to the pushing of the sale of the Association's publications, to negotiations with other publishers for issuing the works of Unitarian writers, and to the extension of the retail business now carried on."[9] From this staff position, Beacon Press ultimately developed.[10]

In due course, the four "departments" increased to twelve, several of them headed by full-time staff members. In a formal sense, the paid staff worked under standing committees of the Board, while the general officers were intended "as agents of unification and co-operation" in the department work, without vote in the standing committees.[11] But one can hardly doubt that the intermittent guidance of a standing committee was of less consequence than the daily activity of the president and other full-time officers.

Administrative reform at headquarters was for the sake of more effective missionary activity in the field. Eliot regarded it as his primary task to energize the denomination at large into more vigorous missionary activity. Field secretaries reporting to headquarters were more regularly appointed; the National Conference had been advocating them for a decade or more, but the positions had often remained unfilled. Field secretaries were given regional jurisdiction—as, for example, New England, or Middle States and Canada, or Pacific Coast—and regional "missionary councils," made up of the representatives of state or local conferences, were established to advise the board committee concerned with church extension.[12] Both president and secretary spent much of their time on the road, visiting the churches, exhorting them to fresh exertions, preaching almost every Sunday, "more often than not preaching in two different churches on Sunday."[13]

A tendency to concentrate authority was apparent. The semi-autonomous trustees of the Building Loan Fund became a board committee in 1903. But the biggest single enlargement of the scope of activities of the Association was the development in 1912 of a Department of Religious Education, which promptly took over the work of the Unitarian Sunday School Society. After the resuscitation of that society in the 1870s and 1880s, it had undertaken an extensive program of publication of manuals and lesson helps for Sunday school teachers. It was given office space and a bookroom at Unitarian headquarters, and it employed its own clerical staff. Its president came to be a sort of field secretary, making visits to churches for consultation and the promotion of the cause. Like the AUA, it depended on churches and individuals for financial support, and ultimately it was governed by an annual meeting made up of both delegates from the churches and individual members.

The Society's finances were inadequate, however, and the solution to its problems was to appoint its president as the secretary of the new Department of Religious Education. For twenty-five years, the Society and the Association jointly sponsored the work of the department. But the Association increasingly underwrote the budgets, and in 1937 a complete merger was effected. The Society did not disband, but its annual meetings became simply occasions for discussion of issues relating to religious education.[14]

In 1900, the headquarters staff consisted of the president, the secretary, an assistant secretary, the treasurer, and three field agents. Ten years later, three full-time department secretaries, a publication agent, and a clerical staff of ten had been added. In another five years, after the absorption of the Sunday School Society's work, the professional staff numbered eleven, supported by a clerical staff of thirteen. This expansion did not proceed without criticism. At the annual meeting in 1911, a resolution was offered critical of Eliot's policy of capitalizing all bequests, and underlying discontent emerged. Eliot's administration was attacked as being more concerned with the accumulation of large endowments than in using money for the church extension. The Reverend John Haynes Holmes was particularly aggressive in criticism. This is the conflict, he asserted, "between the business man and the prophet." He had wanted to follow the leadership of the president, but he could do so no longer. "I am not looking for the business man who can accumulate funds," he continued. "I am looking for a prophet of the soul who can lead us on. . . . And alas! The prophet does not appear, but always the calculation of dollars and cents, always the restriction of funds, always the piling up of endowments."[15] A year later, at the annual meeting in 1912, an attempt was made, unsuccessfully, to find a candidate to run against Dr. Eliot, but he was re-elected overwhelmingly.[16]

One consequence of the vigorous administration of Eliot was an acceleration of a tendency to make the AUA the important focus of denominational activity and to relegate the National Conference to a secondary role. As long as Bellows was alive, major initiatives in the denomination came from the National Conference, while the AUA carried on activities of limited scope in the familiar way. Bellows conceived of the Conference as the central deliberative body for the Unitarian churches, and the AUA as one of several instruments through which its initiatives would be made effective. His death in 1882, followed in 1884 by the decision to give the churches the right to be represented in meetings of the AUA, changed the scope of the two organizations and shifted the balance between them.

In 1905, the chairman of the Council of the National Conference acknowledged that he could no longer make to the assembled delegates a report of the kind originally intended. "The council no longer performs the duties once assigned to it," George Batchelor declared, "because responsibility for our work has been divided among other organizations, and the Conference has divested itself of the power which it claimed at the beginning."

> When the Unitarian Association became a representative body, the Conference surrendered nearly all its executive functions. It now neither asks nor receives reports from the churches; it publishes no list of them, and has ceased to attend to their special needs.[17]

One surviving responsibility was the work of the Fellowship Committee, which continued to supervise the list of ministers for publication in the *Year Book.* This was in keeping with the concept of the Conference as an ecclesiastical body, not an administrative body like the AUA. Batchelor defended the retention of this authority as a protection against ecclesiastical politics, the bane of denominational bureaucracies:

With some instinct of wisdom the Conference retained control of this committee, thinking it to be wholly undesirable that our missionary society, the American Unitarian Association, should be tempted by the control of patronage to exercise undue authority over the ministers of our body, to control their fortunes, to say who should or who should not be admitted to fellowship, who should be allowed to preach as candidates in vacant pulpits and in what pulpits they should appear, or decide when they had completed their period of usefulness, and when, if ever, their names should be dropped from the list of ministers in good and regular standing in the Unitarian body.[18]

As with the programs administered by the AUA, the work of the Fellowship Committee was becoming more thoroughly organized and its rules more elaborate—in short, showing signs of becoming itself more bureaucratic. Originally there had been four regional committees of three members each. The number was increased to five in 1897, and an executive committee to coordinate their work was established in 1903. In 1909, the number of subcommittees was increased to six, and procedures for the executive committee and subcommittees was spelled out in much greater detail. Six criteria for the removal of names from the list by the executive committee were given; the need for subcommittees to pursue careful investigation of applicants for recognition was emphasized; and churches were not to settle ministers who had not received the approval of the Fellowship Committee.[19]

By this time, most of the sessions of the biennial National Conference were given over to informational reports from various organizations, such as the Sunday School Society and the Women's Alliance, and to prepared papers on general themes, such as "The Emphasis Needed in Religion." In 1905, the only matter of a substantive nature considered was a series of amendments to the rules of the Committee on Fellowship.

Power had gone to the AUA, where there was money to spend, a growing staff to spend it, and leadership ready to do so.

THE CHURCHES AND THE MINISTRY

Young President Eliot seems to have had an impulse to tidy up the denomination at large as well as to reform headquarters at 25 Beacon Street. If he did not presume to prescribe for the churches what they would be required to do—and he was actually very careful not to invade local autonomy—he was ready to explain to them what they ought to do in order to regularize their procedures and practices. In 1900–1901 he chaired two committees, one to "collect and codify the church covenants and statements of faith now in use," the other to prepare a *Handbook for Unitarian Congregational Churches.*

The first of these committees sent out a questionnaire to all 459 churches listed in the *Year Book* and received responses from 250 of them. The responses were of varying usefulness; some were dismissed as "too hypothetical or theoretical to be taken as serious statements of existing conditions." But they indicate "the conditions and tendencies" that prevailed in the local churches.[20]

The opening query related to the use of a covenant, or bond of fellowship, or similar organizing statement for the church or society. It appeared that ninety churches had adopted some variant of the wording composed by Charles G. Ames, often referred to as the "Spring Garden Covenant," which the National Conference had recommended to the churches in 1899.[21] Another 111 cases reported some other covenant or preamble or locally devised wording. Some of these were highly theological, others purely business in character having no spiritual purpose, and still others "evidently resurrected from the tomb of oblivion for the benefit of the Committee."[22] None, however, was identified as imposing creedal restrictions on membership. Forty-one churches reported no statement of any kind.

Next the committee inquired as to the number of organizations constituting the local body—that is to say, was there a distinction between church and parish or society, or indeed, was there still a third group of proprietors holding title to the real property. Only one organization, variously termed "Church," or "Parish," or "Society," was reported in 148 cases. The tendency was clearly to discard the dual organization, a tendency Eliot and his committee were eager to encourage.

The third query related to the manner of admission to the church or society. Forty-five required only a signature in the record book. Ninety-six reported a ceremony of some kind. Twenty-one included financial support as a condition. Forty-three seemed to have no form of admission at all. The Committee discerned a considerable reluctance on the part of "elderly people" to participate in a ceremony of admission or to encourage their children to do so, perhaps because of a lingering association with exclusive regenerate membership in the orthodox churches.

Other queries concerned the encouragement to young people to become members of the church, the need for definite and accurate membership lists, and the practice of holding confirmation classes. It was apparent that there was strong reaction against the Episcopalian flavor of the term "confirmation class," though a number of respondents approved of some sort of preparatory class for young people joining the church. This meant an explicit recognition that Unitarian churches had long since acknowledged "birthright membership," as contrasted with the Puritan and evangelical concept of the church as composed of regenerate Christians who have had some sort of conversion experience in mature years. Children were to be "received and dedicated into the church as [their] birthright"; they were to be guided and counseled through the years of religious training; and they were finally to be welcomed "to the full privileges and responsibilities of the church into which he or she was born."[23]

The Committee's report ended with a series of recommendations, such as the elimination of the obsolescent church/ parish dualism, the use of a covenant or bond of fellowship to sharpen the identity of the church, and an accurate listing of those who become members by subscribing to the covenant.[24] Eliot's other committee promptly incorporated these recommendations into the *Handbook for Unitarian Congregational Churches* issued the same year.[25]

The *Handbook* replaced an earlier pamphlet, by then both out of date and out of print.[26] It was intended especially as a guide for those forming new churches, but its compilers hoped that established churches would take heed also, since greater conformity of operation would bring the churches "into closer and more sympathetic fellowship."[27] It specified procedures for initial organization, including a model form for constitution and bylaws, which made it clear that no theological test or confession of spiritual experience is requisite for membership in a Unitarian church. Yet "it may wisely be provided that a proper committee first assure itself of the moral probity and serious intention of all persons applying for membership before they are received into full enrollment."[28] It outlined the method for calling and installing a minister, with advice as to the procedure for candidating; it gave instructions as to business methods and urged their importance; it explained how to organize the Sunday school, the branch Women's Alliance, and the local Young People's Religious Union; and it discussed in some detail, with illustrative models, the practice of public worship.

One concern characteristic of Eliot crops up from time to time in the *Handbook*. It is that sound procedures generally accepted are essential to avoid blunders that may disrupt the harmony of a church and jeopardize its life. Proper procedures for candidating will "protect the pulpit against clerical adventurers and vagrants." Membership should be clearly defined "for the peace and security of the church." The clerk must be held "to the strict and scrupulous" discharge of duty, since in more than one case, "the whole property of a church has been imperilled by a careless keeping of its corporate records." Such admonitions suggest that a good deal of informality actually prevailed in the way churches handled their business affairs.[29]

The compilers were thoroughly conversant with the history and essential principles of congregational polity, which they praised as "a noble heritage of independence, made effective for human welfare by co-operation and fellowship." Their recommendations accorded well with basic congregational principles; indeed they claimed that the Unitarian churches, "almost alone among Christian churches, hold to the democratic principle of self-government in its purity and integrity."[30]

In significant respects, the congregationalism of the *Handbook* is purer than what has been accepted since. It states as long tradition that "a man is not properly a candidate for ordination until he has received and accepted a call to the pastorate of some church or has been commissioned by some competent body to undertake missionary or other ministerial work."[31] It recognizes as "long established (though not invariable) custom" the role of ordaining councils; and it explains with care how the traditional elements of an ordination service represent a liturgical or ritual expression of the central meaning of congregational polity.[32] Though prepared under the direction of a denominational administrator, and with his very active involvement, it is scrupulous in respecting the freedom and independence of the local church. "The churches thus co-operating have no power to control the action of any particular church. Their association is purely voluntary, and does not comprehend the assumption or exercise of any authority."[33] Eliot thought the denomination had found the way "to sustain a strong national association which shall serve its constituents rather than seek to make itself their master."[34] In 1901, Eliot eschewed hierarchical authority. But he seems to have had little awareness of the ways in which the bureaucratic machinery he was eager to build would later be used to coerce both ministers and churches.

Apart from detailed instructions for settling and installing the minister, the *Handbook* has little to say about his relationship to the congregation. It states that he should be a member of the Sunday school committee *ex officio* if he is not acting as superintendent. The only reference to business matters is the injunction that the minister should be paid regularly on the first of the month along with the choir and sexton. He might possibly be the person to issue a printed request for gifts for the charitable work of the church, though preferably this matter should be handled by the officers of the church.[35]

The *Handbook* assumes a traditional ministry of preaching and pastoral care, with little or no involvement in parish administration. It assumes as normal one minister in each church, in which administration is carried on by lay volunteers. But other voices soon insisted that this model was no longer adequate. Especially in urban churches, the demand was increasing for churches to provide a variety of social and philanthropic services for less and less homogeneous communities.[36] "Our parish committees tacitly assume a leisure now unknown to volunteer workers," wrote Louis C. Cornish in 1912, "and a non-existent social and intellectual community of interests." The result was an impossible burden placed on the minister, left to do what volunteers no longer could. "Both to preach well and to ably administer he would need the strength of more than one man and the wits of at least several men."[37] The inevitable result was a weakening either of the pulpit or of the administration.

To address this problem, Eliot recommended the organization of training schools for parish workers. There is, he believed, a "rare opportunity in our body for educating and employing the services of talented and consecrated young women who do not wish to devote themselves to the work of the pulpit, but who are ready, if they can secure the adequate training, for service as parish assistants, Sunday-school superintendents and teachers, parish visitors, and managers of the philanthropic or educational activities of our churches."[38] On Eliot's initiative, the Board of the AUA authorized the establishment of such a school in 1907, naming it in honor of Joseph Tuckerman, the early minister-at-large in Boston. The school was set up with an independent board of trustees, not as a part of headquarters operations. Its two-year program combined work at the School for Social Workers, under the joint auspices of Harvard University and Simmons College,[39] with instruction in such fields as Sunday school methods, parish administration, the use of the Bible in teaching, church history, and the like.[40] The Tuckerman School, with quarters on Beacon Hill, lasted for about thirty years but was a casualty of the Great Depression. Its program was a recognition of the fact that many churches needed an enlarged professional staff. But it also pointed to a future day when directors of religious education would insist on status as a recognized professional group and eventually would seek ordination.

By 1912, Eliot had placed his own firm imprint on the denomination. His early reforms of financial policy were well established, though a few critics still argued that bequests might properly be used for aggressive missionary work.[41] The scope of the Association's activities had been enlarged by the organization of new departments, the final step being the absorption of the Sunday School Society's operations. A bureaucratic staff had been assembled to carry on the enlarged work with greater efficiency.

Throughout these fourteen years as the chief executive officer, Eliot had been concerned as well for the development of a sharper denominational consciousness and loyalty. If the churches are to win the battle with paganism and materialism, he declared, they must get closer together. His extensive trips throughout the country, with speaking engagements in many churches, were intended to promote a sense of common endeavor among scattered Unitarians. One reflection of this concern was the preparation, by three committees, of a new ministers' handbook, a new book of services for congregational worship, and a new hymnal. Eliot served on the three committees. These publications were thought of as promoting an increased sense of community throughout the denomination. As John Howland Lathrop put it in reporting for the committee on the service book:

> I look forward to the day when we can go from one to another of our churches and feel at home because of the familiar utterances at the beginning of our services. Nothing could contribute more to the sense of membership in a body reaching beyond the limits of the single parish than the ability to lose oneself at once in the church where we may chance to be, by the use of phrases endeared at home.[42]

Eliot stood for "collective efficiency" in the administration of 25 Beacon Street, but he always understood the AUA to be the servant of the churches, not their master exercising authority over them. Deeply rooted in the tradition of New England congregationalism, and knowledgeable of its history as few administrators have been since, he respected the autonomy of the local church, and he was careful not to use administrative power for coercion or control.

At the same time, he was well aware of the tendency of local churches to be very parochial in their outlook. The Universalists sought to counterbalance this tendency by attempting, quite unsuccessfully, to construct a hierarchical polity. Eliot's way was to encourage cooperative endeavor and to develop a clearer shared identity for the denomination. In this, he was true to a basic principle of the polity he clearly understood and believed in: that congregational polity means, not the autonomy of the particular church, but the communion of autonomous churches.[43]

THE UNIVERSALIST GENERAL SUPERINTENDENCY

The ecclesiastical structure adopted by the Universalists in 1870 continued basically unchanged to the close of the century. As outlined earlier, the "General Plan of Organization" provided for a General Convention with jurisdiction over all clergy and denominational organizations. State conventions exercised similar jurisdiction within their bounds, subject to the General Convention, to which they sent delegates. Local parishes, organized for religious improvement and the support of public worship, were entitled to representation in their state conventions. In a territory where no state convention existed, the parishes might unite to send two delegates directly to the General Convention. In a number of states, the associations of churches dating back to the early decades of the century continued to meet for sociability, but they did not exercise disciplinary power.

In this structure, the state conventions were of far greater importance than the General Convention. They admitted ministers to fellowship and ordained them at their annual sessions. They exercised original jurisdiction in cases of discipline of clergy, and only in cases of appeal would the matter be referred to a special board appointed by the Trustees of the General Convention. The *Manual* of the General Convention strongly recommended that the property of individual parishes be deeded either to the state convention or to the General Convention, "receiving back a conveyance with such conditions that the property can never be alienated from the purpose to which it was originally dedicated."[44] In this way, it was thought, if a parish should be dissolved, its property would be held in trust for the benefit of some future parish in the same neighborhood. This procedure was widely accepted, with the result that over the years the larger state conventions, such as New York and Massachusetts, built up substantial endowments from the dissolution of churches within their borders.

The annual sessions of state conventions, two or three days in length, were often well attended and fully reported in the *Christian Leader* (after 1897, the *Universalist Leader*). The General Convention began by meeting annually, but in 1889 a change was made to biennial sessions. Its discussions of revising the Winchester Confession attracted attention, but on the whole, its sessions aroused no more interest than the more frequent meetings of the state conventions. Its Board of Trustees needed only three meetings a year to transact its business. The only full-time officer was the secretary of the Convention, responsible for keeping its records, compiling the register of ministers and parishes, enrolling the delegates to the Convention, preparing the report of the Convention for publication, and conducting whatever correspondence was required.[45]

What had been conceived as an orderly hierarchical structure had failed to produce a denomination with a central focus of loyalty and locus of authority. Voices of complaint began to be heard, especially in the late nineties. In October 1896, Dr. Willard C. Selleck argued for the appointment of one or more men to supervise the churches, especially the smaller ones, to give them the inspiration and encouragement to continue; this was, in effect, a revival of the position of General Secretary that had earlier been authorized but never implemented. In January 1897, the Reverend Fred W. Dillingham complained: "Our polity, such as we have had, has been ill adapted to individual Christian development, parish prosperity, or denominational growth." It had failed to reconcile divergent interests of particular churches; incompetent ministers, laymen, and churches could not be checked; there was no satisfactory increase of numbers; the best power was going to waste; the polity was not conducive to the prosecution of missionary enterprises; ministerial fellowship was deficient. In October 1898, Dr. Almon Gunnison declared: "We have State Conventions but they are not heartily supported; we have a General Convention but its petitions are unheeded and its policies are supported or neglected according to the mood or whim of those who tentatively recognize its authority."[46]

In response to such widely expressed concerns, about seventy ministers gathered in Chicago, just prior to the General Convention meeting in October 1897, and prepared a memorial to the Convention urging the appointment of a general field secretary "to stimulate and supervise the spiritual activities of the churches." The appointment of salaried state superintendents, already found in some states, should be encouraged, and together with the field secretary they should constitute a Council of Administration to promote "pastoral efficiency and continuity," ensure "the suitable settlement of pastors," and "devise and put into execution a general system of evangelism within and beyond the churches."[47] The delegates approved the proposal and instructed the Board of Trustees to perfect the details and put the scheme into operation. After much discussion in three successive committees of the Board, agreement was finally reached. The term "Field Secretary" was discarded, however, as was "Bishop," which had been suggested more than once in articles in the *Leader*. In October 1898, the Board appointed Dr. Isaac M. Atwood of the St. Lawrence Theological School as the first General Superintendent of the Universalist Church.[48]

Dr. Atwood was not an administrator, nor was it intended that he would be. The role was ecclesiastical, not executive. The Board of Trustees of the General Convention recognized him as "Arbitrator, Adviser, Conciliator, Inspirer General!" Widely known and respected in the denomination, Atwood fitted the position well. He traveled widely—32,000 miles the first year—attending state conventions when possible, but focusing his attention especially on local parishes, which he regarded as "the true unit and motor of our denominational life." He found a new and hopeful spirit, but he also found "almost everywhere evidences of unwise administration in former years, of strife and the desolations they never fail to make." Cases both of ministers and of parishes "requiring investigation" came to his attention.[49]

Though Atwood was personally highly regarded, disagreement continued over the nature and usefulness of the office. The Reverend Marion Crosley argued that the general superintendent needed more authority. "We have a General Superintendent; he crosses the continent, he consults, counsels, suggests and passes on from place to place. With what is he invested? With no power to act, certainly. He is not invested with one grain of authority." We are "delighted with his words of wisdom and charmed with his general agreeableness, but then he changes nothing." On the other hand, reflecting the long-standing Universalist dislike of ecclesiastical authority, the Reverend Frederick W. Hamilton protested that the office was an encroachment on the sphere of the state conventions, "a field which . . . the General Convention has no right to enter." The general superintendent had no more right to take part in retiring a minister or adjusting a parish dispute than any other minister in the denomination. "The moment he is invested with more, the fundamental principle of our polity is attacked." Besides, after three years, Hamilton felt, the results did not justify continuance of "a costly experiment."[50]

It would seem that Atwood was attempting far too much for one man, with far too little denominational support. In 1905, a majority of the trustees recommended abolishing the post, and only by a narrow margin did the General Convention reject the recommendation. Atwood resigned that year to become General Secretary of the Convention, but the position of General Superintendent was not filled, and for two more years he served on an interim basis until the Reverend William McGlauflin was chosen as his successor in 1907.

What no one was ready to recognize was that the denomination needed a bureaucracy to administer its affairs—that is, a permanent paid staff, with a permanent address, with an opportunity to formulate long-range plans and an assurance of continuity to carry them out, prepared to keep adequate records and foster an institutional memory, and with money to spend. Administration entrusted to committees of unpaid volunteers is never successful over the long haul. Administration entrusted to a single individual will not be done reliably unless the job is big enough to require the primary attention of whoever may be appointed; even so, continuity is jeopardized when a successor must be chosen.

The denomination did have one segment of such an operation in the Universalist Publishing House, which compiled the *Universalist Register*, published the weekly *Universalist Leader* and other journals, and kept in print doctrinal, biblical, historical, and biographical works by Universalist writers.[51] But there was no comparable organization to coordinate and administer the missionary work of the denomination, which was spread out through many separate organizations, and spread so thin that many of the available resources were wasted. The General Convention authorized the Japan Mission in a burst of enthusiasm in 1890, but struggled thereafter to persuade Universalists to support it. The trustees of the General Convention were responsible for the missionary work of Quillen Shinn, who was actually a sort of individual operator, traveling hither and yon as opportunities to preach arose, especially in the southern states. Sometimes he planted the seeds of a new church, but the nurture of the new enterprise was left to chance. There is a romantic myth about Shinn's missionary travels, but many of the churches he started were short lived.[52] When he died in 1907, no one took his place as a field worker, and the general superintendent and state superintendents were expected to assume his responsibilities.

State conventions were supposed to promote missionary work in their own jurisdictions, and some of them did. When the office of General Superintendent was established in 1897, it was widely urged that state superintendents were also needed. By 1900, there were fourteen of them. The Massachusetts and New York conventions had the best chance of success, but even there the results were discouraging. Appointments were delayed when no funds could be found. Tenures were brief, terminated by early resignations or death. Long gaps between appointments were common. The conventions resorted to temporary expedients, such as asking the secretary of the convention to perform the duties of superintendent also. False starts and no continuity resulted.[53]

The independent organizations sponsored missionary projects of their own. The Women's Centenary Aid Association (1869) continued as the Women's Centenary Association, not only to raise money but to distribute funds itself. It contributed to Lombard College in Galesburg, Illinois, and other educational institutions; it sponsored a missionary effort for a few years in Scotland; it gave support to the Japan Mission; it doled out subsidies to struggling churches; it published tracts. The Young People's Christian Union, organized in 1889, likewise published tracts and undertook missionary work, including major efforts in Harriman, Tennessee, and Atlanta, Georgia.[54]

The hierarchical polity of the denomination, as prescribed in the "General Plan of Organization," was ecclesiastical rather than administrative. For the limited purposes of ecclesiastical discipline, such as the ordination and fellowshiping of ministers, it was perhaps a plausible structure. But it was wholly unsuited for the administration of affairs: church extension, aid to struggling churches, ministerial settlement, and the like. Instead of concentrating resources to produce a critical mass that would justify professional administration, the denomination parceled out the work in bits and pieces to state conventions, not even the strongest of which was in a position to create for itself an administrative arm or auxiliary.

The usual complaint was lack of funds to do a better job. One could argue that Universalists were not eager to contribute to denominational work because the administration of affairs was not done well enough to inspire confidence and loyalty. Had there been a Universalist equivalent of the AUA, organized on a denominational basis without reference to state conventions, the story might have been different.

THE AUA AND THE GENERAL CONFERENCE

Dr. Eliot's reorganization of the AUA was largely completed by 1912, and the administrative structure he developed remained substantially unchanged as long as he served in office. His reforms were administrative rather than ecclesiastical and did not directly alter the ecclesiology of the denomination. But the increased scope of the work of the AUA and the weight of the bureaucratic structure he erected to maintain enlarged activities inevitably warped the traditional polity. The diminished role and eventual disappearance of the National Conference (renamed the General Conference in 1911) is the most obvious evidence.

Problems of polity were involved, furthermore, in some continuing discussion of the relationship of the AUA to the churches. The question first arose in connection with the status of voting life members in an organization now thought to be responsible to the churches. In 1884, when delegates from the churches were admitted as voting members of the Association, individual life memberships were not abolished, since it was felt that voting rights, once granted, could not be revoked. It was assumed that the number of life members would not increase; and in any event, life members who were deeply interested in the work of the Association most likely would attend as delegates from the churches. Instead the number grew steadily, from 1,511 in 1884 to 2,342 in 1900, and to 2,600 in 1914. Some churches were using their annual contributions to the AUA to create voting life memberships for their ministers and prominent lay members.

The representative character of the Association was thereby compromised. Theoretically, the delegates from the churches could be outvoted by individuals who had bought their voting rights by a one-time payment of fifty dollars. In 1908, the anomalous position of the life members was referred to as "a stumbling block" and "the one thing on which there is criticism" when the procedure for nomination of officers and directors was under review. In 1909, a proposal was offered at the annual meeting to limit the number of new life members to one per year per church, but the following year it was agreed to take no action in view of "the small gain, if any, over the present practice, to be obtained in any change of the by-laws which can be made without legislative action."[55]

In 1913, Lewis G. Wilson returned to the question in his annual report as secretary of the Association. In accordance with the bylaws, he argued, life members had the same rights as delegates, yet they had been effectively excluded from the process of nominating officers and directors. The life members, furthermore, were presumably active and loyal Unitarians, yet the Association was failing to mobilize their talents and influence. At his urging, a special commission was established to review the legal status of membership and related questions.[56] The Commission's report to the annual meeting in 1914 found no legal difficulty with respect to the provisions for two classes of membership, delegate and life, or the mechanism for the nomination of officers. It recommended only minor changes in the bylaws with respect to life members, which were accepted without debate when they came up for approval the following year.[57]

A separate issue emerged in the course of the Commission's work, namely the relationship of the Association to aided churches. The propriety of such expenditures of the Association's funds, the report noted, "must depend upon the Unitarian character of the institution so assisted." The question of the boundaries of the denomination—how it is to be defined and who is to determine whether a particular local church is properly within the Unitarian denomination—is a basic question of ecclesiology. The Commission's judgment was that this was a theological problem, not within the competence of the AUA, which was incorporated to administer missionary work, not as an ecclesiastical tribunal. The report declared that "matters which are distinctly theological or denominational are the business, not of the Association, but of the 'General Conference.'" If the issues are inadequately addressed, "the remedy must be sought in that organization and not by attempting to clothe the American Unitarian Association with power and duties that are at variance with the objects of its incorporation." It does not appear that the matter was pursued further or that there was any occasion for the General Conference to assume the jurisdiction that the report had assigned to it.[58]

The reluctance to pursue the matter left the situation as the editor of the *Register* had described it earlier in outlining basic principles of congregational polity: A church "does not derive its existence from, and it owes no allegiance to, any other ecclesiastical body. . . . Neither the American Unitarian Association, nor the National Conference, nor the Western Conference, nor any other organized body has any right whatever to decide authoritatively what is a Unitarian church. There may be Unitarian churches outside of any of these organizations."[59]

The question of the relationship between the AUA and aided churches reappeared in a different way in 1918, involving an issue that might equally well apply to all the churches. Once again, basic principles of congregational polity were involved, this time because of an action taken by the AUA Board. In April 1918, it voted that "any society which engages a minister who is not a willing, earnest, and outspoken supporter of the United States in the vigorous and resolute prosecution of the war cannot be considered eligible for aid from the Association."[60] Several ministers were forced or felt obliged to leave their pulpits in consequence. The Reverend John Haynes Holmes withdrew from Fellowship with the Association, though he continued as minister of the Church of the Messiah in New York. The vote was recognized in a later and more sober time as an egregious violation of the right of the local church to choose its own leadership without control or coercion from denominational authorities. In 1936, the annual meeting by formal resolution repudiated the earlier action: "The American Unitarian Association regrets the action of the board as contrary to the fundamental principle of freedom of thought and conscience, and insists that never in the future shall the economic power of the organization be used to influence the opinion or conduct of any minister or society."[61]

The years following the Great War saw a spurt of denominational activity. But the most obvious indications of fresh vitality—the formation of the Laymen's League in 1919 and the unified campaign for funds the following year—were quite separate from either the AUA or the General Conference. The adequacy of the prevailing denominational structure came into question, with the result that a Commission on Polity was appointed in 1921. The final outcome was the absorption by the AUA of the functions of the General Conference, which met for the last time in 1925. In the process, the problem of voting life members of the AUA was finally resolved.

The Unitarian Laymen's League was organized in April 1919. Within a year it had 7,850 members in 194 chapters throughout the country. It undertook a vigorous missionary program, securing the cooperation of prominent ministers to go on extended preaching tours. Even before it had been in existence a year, it had received the gift of a building in Boston, renamed "Unity House." It was used both for office headquarters and as a clubhouse, equipped with assembly hall, library, refectory, and bedrooms. In 1922, the Reverend William L. Sullivan resigned his pastorate in New York to become the "Missionary Minister" of the League. Whether the League's evangelical enthusiasms were more effective than the AUA's bureaucratic routine would be hard to say; the League certainly was making a bigger splash, as evidenced in the pages of the *Christian Register*.[62]

Also in 1919, a unified campaign to raise a large sum of money for a variety of denominational causes was suggested. The Board of the AUA voted to authorize it, but the initiative had come from outside the Board, and it was run by a separate committee in which the AUA was but one of several denominational organizations represented. The energizing leader of the campaign was a layman, not an officer of the AUA. The intensive period of the drive was November 1920; the goal was $3,000,000, of which almost $2,500,000 had been pledged by the time of May Meetings in 1921.[63]

These stirrings of vitality were encouraging, but diffuse, and they gave no assurance of continued activity once the initial enthusiasm died down. The lack of a common vision and any mechanism for ongoing cooperation among independent denominational organizations especially concerned the Council of the General Conference in its report to the meetings of the Conference in Detroit in September 1921. The AUA, it granted, was doing admirable work, but it was still primarily a missionary organization, even though by default it had taken on some of the functions of a general convention. The Conference was expected to deal with issues of broad policy, but "we only have a biennial meeting." Hence the decision to appoint a Commission on Polity, authorized by the Conference "to consider and recommend action which shall bring the Conference into more intimate and effective relations with all other denominational organizations."[64]

The Commission reported to the General Conference in September 1923 at New Haven. It posed the question: "How can these many and mutually sympathetic churches and societies improve their organization so that they may be more effective in their common endeavors?" Its basic proposal was to merge the General Conference into the AUA, by a revision of the latter's bylaws.[65]

Three proposed changes in the bylaws were the crux of the proposal. One was the elimination of the right to vote of persons who might become life members in the future. This would mean a gradual phase-out of voting life members, so as to make the AUA eventually a completely delegate body, as the General Conference had always been.[66] The second was a provision for larger churches to have proportionately more delegates—this in contrast to the equal representation that had prevailed in the National Conference from the beginning. The third was a provision that the AUA hold a meeting away from Boston in the fall of each alternate year. This would serve as a continuation of the biennial General Conference meetings. While it would be a full legal meeting of the Association, its sessions should be devoted to general discussion, while the regular business would be transacted at the annual meeting in Boston, in accordance with the charter of incorporation. Hence: "No business requiring the appropriation of money, transacted at any meeting other than the annual meeting, shall become effective until ratified by the Board of Directors or the Association at its next annual meeting."[67]

The report recommended other changes, some of them to bring the bylaws into line with the new understanding of the nature and functions of the Association, others to address long-standing deficiencies. A revision of the statement of purpose expressed the enlarged scope of the Association by incorporating some of the language of the Preamble of the Conference. One or more administrative vice presidents were authorized to take over many of the duties previously assigned to the secretary; officers were given four-year terms to encourage long-range planning. The Board of Directors was enlarged from eighteen to twenty-four by the addition of representatives of the Ministerial Union, the Women's Alliance, the Laymen's League, the Young People's Religious Union, the educational institutions related to the denomination, and the societies devoted to the social expression of religion. The work of the Fellowship Committee would continue unchanged, now a responsibility of the Association, but elected at the biennial "General Conference" meetings.

The merger of the General Conference and the AUA was an important turning point for the denomination. For a quarter of a century, the administrative machinery of the AUA had been growing in importance at the expense of the ecclesiastical body representative of the churches. Dr. Eliot repeatedly insisted that the AUA was simply the agent of the churches, having no ecclesiastical authority over them. But concern for the growing impact of bureaucratic decision-making on a religious body was expressed from time to time, most notably by John Haynes Holmes even before the episode in 1918 that led to his withdrawal from the Unitarian fellowship. In 1905, George Batchelor had pointedly indicated the danger in mixing bureaucratic and ecclesiastical structures. But the merger accomplished just that.

To be sure, the Commission on Polity had tried to assure that the special value of the General Conference meetings would survive. All its essential features—the biennial sessions in different parts of the country, the Fellowship Committee, its character as a delegate body, the opportunity for discussion over a period of several days—were continued, "so that if the plan is adopted and carried into effect, there is not one good or essential feature of the Conference which will be lost."[68]

How much the denomination owed to the General Conference was eloquently stated by the editor of the *Christian Register:*

> It was and is the Conference from which the principal creative thought and action of the free churches has emanated. It has ever been the guardian of our religious liberty, the foe of denominationalism, the doctrinal fount at which our leaders have drunk deep of the purest spiritual truth, the forum of unrestrained practical discussion and doctrinal disputation, and best of all, it may be, the quickening heart and will from which have largely come the missionary activity and

the financial resources that have builded our name in heroic size throughout our country and indeed around the world.[69]

It remained to be seen whether two structures with very different purposes and value systems could be combined without loss on one side or the other. Given the vigor of the bureaucracy Dr. Eliot had constructed, whether the special contribution of the Conference to the denomination would survive was for the future to determine.

Meanwhile, the Conference unanimously approved the report in 1923. Earlier that year, the proposed new bylaws had been officially introduced at the annual meeting of the AUA, so as to make possible final action a year later. The Association approved the changes at May Meetings in 1924, and the Conference met for the last time in Cleveland in 1925.

Dr. Samuel A. Eliot resigned as president in 1927, halfway through a four-year term, to return to the parish ministry. The major initiatives of his administration had been in the first decade and a half of his twenty-nine years as chief executive officer. He left behind an experienced staff, which, under his successor, Dr. Louis C. Cornish, continued in routine bureaucratic ways. "I have nothing startlingly new to propose," Dr. Cornish announced following his election to a regular four-year term in 1929. Unfortunately that was not adequate when the Great Depression struck. Straightened finances were one obvious result; more significant was the severe loss of morale. There were those who wondered whether religious liberalism had had its day. The appointment of a Commission of Appraisal in 1934, its report to the denomination in 1936, and the election of Dr. Frederick May Eliot as president of the AUA in 1937 were crucial to the resuscitation of an ailing denomination.

UNIVERSALISTS: FROM "CONVENTION" TO "CHURCH"

In 1908, Dr. Atwood took occasion to review the state of the denomination he had been serving as general superintendent. He recognized that there was continuing disappointment with missionary efforts and widespread feeling that "something must be done." But he rejected the arguments of some that the denomination's plan of organization was part of the problem. It is "as sound in theory," he wrote, "as suitable to its constituency, and as practical in operation as any denomination has, or as we could devise if we tried again." It had not disappointed reasonable expectation. "No material improvement is to be looked for . . . by any change of organization, or of policies, or of the personnel of boards and officers." The failure to grow was rather to be attributed to "incapacity on the part of people generally, to appreciate the ethical and spiritual principle underlying Universalism."[70]

Atwood's mixture of concern over the condition of the denomination, and inability to conceive of any other way of organizing its affairs, was all too common. By way of contrast, Dr. Frederic W. Perkins of Lynn, Massachusetts, was a persistent advocate of organizational reform. In 1905, he proposed an amendment to the Constitution to make the general superintendent the chairman of the Board of Trustees; it was widely supported but failed to get the required two-thirds vote.

In 1907, his proposal was to make the president of the Convention the chairman of the board as well; it received preliminary approval that year, but was withdrawn in 1909 because of legal technicalities. In its place, he proposed that the presiding officer of the Convention be designated its moderator, and that the president of the Convention be the chairman of the board and the chief executive officer of the denomination. His expectation was that the work done by the general superintendent would come under the jurisdiction of the president. Once again, the proposal was supported by a majority of those present at the convention, but failed to receive the necessary two-thirds vote.[71]

Yet even Perkins's proposals did not really address the question of what it would mean to make the president an executive officer. The denominational structure established in 1870 was ecclesiastical, with detailed provisions for the resolution of disciplinary problems. The efficient organization of programs to benefit the denomination at large required not only a different kind of structure, but a different mentality. The Convention was aware that there were jobs to be done, but left them to committees of volunteers. Committees can set policy, but they cannot administer programs, and the results were inevitable. In 1909, the Detroit convention authorized the trustees to appoint four nonsalaried commissions: Increase of the Ministry, Social Service, Sunday Schools, and the Relation of Pastors and Churches. It further recommended the appointment of a salaried Sunday school executive, or secretary. The commissions were appointed, but the secretary was not. At the next convention, the Sunday School Commission complained: "Without an executive officer but wholly dependent on the voluntary services of men already busy with other things and without money to realize its plans your commission is unable to report very much actually accomplished."[72]

Unready to create an administrative structure, the members of the General Convention were nevertheless receptive to a strengthening of the Convention itself. At the Detroit convention (1909), proposals were floated to make the general superintendent and all state superintendents regular members of the General Convention; to eliminate delegates from state conventions, substituting one delegate directly from each parish; and to make all ministers in fellowship members of the General Convention. This might be expected to encourage Universalists at large to focus more attention on the denomination as a whole, instead of limiting their horizons to their particular state conventions. It would be a modification of the quasi-presbyterian polity adopted in 1870, by giving local parishes and their ministers direct participation in the General Convention. A revision of the proposals was presented in 1911, a formal vote was passed in 1913, and final approval came in 1915. These changes did not arouse particular controversy, and their practical effect may not have been immediate or great, but they at least gave enhanced recognition to the role of the general superintendent as an officer of the denomination at large.[73]

An emphatic editorial in the *Leader* just before the 1911 convention in Springfield, Massachusetts, raised the issue of executive authority once more. No advance would be possible, it asserted, "under our many-headed, or no-headed policy." We can never have "a real, progressive and growing church, until we have a real, executive head." A general superintendency had proved its worth in providing an inspirational guide to ministers and churches, but that was not all that was needed. The "biggest, and brainiest and best man" of the denomination should be chosen, either as president or secretary, and given "authority, and liberty and help" to lead the denomination. "It will cost money, but it is the best paying investment we can make. It is the key to the situation."[74]

The immediate result fell far short of what the editorial in the *Leader* suggested. The Convention voted to redefine the role of the president "to advise, counsel, and inspire the Church, and to discharge such duties as the Board of Trustees shall direct." Often referred to as the "Springfield Plan," this was considered to be the creation of a "new Presidency" in which the president of the Convention was made "an administrative leader rather than a parliamentary moderator." But the administrative leader was not to be an executive officer. Dr. Marion D. Shutter was elected president at that convention and made a member of the Board of Trustees. He accepted the post with the clear understanding that he would do what he could "without impairing the work of his own parish" in Minneapolis. He devoted what time he could spare to speaking at state conventions and other denominational meetings, with the object of promoting unity in the denomination and loyalty to the General Convention; he encouraged coordination among the various independent organizations, such as the Women's National Missionary Association and the Young People's Christian Union (YPCU), in order to prevent overlapping activity or working at cross-purposes. But he had no thought of seeking executive authority, or developing a professional staff, or spending any money except for travel expenses. The general superintendent, he argued, should be the only salaried officer of the Convention, while "the Presidency must continue a position of honor and a labor of love." After two years he sought to withdraw, noting that the many demands on his time in his own parish had meant that he had imperfectly discharged the duties of the presidency. Persuaded to continue, he finally withdrew two years later, in 1915.[75]

Lee S. McCollester, Shutter's successor, argued that the "Springfield Plan" required a much more activist role for the president, and it may well be that his example changed perceptions of it. Reporting in 1917 after two years in office, he frankly acknowledged: "I have done many things I had no direct authority to do but the opportunity seemed a duty, and I have dared to assume the responsibility to do the things, or to devise their doing, and to obtain permission afterwards." The presidency, he insisted, should be made a full-time position: "no man, however strong, can carry on an important parish or a similar work, and adequately administer the presidency of the Universalist General Convention." What was required was "a better executive administration," or professional staff, including the secretary, the general superintendent, the president of the Sunday School Association, and a "business manager or executive president," all located in a central headquarters "where all departments might confer and co-operate in policies." Because of the duplication and overlapping among the several independent organizations, such as the Women's National Missionary Association and the YPCU, he pointed to the need for some "Executive Committee, or some executive officer with a genius of co-ordinating and initiating, which shall eliminate waste and increase efficiency and carry out policies."[76]

McCollester's report, together with the report of the Board of Trustees, pointed out the direction in which the denomination had long needed to move. By the time of the next convention, at Baltimore in 1919, the denomination had at last established a headquarters, in the building owned by the Universalist Publishing House in Boston at 359 Boylston Street, where the *Leader* was edited and where the Massachusetts Convention had an office. Here were established the offices of the secretary of the Convention, the general superintendent, the president of the Sunday School Association, the YPCU director, and the Women's National Missionary Association.[77]

To bring these officers together in one location, with a common mailing address, was probably more important in the life of the denomination than all the discussions in convention as to the proper role of the president, or the secretary of the Convention, or the general superintendent. To be sure, the auxiliary organizations had their own corporate identities and their traditions of having served the denomination, each in its own way. A true consolidation of such activities as aid to struggling churches was too radical a solution even to be considered, and the headquarters staff of the General Convention was the bare beginnings of an administrative structure.

More than coordination was needed, but coordination was all that could be envisioned. The 1925 Convention approved a plan of reorganization, which provided that policies of the auxiliary organizations should be determined in consultation with the Board of Trustees, and that the Board should have power, within limitations, to veto measures adopted by an auxiliary organization or its executive body. The plan even required the organizations to submit their plans for the pub-lication of literature to a denominational "Commission on Literature." In 1927, the Constitution of the General Convention was amended to specify that it had "jurisdiction over all organizations, including all general denominational bodies, wherever located." But it is hard to see how a Board of Trustees meeting only three times a year, and having little money to spend, would have clout enough to affect the work of the auxiliary bodies and give focused leadership to the denomination.[78]

The chief development of the 1930s was the emergence of the general superintendent as the real executive leader of the denomination. This came about more by default than by design. Despite Dr. McCollester's attempts to create an executive presidency, that was impossible so long as the position was part-time and unpaid. The secretary and the general superintendent were the only salaried full-time officers of the Convention (though the Convention also underwrote the salary of the president of the Sunday School Association).

In 1928, John Smith Lowe resigned as general superintendent, and Roger F. Etz, the secretary, agreed as an interim measure to take on the duties of that office in addition to his own. The Board of Trustees, chronically short of funds, showed no eagerness to make a permanent appointment. Finally, in 1930, Etz was appointed to the position and continued to hold both offices. Russell Miller has noted that, "overwhelmed with administrative details," he could "do little more than conduct a holding operation until his resignation in 1938." By the time Robert Cummins was chosen as his successor, the general superintendent rather than the secretary was regarded as the chief administrative officer of the denomination.[79]

Progress toward a more efficient administration had been painfully slow, despite recurrent criticism of the prevailing denominational structure. Part of the problem was inertia, some of it was financial, much of it was traditional parochialism. In some quarters the fear was expressed that the general superintendent would become a little dictator, at liberty to move into a parish where a problem existed and assume authority to dismiss the minister. Indeed, some critics argued that it was necessary to give the superintendent precisely that kind of authority.

The problem was that, unlike the Unitarians, who had made a clear distinction—at least until 1925—between their ecclesiastical structure and their administrative bureaucracy, the denominational administration the Universalists sought to develop was part of the ecclesiastical or disciplinary structure. Dr. Samuel Eliot was free to develop a bureaucracy because he repeatedly took the position that the AUA existed to serve the churches and had no hierarchical control over them. Unitarian churches that insisted on being parochial-minded—and there were many of them—could take or leave what the AUA had to offer without exposing themselves to formal sanctions from headquarters. But the Universalists feared the growth of the necessary bureaucracy because they saw administrative development as an increase of centralized disciplinary authority, and there was wide disagreement as to whether that would be desirable.

Yet the continued decline in membership and the loss of churches made inescapable the conclusion that a more vigorous administration and more imaginative leadership at the top was needed. In 1938, Robert Cummins, somewhat reluctantly persuaded to become general superintendent, sought to do what should have been attempted twenty—or forty—years earlier. Probably it was already too late. For generations, the General Convention had tried to solve problems by passing resolutions and tinkering with the bylaws. Now it sought to persuade itself that it would be taking a step toward integration if it changed the name of the Universalist General Convention to the Universalist Church of America.[80]

THE LOCAL CHURCH AND ITS MINISTER

The decades following the Great War saw many changes in American life, with consequences for the churches that historians have been slow to consider. In the most general terms, one may argue that the sense of community in small towns and urban neighborhoods was eroding, resulting in a weakening of some of the cohesive forces undergirding churches and other institutions that had a local constituency and concern. The automobile had much to do with it, if only because it made possible larger opportunities for recreation on Sunday as an alternative to going to church. Suburban communities, which had begun as relatively compact settlements along rail or streetcar lines, could now spread out.

Curiously enough, just as this sense of community was eroding, a prominent minister urged the organization of churches on a community basis. In 1919, John Haynes Holmes persuaded the Church of the Messiah to change its name to the Community Church of New York. In a series of articles in the magazine *Unity*, and in 1922 in a book entitled *New Churches for Old*, he outlined his preferred ecclesiology. Churches should find their identity, not in relationship to a denomination, but in representing the religious concerns of the political entity of which they are the spiritual focus, especially in respect to the social application of religion. The theology of the denominations is divisive; social concerns unite.

Unfortunately, his proposal was an exercise in nostalgia; the kind of community on which his ecclesiology was predicated did not exist in urban America. (In rural America, the "community church movement" took a quite different turn in the federation of churches of different denominations.) Something like what Holmes advocated had indeed once existed, in the Standing Order of the churches in New England in the eighteenth century. But that had self-destructed long ago. So far as polity is concerned, Holmes's proposals had no effect then or consequences thereafter, even in his own church, which continued to be a part of the AUA despite his vigorous condemnation of denominationalism.[81]

More representative of prevailing tendencies was a book entitled *The Minister and His Parish*, published in 1923, which provides a useful picture of church life in the early decades of the century.[82] By Henry Wilder Foote, it was based on his teaching from 1914 to 1924 as professor of preaching and parish administration at the Harvard Divinity School. Not intended as a purely denominational manual for Unitarian churches, its focus nevertheless is on churches of congregational polity. It discusses how churches should be organized and administered for the greatest effectiveness, and what the role of the minister should be. Its comments on the unhappy consequences of failure to do things properly suggest that actual practice as the author knew it was often careless and inefficient.

Legal title to church property, the book insists, should be vested in the whole body of members. In some cases, the dual organization of church and parish may survive, or separate trustees rather than the membership at large may be the body corporate; but such arrangements lead "to confusion, controversy and inefficiency, and should be done away with." Membership carries with it the right to vote, though conditions may be imposed with respect to age or financial support. The bylaws should include a provision for the dismissal or expulsion of members, though no one should be expelled without due notice and an opportunity to be heard. The governing board should be elected at the annual meeting by all qualified voting members. It has the power to transact all the ordinary business of the church, subject to instruction from the society; but the authority to call or dismiss the minister rests with the whole membership.[83]

There is no novelty or departure from familiar congregation practice in these arrangements, unless it is the emphasis on efficient operation and sound business methods, so different from earlier, less complicated times. Foote was quick to insist that sound administration is not an end in itself. The church does not exist for its own sake, but for the community in which it is placed and the souls it serves. But: "Business-like methods in the financial administration of a church are of vital importance to its welfare,"[84] and that is where the emphasis of much of the book rests.

Ministry is defined as "a sacred calling of standing and dignity." The minister is not an employee, "hired" to do a particular piece of work—though appropriate provision for his support must be agreed to and paid regularly without fail. He is granted a "living," so he can be freed from "the necessity of worldly pursuits in order that he may give his whole time and thought to his charge." The church that affords him a fair salary has a claim on his full time and strength. Unless by special arrangement, he has no right "to add other remunerative employment to his ministry—teaching, lecturing, selling books or life insurance." Within the church, his duties are to conduct worship, to administer the sacraments in accordance with the practice of the particular church, to preach "with as much unction as the Lord gives him," to meet his pastoral obligations, and to "exercise a general supervision over the educational and administrative activities of the parish." While he should be informed as to the church's financial affairs and may on occasion meet with the governing board—and may indeed sometimes have to suggest better ways of carrying on the business affairs of the parish—the temporalities of the parish are the responsibility of the members. Preaching and parish calling are the minister's central concerns.[85]

The ethical standards of the ministry are no different than those of other honorable men, yet the minister is expected to be scrupulous in adhering to them. He "has openly devoted himself to the ideals of the Christian life, and may properly be required to practice, so far as the grace of God permits, what he preaches." An "unblemished character is the first requirement for his entrance into and continuance in the ministry." The prime moral requirement is integrity, particularly in financial matters. In his relationship with women, he must "maintain that outward demeanor of courtesy and respect which is the genuine expression of an inner chastity of soul." Sexual immorality is "an absolute disqualification" for continuance in the profession. In other matters, such as indulgence in frivolous forms of amusement, such as dancing and cards, the minister will be judged more strictly than a layman. He must neither copy the fashionable attire of a man of the world, nor adopt "defiant unconventionality" of dress. He will avoid profanity and "broad stories." He should not drink alcoholic beverages—quite apart from the fact that prohibition was then the law of the land.[86]

But while the minister should conform to the conventions of his community in such matters, he remains the master of his own pulpit and the sole judge "of what and how he shall preach." Even if his criticisms of the social order seem foolish or unacceptable to the majority, he cannot be excluded from his pulpit, and he must not be coerced by the threat of reduction of his salary. To be sure, he may not advocate illegal or immoral conduct, nor preach contrary to the accepted tenets of his church. He must preach the truth in love and never forget that "his primary duty is to minister to the moral and spiritual needs of his flock." But he "must insist upon his liberty in the pulpit or quit his ministry."[87]

The book assumes that in the great majority of cases, there will be but one minister serving a given parish, but it acknowledges other possibilities. An "associate minister" may be called and settled by the church as the equivalent of what an earlier generation meant by a junior colleague. That is to say, he is the partner of the senior minister, not his assistant, and if the senior minister resigns or dies, "the associate remains the minister of the church, without any further action on his part or that of the parish, and is, both by law and custom, entitled to all the rights of that position." An "assistant minister," by contrast, should be ordained but not installed, "since he is not a settled minister of the parish, but strictly an assistant to the minister." This clear distinction between associate minister and assistant minister, Foote wrote, admittedly is often, through ignorance, overlooked by parishes, which engage as "associate" someone they intend to be "assistant." The book also recognizes the status of a "stated supply," that is, the filling of a vacant pulpit for a longer or shorter time with no intention of a permanent settlement.[88]

The book recommends a more formal or regularized procedure than was then common for the calling and settlement of the minister. Often, it appears, candidates seeking a settlement would ask personal friends to recommend them to vacant churches, or they would even write directly to a church to solicit a hearing.[89] Churches, in turn, would hear a parade of candidates on successive Sundays. "This method involves a maximum amount of competition between candidates, odious comparisons between this and that man, and results in confusing and often splitting the congregation."[90] The results would often be a decision based on very superficial impressions of the candidate.

A better method, the book argues, is to request of the denominational officers a list of ministers seeking pulpits, and to winnow the list with the help of the denominational intermediary, until it has been reduced to two or three candidates of largest promise who might be willing to consider a call. These finalists should be reviewed by the committee on pulpit supply on several occasions and their qualifications carefully considered, until it would be possible to present a single candidate for recommendation to the church.

These procedures clearly would be an improvement over the primitive and inefficient ways of bringing church and candidate together that widely prevailed. It is not supposed, however, that they were promptly and universally adopted. To hear as many as three finalists on successive Sundays continued to be common.[91] In any event, it was considered desirable that a church whose pulpit became vacant should settle the successor as promptly as possible—within a few months, at most. Two instances at least may be cited in which the successor was chosen prior to the retirement of the settled minister.[92] Foote's suggestions envisaged a somewhat enlarged role for the denominational representative, but the purpose was not denominational control, and there were no sanctions on either church or candidate if their happy union was of their own devising. It was left to the churches to accept as much or as little help as seemed best to them.

UNITARIANS AND UNIVERSALISTS IN 1937

In 1899, when Dr. Samuel A. Eliot declared that "the time has come for a closer and more cordial co-operation with our brethren of the Universalist fellowship," he was restating a concern that had been expressed before and that was to be heard periodically in the years to come. The immediate result was the appointment of a joint committee which met from time to time with minimal accomplishment until it petered out in 1907. The assurances of the committee that it sought "co-operation, not consolidation" were not enough to satisfy strongly Christian Universalists, who were dismayed by the element of "radicalism" or Free Religion among the Unitarians.[93]

Differences in polity between the two denominations continued to be a barrier. The hierarchical structure of the Universalists, with the entrenched role of state conventions, may have been the most obvious problem, but there were more subtle ones as well. The Universalists asserted a more ecclesiastical concept of the ministry than the more congregational Unitarians. For the Unitarians, the power to ordain remained with the local church, though the advice of an ecclesiastical council or the Fellowship Committee should be sought. For the Universalists, authority to ordain rested with the state conventions, and ordinations sometimes took place at meetings of the conventions. For the Unitarians, the essential work of the Fellowship Committee was "credentialing"—assuring parishes seeking ministerial leadership that those listed by it had appropriate qualifications for settlement. For the Universalists, fellowshiping was set in a disciplinary context, with specific vows of faithfulness to the denomination, with stipulations as to the nature of the examination of candidates, and with requirements to be met and procedures to be followed for those seeking reinstatement after being disfellowshiped for moral lapses.

The Unitarians recommended that churches call only ministers approved by the Fellowship Committee, but no church suffered penalty if it did not; the Universalists limited the choice to those in fellowship, and the church itself was liable to be disfellowshiped if it settled anyone else. The Unitarians assumed that ordained ministers would administer the ordinances: communion, and baptism or christening; the Universalists provided specifically that while persons preparing for the ministry or lay preachers might be granted license to preach, they should not "administer any Christian ordinance."

Pressures were developing, however, that in the long run forced closer relationships between the two denominations, regardless of such differences. Universalist polity had originally established a sharp sectarian boundary line around the denomination. As late as 1916, the Laws of Fellowship prescribed the withdrawal of fellowship from any minister "entering upon ministerial labor under the auspices of, or into Fellowship with, any other denomination." Likewise fellowship should be withdrawn from any parish settling a minister not in fellowship. But when federation became a solution to the problem of weak and dying churches, especially in rural areas, the rigid boundaries of Universalist polity could not be maintained.[94]

In 1917, the Laws of Fellowship were amended to provide: "Any denomination permitting clergymen in the fellowship of this convention to be settled as pastors over its parishes, without surrender of Universalist fellowship, shall be accorded similar recognition by the Universalist General Convention." Ministers availing themselves of reciprocal fellowship would not forfeit their Universalist fellowship, though they would lose the right to vote or hold office either in the General Convention or their state convention "so long as they are pastors of parishes in other denominations." A decade later, an equivalent amendment with respect to federated churches was adopted.[95]

While these provisions could apply to any denomination, and reciprocal fellowship of ministers or federated churches involving the Congregationalists sometimes resulted, in practice it was the relationship between Unitarians and Universalists that was affected. This was a time when formal discussions looking to closer relationships between Universalists and Congregationalists were more active than between Universalists and Unitarians.[96] Yet the Universalist Year Book for 1930 lists eighty-one ministers holding dual Universalist-Unitarian fellowship, but only eighteen holding Universalist-Congregational fellowship.[97] It may be argued that the changes in the Universalist Laws of Fellowship at the parish level, with dual ministerial fellowship more and more a common result, were more significant than negotiations or conversations at the denominational level, and indeed they were what made eventual merger inevitable.

Parallel Routes to Merger, 1937–1961

Frederick May Eliot was elected president of the American Unitarian Association in May 1937; Robert Cummins became the general superintendent of the Universalist General Convention in August 1938. Neither one was then advocating merger, except as a remote possibility. But they were ready for such cooperation as circumstances from time to time made possible. In hindsight, eventual merger was probably inevitable; their eagerness to encourage cooperative activity helped prepare the way.

More immediately, each had the task of rallying a dispirited denomination. Both had demonstrated capacities for leadership and each possessed a vision extending beyond bureaucratic routine. Both were energetic administrators with a clear sense of the needs of their denominations. But both were confronted by pressing problems of organization and administration.

"UNITARIANS FACE A NEW AGE"

"The presidency of the American Unitarian Association was [Eliot's] great public labor," declared Wallace Robbins in 1958, "and few now remember at what a lowly point it began. Eight years of national depression had been a coarse abrasive on the churches: financially and spiritually they were scratched and worn."[1] Dr. Louis C. Cornish, president of the

AUA since 1927, had shown little capacity for imaginative leadership in time of adversity. A member of the headquarters staff for a dozen years previously, he led an administration that maintained familiar bureaucratic ways. There is "really no room for very much that is new," he reported to the annual meeting in 1929. "Our work has always progressed in an orderly fashion." Two years later, he remarked: "It is good sometimes just to repeat."[2]

The response of those Unitarians who were not ready to give up was the appointment in 1934 of a Commission of Appraisal, which Eliot headed. Its findings were discussed at the General Conference meeting in October 1935, and the final report and recommendations—a book of 348 pages, entitled *Unitarians Face a New Age*—appeared in time for the annual meeting in May 1936. Recommended amendments to the bylaws were approved in May 1937, at the annual meeting that elected Eliot as president.[3]

Integration. When the Commission on Polity (1923–25) had recommended the merger of the AUA and the General Conference, it had sought to assure that the distinctive values of the Conference would survive. The technical staff of the Commission of Appraisal reported that that had not happened. The AUA was the "stronger and more stubborn of the two bodies"; it had property and a paid staff; it had developed "a peculiar defensive strength."

> Consequently, when the reorganization was over, and in spite of the fact that the Association had been transformed into an essentially ecclesiastical body, its old characteristics dominated. It did not equally perpetuate its own values and those of the General Conference to which it had succeeded.

Furthermore, the Association failed "to carry over to itself the regard and affection in which the General Conference had been held by its constituency."[4]

The Commission recommended a serious attempt to regain the values centering in the old General Conference. It recommended the passage of a "declaratory resolution," by which the Association would specifically acknowledge that it had assumed the functions once exercised by the General Conference. It proposed a new office—that of Moderator—to give to the fellowship "a titular head apart from the administrative work," thereby enhancing "the importance of spiritual leadership as distinct from administrative control." It proposed a standing Commission on Planning and Review, with the primary duty of fostering "the cooperative functioning of all Unitarian agencies within a common purpose and plan." In order to enhance the importance of the biennial General Conference meetings, it proposed that they should nominate the moderator and elect the Nominating Committee and the Commission on Planning and Review.[5] In response to these recommendations, a "Declaratory Resolution" was adopted at the annual meeting in 1936, defining the scope of the AUA as "a general council," to undertake such functions on behalf of all the churches as they might from time to time entrust to it.[6]

Other proposals of the Commission were implemented in 1937 by changes in the bylaws. The moderator was defined as an unsalaried officer, to serve for two years, not eligible for re-election. He or she would preside at the biennial fall meetings of the Association (but not necessarily at the annual meeting in May); he would be the representative of the denomination "in fraternal and non-administrative relations with other religious bodies"; he would be an *ex officio* member of the Commission on Planning and Review and the Board of Directors, "but have no other responsibility for its administrative affairs."[7] It was the obvious intention to make the position one of nonadministrative leadership within the denomination and visibility in the country at large. Behind it was the recollection of former US President William Howard Taft, once the presiding officer of the old General Conference, who brought the denomination to the attention of many Americans who otherwise would scarcely have known it existed.

An obvious attempt was made in the years that followed to choose persons with name recognition beyond the boundaries of the denomination. The first moderator was Sanford Bates, the leading penologist of the day, who had once been superintendent of Federal prisons. College and university presidents followed: Aurelia Henry Reinhardt of Mills College, Philip Nash of the University of Toledo, George D. Stoddard of the University of Illinois. Senator Harold H. Burton of Ohio was chosen in 1944, but he felt obliged to resign when appointed to the Supreme Court. But it may be questioned whether the position of moderator ever fully became what was intended. Former presidents of the United States were in short supply in the denomination. Because Frederick Eliot was the person elected president of the Association, that office became one of ecclesiastical leadership as well as bureaucratic administration, and the role of moderator was somewhat eclipsed.

The General Conference meetings of the Association were structured to encourage consideration of large matters of general denominational concern. They were scheduled for the fall of alternate years, "but not at the place at which the last annual meeting was held." Their charge was to review the "outlook and work" of the denomination as a whole, including auxiliary agencies such as the Laymen's League, the Women's Alliance, and the Young People's Religious Union. They would be fully competent to define policy for the Association, except that no matter requiring the appropriation of money would be effective unless ratified by the Board of Directors or by the next annual meeting. At its meetings, the moderator would be nominated—to be elected by the annual meeting in order to conform to legal requirements—and the Nominating Committee, the Commission on Planning and Review, and its own Program Committee elected.[8] The biennial sessions turned out to be moderately successful at best in taking the larger view of the denomination, but they were very important in the discussions leading to merger. It was at the General Conference meeting at Syracuse in 1959, not at an annual meeting of the Association, that the crucial decisions were made.

The Commission on Planning and Review was to be elected by and report to the General Conference. It was established as a body of five members, including the moderator but excluding officers of the AUA or major denominational organizations. It was to present to the General Conference "a unified report on the total work of the Unitarian fellowship through its national and regional organizations." The new bylaw went so far as to provide that the Commission should prepare "a consolidated budget covering the whole scope of the work, its items to be effective when accepted by the several agencies." It does not appear that this provision was ever implemented.[9] The suggested unified report is an echo of the general assessments of the state of the denomination prepared by the Council of the old National Conference when Bellows headed it and wrote them himself. The Commission on Planning and Review never became the coordinating agent of the denomination it was intended to be, though it was a precedent for the Commission on Appraisal of the UUA established at the time of merger.

Decentralization. Dr. Samuel A. Eliot understood the AUA to be a service agency to do for the Unitarian community many practical things the churches were not in a position to do for themselves. As its chief executive officer, he initially advocated a plan of decentralized responsibility and administration. "After a trial of five or six years," he later recalled, "it became necessary for me to surrender my hope and expectation of decentralization and admit defeat." Failing to secure self-governing and self-supporting "centers of administration," the Eliot administration itself established offices in New York City, San Francisco, and Salt Lake City, and it joined with the Western Conference in maintaining an office in Chicago. The field secretaries of the Association worked out of these regional offices, and they were identified with their regions. Furthermore, the Board of Directors continued to have territorial subcommittees "charged with the consideration of church extension affairs in their respective areas." "I do not hesitate to say that this plan worked well," Eliot advised the Appraisal Commission. "There was a centralized authority, but at the same time there was a sense of regional or local responsibility."[10]

In 1925, aware that a merger of the AUA and the General Conference would accentuate centralization, the Commission on Polity sought to provide balance by reinvigorating the regional conferences. Its recommendations, the Appraisal Commission reported, "have conspicuously failed of adoption." By 1935, even the regional offices established by Dr. Samuel Eliot had lost most of their functions. "All field secretaries have been withdrawn and field work is concentrated in the hands of administrative vice-presidents and other officers, with headquarters in Boston." This concentration was warmly defended by the leading officers of the AUA as "wise and economical," but Dr. Eliot responded: "The present concentration of our denominational offices in Boston is thoroughly unsound and inefficient."[11]

In 1936, the Commission of Appraisal once again tried to revive "partial decentralization of administrative centers and responsibility." It suggested as a first step a revival of the practice of locating administrative officers in three or four regional centers. Regional advisory committees should be set up to consider requests for financial aid in their territories and to advise on all major regional problems—these would seem to be a functional equivalent of the regional Board committees of earlier times. Auxiliary bodies, such as the Alliance and the League, should be encouraged to join in the support of regional offices.[12]

The Appraisal Commission understood that such a program of decentralized administration would have to be implemented gradually. A start was made in the first year of the new administration, building on existing structures such as the Maine Unitarian Association and the Western Conference. After one year, the director of the Department of Unitarian Extension and Church Maintenance could report that "there are now only a few widely scattered churches that are not included in some regional organization and who will not have during the coming year at least the part-time service of a Regional Director." By December 1938, the local conferences in the Middle Atlantic states could report full organization of a regional council in accordance with the proposals of the Appraisal Commission, the first region to do so. They had appointed a full-time director, established an office, solicited funds to support their own activities, and begun to develop plans for student work, religious education, the strengthening of weak churches, and the establishment of new ones. Not subdivisions of the AUA, the regional councils were to be "entirely independent" but "cooperate fully."[13]

These arrangements were much more than a revival of the regional field offices of the AUA that had been part of the administration of Dr. Samuel Eliot. The intention was to stimulate regional responsibility and to expand the circle of Unitarians, lay and ministerial both, who would be drawn into active work beyond the local parish. But implementation of the program came slowly, partly for financial reasons, partly because the geographical distribution of churches was uneven, and "in some part because our people have not caught the idea at all."[14]

Internal organization. As the Appraisal Commission saw it, the "marked and accelerating tendency toward centralization" was especially apparent in headquarters operations, which had become staff-driven to an extraordinary degree. Five paid officers of the Association were on the Board of Directors. There was an increase in the proportion of staff members on subcommittees of the Board, indeed chairing them. At the same time, the numbers and activities of sub-committees decreased—no doubt because staff members were in a position to decide many matters themselves without the nuisance of consulting the subcommittees they chaired. Recommendations to the Board came chiefly from the staff—that is, from "persons who are inevitably bound to present matters in ways favorable to their own action on any particular issue." The Executive Committee, authorized by the bylaws to deal with necessary business between meetings of the Board, consisted of "the President and three other paid officers, leaving only three places of un-paid Board members." In practice, an Administrative Council had largely taken over the Executive Committee's functions. The Council consisted entirely of the chief paid officers and had become "the central body of the administrative system." It met frequently as a budget committee; it dealt with matters affecting local churches; and it even made recommendations for appointment to Board committees.[15]

Concentration of authority at headquarters should not be understood as simply representing a thirst for power on the part of officers and staff. It was the result of the tendency of all bureaucracies to acquire increasing authority because they have the advantages of institutional continuity and access to more complete information than the constituencies they exist to serve. They can reach decisions more quickly and efficiently than is possible with wider participation. Furthermore, the need to economize in hard times had reinforced the natural tendency to centralize. But the Commission argued that "this process of centralization has been carried to a point where it endangers the fundamental values and the healthy functioning of our denomination." Congregational polity, it seems, can be undercut as readily by bureaucratic hierarchy as by ecclesiastical hierarchy.[16]

Implementation of the proposals of the Appraisal Commission with respect to integration and decentralization proved difficult; to address problems of internal organization was easier and results came more quickly. In his first report after one year in office, Frederick Eliot noted the effective work being done by departmental committees, involving the active participation of large numbers of persons who were not members of the Board. The committees introduced into policy decisions perspectives from outside the administrative staff. Business before the Board was now presented, not by the paid staff "but by the chairmen of the departmental and standing committees, following consideration by the respective committees." Routine matters could be handled quickly, allowing the Board "to devote considerable periods of time to questions of broad general policy brought to the attention of the Board by individual members." In due course, the departmental structure was reorganized into a Division of Churches, a Division of Education, and a Division of Promotion and Publications. To these familiar areas of responsibility was added the Service Committee, initially a response to the problem of refugees from Nazi persecution. Eliot considered it to be the most significant event of his first four years, "its promise for the future the most exciting and reassuring."[17]

In 1941, reviewing the first four years, Eliot took particular satisfaction in the great increase of lay participation in the formulation of policy. It had been achieved "not only by increasing the number of working committees but by developing the habit of mind that makes the distinction between the executive function and the policy-making function." In the yearbook for 1940–41, there were 153 men and women listed as serving on Association committees.[18]

The Christian Register. One "conspicuous and serious failure" of Eliot's first term involved the *Christian Register,* the independent denominational weekly journal of news and views. Eliot thought of it as a "failure to persuade the members of our Unitarian fellowship to support in even decent fashion our denominational journal."[19] It may be argued, as some did very vigorously at the time, that Eliot's real failure was a more significant one. It was his unwillingness to acknowledge that a takeover of the *Register* by the AUA, though plausible on financial grounds, would weaken the democratic processes in the denomination that he sought to energize, and which congregational polity seeks to embody.

"It is difficult today to develop the financial support for the general religious journal of ideas," the report of the Appraisal Commission had stated. "No denomination has found a satisfactorily right answer to the problems."[20] The *Register* had been a profitable business venture for its founder and first owner, David Reed. After the Civil War, it paid its own way for a time, but it never made any money for its new publisher, George H. Ellis. Toward the end of the century, the coming of low-priced magazines drained religious journals of their advertising revenues, and all such papers ran into financial difficulty. For a number of years, until his retirement from business in 1917, Ellis himself covered the losses. After he turned the paper over to a board of trustees, modest subsidies were granted by the AUA. This was no more than proper, Ellis insisted, in view of the service the paper rendered to the denomination. Indeed, beginning in 1924, the AUA house organ, entitled *Word and Work*, was incorporated into the *Register* and allotted a given number of pages each month for material edited at headquarters.[21]

The financial situation reached a point of crisis with the onslaught of the depression. In 1932, the trustees felt compelled to dispense with the paid services of a full-time editor-in-chief. Dr. Albert C. Dieffenbach, who had conducted the paper for fifteen years with notable success, was dropped; as a temporary expedient, an editorial staff of volunteers undertook to carry on. When the Appraisal Commission reviewed the situation in 1935, it accepted these arrangements as necessary "until the budget may permit a full-time editor," and the trustees were encouraged to make a fresh campaign for subscriptions. The Commission went on to underline the importance of the *Register* as "a journal of opinion and distributor of denominational plans and news," which should continue to be directed by an independent board of trustees. "As a journal of discussion, it would be handicapped if it became marked as an institutional organ merely."[22]

Following a succession of part-time editors, Llewellyn Jones was appointed full-time editor in 1938. With vigorous support from Frederick Eliot, the trustees sought to increase the subscription list, though with only modest success. In October 1939, faced with the prospect of continuing subsidies, the AUA took over the journal from the board of trustees. Eliot was firm in insisting that "the usefulness of the paper as a channel for the expression of widely diverging views" would not be impaired. But a letter to the editor of the *Register* asked:

> Can you see a house organ making room for searching criticism of either an administration or its departments? Must there not be some place for public presentation and discussion of criticism of that sort if we are not to lapse into the smug bureaucracy toward which we were tending before the reorganization which brought the present administration to power? Does the present administration realize how important the independence of *The Register* was during that period?[23]

Under the new arrangement, Jones continued as editor at a reduced salary, and an advisory committee was appointed, representing the several agencies of the denomination. The publication schedule was changed from weekly to semi-monthly. The subscription rate was reduced, although Jones warned against that step. It soon became apparent that the AUA was no more able to make the journal self-supporting than the independent trustees had been. In March 1941, the directors of the AUA voted to issue the *Register* once a month, and to "make such reductions and changes in the editorial personnel and publishing costs" as would reduce the annual deficit to $2,500. This meant the dismissal of Jones and publication under the direction of an editorial board of headquarters staff members, headed by Eliot.[24] Subsidy by the Association was now hidden in the salaries of staff members who devoted time to the journal.

Throughout the successive steps by which the bureaucracy took over control of the journal, the official position, repeatedly stated by Eliot, was that the *Register* would continue to be "a free journal of opinion and news of the Unitarian fellowship."[25] But it became clear that adverse criticism of the administration was not welcome. The *Register* under Dieffenbach had not hesitated to comment, sometimes favorably, sometimes not, on administration policy. During the period of part-time editors, the paper had been available to the Commission on Appraisal for extended discussion of its findings, critical by implication of the Cornish regime. The contested election of 1937 had been resolved a month before the actual voting by full presentation of the views of the candidates in its pages. Jones continued to admit critical comment. But he was told, according to his account of the matter, that in the meeting of the directors in March 1941, "the feeling was quite general that a paper in which denominational 'dirty linen' was publicly washed was a bad thing and the determination was made that in the reconstituted 'house organ' the Family Circle would be available only to people who had 'constructive suggestions to make.'"[26]

The decision taken in March 1941 to put the *Register* under the direction of headquarters staff members led to widespread criticism, some of which Jones rather enthusiastically published in the few issues remaining to him. Even close friends of Eliot and loyal supporters of the administration, such as Leslie Pennington, argued that the AUA directors had "acted unwisely and undemocratically."[27] An attempt was made at the annual meeting in May 1942 to amend the bylaws so as to establish an independent editorial board, but after some rather animated debate it was rejected. As a monthly, the *Register* published more photographs, but considerably less news of the churches, and decidedly less unsolicited comment on administrative policy.

Robert Cummins became general superintendent of the Universalist General Convention on August 1, 1938. At the time, and in the course of the following year, there was ongoing discussion in the *Christian Leader* of the need to give the general superintendent more authority. Usually what was meant was more ecclesiastical or disciplinary authority to curb the irresponsible exercise of independence by both ministers and churches.[28] Cummins knew that it was altogether too common for ministers or churches to go their own ways, whether by action taken in disregard of the well-being of the whole denomination, or by lack of cooperation with denominational officials, or by giving feeble financial support. Whether the General Convention and its superintendent had enough power was for him an open question; what was clear was that "such power has never been used." Instead of pressing for formal changes in the established polity, he sought to enhance the role of the central administration by making it more effective and hence more focal in the life of the denomination.[29]

By aggressive leadership in attacking long-standing problems of administration, by rallying the troops at countless state conventions and other Universalist gatherings, and by the force of his personality, Cummins transformed the office of General Superintendent. He made the position visible as it never had been before, offering proposals for reform and urging support both in committee and in public. In a real sense he was doing for the Universalists what Frederick Eliot did for the Unitarians. Both men restored morale after periods of discouragement. By the quality of their leadership they placed an imprint on the positions they held that was at least as important as the formal definition of powers in denominational bylaws.

"Forward Together" was Cummins's rallying cry for the program of his administration. He stated four objectives in an address to the Convention meeting in Washington in 1939: (1) a detailed evaluation of all the programs and churches receiving financial aid in order to end much needless duplication, perpetual grants spread so thin as to be wasted, and poor supervision; (2) the institution of "general field work"—that is, the appointment of field workers equipped to work with churches on matters covering the whole range of church life, in place of separate field workers sent out by specialized agencies such as the Sunday School Association; (3) the integration of denominational programs, involving coordination and the elimination of duplicating efforts by the national auxiliary organizations; (4) finally, a proposal to invest some money to make these initiatives possible. Eventually, Cummins suggested, the result might be an integrated administration, with a "departmentalized" church: "a Department of Youth, a Department of the Ministry, a Department of Publication, a Department of Religious Education."[30]

What Dr. Samuel A. Eliot had done for the Unitarians under much more favorable circumstances, Cummins was now trying to do for a denomination that had not only lost 275 churches in twenty-eight years but was doling out financial aid in small amounts to 100 of the 544 remaining. The money received for promotion in 1938, Cummins reported, "was only a little more than half of what was received in 1890."[31]

By the time the General Convention met in September 1941 at Tufts College in Medford, Massachusetts, a start had been made on all four objectives. Several surveys of churches receiving financial support had been completed and more were under way. A full-time general field worker had been busy since the previous November.[32] An amendment to the bylaws was ready for action to create a Central Planning

Council made up of representatives of the General Convention and the auxiliary agencies. Cummins was heartened by these positive accomplishments. But his proposal for the establishment of a Department of Finance had been unanimously rejected by the Board of Trustees, and he felt frustrated by "the stealthy, persistent, barbed opposition of a handful of those from whom one might rightfully hope to receive only the finest team-play." It should be clear, he insisted,

> that "headquarters" is trying neither to "put over" a "project" in which (for some selfish but unknown reasons) only "the administration" is interested, nor in sponsoring a movement leading towards what (in a derogatory sense) has been referred to as "centralization."[33]

Two months later, the country was at war, and Cummins's initiatives lost momentum. Soon the denomination was concerned with civil defense, maintaining contact with those in the service, chaplains, conscientious objectors and other pacifists, and the Universalist War Relief Committee. Forward Together was scarcely heard of.

The 1941 General Convention had authorized application to the New York state legislature for a new charter, changing the name to the Universalist Church of America. This necessitated an abbreviated meeting in 1943, despite travel restrictions, so that the bylaws could be brought into conformity with the new charter and provisions included for the Central Planning Council. Otherwise little progress was made toward reforming the basic organization of the denomination. The 1945 meeting was not held on schedule, but postponed until April 1946.

"UNITARIAN ADVANCE"

Unitarians, like Universalists, were soon engrossed in problems relating to the war. The efforts of the first four years of the Eliot administration to implement the proposals of the Appraisal Commission slackened perceptibly. Travel restrictions meant that the General Conference meetings of 1943 and 1945 were *pro forma* for the nomination of the moderator and the election of committees. The annual meeting of 1944 was abbreviated; the annual meeting of 1945 was *pro forma*.

Preparation for Unitarian extension after the war took the form of a program called Unitarian Advance, developed by three committees appointed by the Board. Committee A sought to define the basic religious values of the denomination; Committee B was to be a "testing and methods" committee; Committee C was to recommend ways of implementation, especially by closer integration of the various denominational agencies. The work of Committee A, chaired by A. Powell Davies, produced controversy within the Board of Directors, on the grounds that its proposed document would be a sort of creedal statement. Frederick Eliot was among those who voted against it on those grounds.[34] Looking back, however, it would seem to have been an attempt at a consensus statement without creedal status.

Following the war, efforts to increase membership became the chief priority, resulting in new initiatives with implications for polity, particularly the Church of the Larger Fellowship and the organization of fellowship units. At the same time, the problem of centralized bureaucracy reappeared in discussions over the *Christian Register* and the Service Committee.

Church of the Larger Fellowship. The Church of the Larger Fellowship was formally authorized by vote of the AUA Board on January 14, 1944, with a view to addressing the needs of isolated Unitarians and drawing them into closer relationship with the denomination. Bylaws were adopted, which provided for administration by a committee appointed by the AUA Board. The Board appropriated funds and designated Dr. Albert C. Dieffenbach as minister. When he resigned five years later, he could report a total membership of more than 1,500 from every state, every Canadian province, and a dozen foreign countries, with whom he kept in touch by monthly ministerial letters.[35]

The work of the Church of the Larger Fellowship was not without precedents. The most obvious of these was the Post Office Mission of the Women's Alliance, carried on for many years by dedicated laywomen in Alliance branches in the local churches.[36] What was new was something called a "church" and the appointment of a "minister" by central bureaucratic action. The work of Dieffenbach and his successors was important, and only the AUA was in a position to organize and support it. To call scattered individuals on a common mailing list a "church" might seem to be a matter of handy nomenclature only. But the effect was to blur the understanding of a congregational church as a covenanted body of worshipers empowered to choose its own leadership. It does not appear that this departure from norms of congregational polity bothered anyone, or stimulated consideration of whether the ecclesiology of the denomination should be reconceived to accommodate this anomaly.

The Fellowship Program. The concept of a congregational church was blurred in a somewhat different way by the development of "fellowships" as lay-led religious communities. Initially they were thought of as instruments for Unitarian extension authorized by the AUA. In March 1945, the Board of Directors voted to explore the possibility of "organizing lay centers in communities where there is no Unitarian church and where there is a sufficient number of individual Unitarians." The idea was not a new one, but earlier attempts of a similar kind had come to nothing. This time, the initiative of Lon Ray Call, "Minister-at-Large" for church extension, and the appointment of Monroe Husbands to direct the program, made the fellowship movement the cutting edge of denominational expansion into new territory.[37]

The key to Husbands's success, as its chief chronicler has argued, was that he did not require the fellowships to conform to a standard pattern or organization prescribed by headquarters. Instead of asserting denominational control, he "let the local group *itself* produce what was wanted." He stood ready to help the group get started and made available materials and suggestions for the fellowships to use, but he expected "each local unit to choose its own leaders and evolve its own purposes, goals, methods of operation, mood, setting, philosophy, and emphasis."[38]

Ecclesiologically, the result was congregational churches of the purest kind. They did not have ministerial leadership; but it is to be remembered that the Cambridge Platform (1648) declared that "there may be the essence & being of a church without any officers, seeing there is both the form and matter of a church." Ministers are not necessary to "the simple being of a church," however much they may be needed for its well-being.

If the word *church* was applied to the Church of the Larger Fellowship, which ecclesiologically was not a church, the word *fellowship* was applied to groups that ecclesiologically were churches. The effect was to establish the image of two kinds of religious groups: *churches* with ministers (and buildings and budgets) and *fellowships* without these defining characteristics. When the question arose of admitting fellowships to membership in the AUA, additional criteria were introduced. In 1955, the Board of Directors prescribed that a fellowship might be recognized "when it has ten resident members," while a church might be recognized "when there is a charter membership roll representing sixty-five or more resident, contributing families and when the regional and continental officers concerned are convinced that the community is large enough to assure very substantial future growth."[39]

It needs to be emphasized that this distinction between a "church" and a "fellowship" was bureaucratic and not ecclesiological. Its practical meaning was that the AUA gave subsidies to nascent churches but not to fellowships. But ecclesiologically, from the point of view of congregational polity, both were churches. Some fellowships, indeed, used the word *church* in their titles, much to the dismay of some bureaucrats, who insisted that they were really "only fellowships." Lon Ray Call, in particular, was concerned by a tendency to regard fellowships as "seedling churches." Acknowledging that some might grow large enough to become churches, he nevertheless insisted that their proper function was to meet the needs of Unitarians located where no church was anticipated. To allow fellowships to think of themselves as future churches would lead to requests for subsidies, thereby undercutting the ongoing work of planting churches in larger metropolitan areas where there would be good hope that they would be self-sustaining.[40]

The distinction between "churches" and "fellowships" soon became embedded in popular understanding, the presence or absence of a minister usually being the defining characteristic. Yet while some fellowships remained small, others became larger than many churches; while some fellowships continued to meet in homes or rented quarters, others decided to buy or build permanent homes; while some fellowships would have nothing to do with a clerical presence, others decided they needed professional leadership. Bylaws of the AUA adopted in 1951 had defined fellowships as groups "organized under the auspices and functioning under a charter granted by the Association for the purpose of extending or promoting the Unitarian movement."[41] This definition made less and less sense as time passed, and a decade later the bylaws of the UUA, adopted at the time of merger, made no such distinction. It survived in the listings of churches and fellowships in the UUA *Directory*, but finally disappeared in 1970. It is fair to say, however, that many Unitarian Universalists still think a "fellowship" is not a church, though they would be hard put to say what the essential distinction is between them, either practically or ecclesiologically.

Congregational ordination. If a denominational committee could organize a church and appoint its minister, and if the minister available to members of a fellowship was a Minister-at-Large from 25 Beacon Street, little wonder that the traditional symbiotic relationship between minister and covenanted church was obscured. The influx of new Unitarians in the 1950s, often from denominations with hierarchical polity, strengthened the existing tendency for ministers to define themselves in terms of their professional status—"in ministerial fellowship" with the denomination—rather than in terms of a congregation's validation of their inner call to ministry. While ordination continued to be by local congregations, its inner meaning was eroded. Some churches (usually big ones) stated that they ordained "with the consent of" Boards of Trustees or Prudential Committees, rather than by vote of the members.[42] Some churches (usually small ones) declared that they ordained "on recommendation of" or "with the approval of" the Fellowship Committee of the AUA.[43] Some candidates were ordained by their home churches, instead of reserving this as a precious privilege of the churches they were to serve.[44]

In these instances, the churches allowed an erosion of their privileges and responsibilities. But there were other cases where churches extended their prerogatives and presumed to ordain ministers at large, without taking responsibility for a continued parochial relationship. Thus some students sought ordination as soon as they received the Bachelor of Divinity degree, even when they had no prospect of serving a church immediately, perhaps for some time to come.[45] In one instance, a local church was asked to ordain a man without theological training, who had never served a parish, who never expected to, and whose career was exclusively bureaucratic.[46] There was one instance where an individual was ordained at the age of eighty-three as a kind of honorary recognition of past services to the cause of liberal religion.[47] In each case, except perhaps the last one, sufficient precedent existed so that the action generally passed without comment, and the Fellowship Committee promptly approved the persons concerned as available for parish ministry.

The Christian Register. When Llewellyn Jones was dismissed as editor of the *Register* in 1941, the attempt by critics of the administration to assure editorial freedom by establishing an independent editorial board was rejected. Control continued to be exercised by an Editorial Board of seven persons, three of them staff members, including the president of the Association. Given such a structure, as long as the editor retained the confidence of the board, he or she would have great freedom to shape the nature of the journal. Jones had discovered that it did not include freedom to make criticisms reflecting unfavorably on the administration. Stephen Fritchman discovered that it did not include freedom to shape the contents in accord with his own vision of social or political policy when prevailing opinion in the denomination disagreed.[48]

Stephen Fritchman became editor of the *Register* on a part-time basis in the fall of 1942. His primary assignment continued to be to coordinate and develop programs with the youth of the denomination. As editor, he did not accept the view that the function of the journal was merely to promote denominational interests and print news of the churches. He conceived of it as a journal of opinion addressing the great social and political issues of the day, expressive of Unitarian concern for the application of religion to social problems. He was a social activist, a socialist for whom the threat of fascism came not only from abroad but also from the failure of the domestic policies of the New Deal to solve problems of depression, unemployment, and oppression of the weak by the strong. "Fascism," he wrote in 1943, "is not only political and economic exploitation, not only the building of a master-slave society; it is also the crucifixion of everything the Christian church represents."[49] He was involved in such organizations as the Joint Anti-Fascist Refugee Committee, the National Council of American-Soviet Friendship, and American Youth for Democracy.

As long as the United States and the Soviet Union were allies in the war against Nazi Germany, these associations presented no particular problem. After the war, when the iron curtain descended, such organizations became suspect. Fritchman had been accustomed to turn to associates in these organizations for contributions to the *Register,* which, as seen by many readers in the incipient cold war era, gave the magazine a left-wing tinge. The most vigorous protests came from political conservatives in the denomination, who charged that Fritchman was using his position for "a studied and deliberate campaign to use the *Christian Register* and other agencies as a means of proselytizing in behalf of the Communist party cause."[50] But there were anticommunist liberals also who were concerned, on the basis of personal experience, over infiltration of liberal organizations, including Unitarian churches and the Service Committee, by Communists or fellow-travelers who were evasive about their identity.[51] After extended investigation, by an overwhelming vote on October 9, 1946, the Board exonerated Fritchman of the charges.[52]

At the same time, an arrangement was worked out whereby the editor would consult regularly with the Editorial Board, "to give Mr. Fritchman the backing and support of the officers in making THE REGISTER as widely representative as possible of the views of the denomination."[53] This did not end the dispute. Dr. Eliot traveled across the continent in December "to discover at first hand the seriousness of this criticism" of the *Register,* which clearly went beyond the very conservative elements in the denomination, and he reached the conclusion that "the criticism is indeed widespread and of a nature to be taken very seriously." Most Unitarians, though, were "pretty solidly behind the present policies of the Association."[54]

For a time the arrangement for consultation with the Editorial Board seemed to work well. Fritchman sent advance proofs of his editorials for comment by those most concerned, and he "frequently asked for an opinion concerning a proposed article."[55] But in April 1947, he prepared an editorial castigating the Truman Doctrine, which sought to assure that Greece would not fall into the Soviet orbit.[56] The editorial may seem innocuous today. But in the spring of 1947, the Editorial Board felt its publication would be injudicious and telegraphed Fritchman—who was away on a speaking trip—for permission to substitute another text or to return to Boston for consultation. He wired back his assent to the substitution, but on his return stated that he would resign as editor. He told the Advisory Board "that he would have to have complete and final freedom of the complete contents of the *Christian Register*" if he were to continue.[57]

The Executive Committee called a special meeting of the Board of Directors, meanwhile suspending him. He asked that his resignation be considered, not by the Board of Directors but by the annual meeting of the Association. After long discussion the board terminated his employment, and at the annual meeting on May 22, 1947, a motion to reinstate him was decisively defeated.[58]

Fritchman's supporters declared that freedom of the press was at stake, and that the Editorial Board was exercising censorship. But the *Register* was a house organ, not an independent journal. The kind of freedom Fritchman insisted on—to take principled stands unpalatable to widespread opinion throughout the constituency to which he was responsible—was divisive and threatened to continue to be so. That is not permitted to editors of house organs, as the *Register* had been since 1939.

The Service Committee. In one instance, the trend toward

centralization at headquarters was reversed. The Unitarian Service Committee was established by a vote of the Board of Directors in May 1940. It gave formal structure and enlarged scope to the relief work begun in 1938 to aid Czech Unitarians fleeing Nazi occupation. It continued as a headquarters operation until December 1948, when it was separately incorporated. The end of the war had brought severe cutbacks in funding, and the scope of activities had been drastically curtailed. Members of the Service Committee board argued that it was necessary to be autonomous in order to appeal for non-Unitarian support, including government support. Frederick Eliot strongly opposed the proposal, desiring that the Service Committee be closely identified with the denomination. The matter came to a vote at a meeting of the AUA Board on October 13; Eliot and two others were the lone dissenters. It was stipulated, however, as part of the vote that the corporate name should remain Unitarian Service Committee.[59]

FINAL MOVEMENT TO MERGER

The conference committee established in 1899 to promote cooperation between the two denominations petered out with no lasting result. Discussions in the 1920s—at one time looking toward closer relations among Congregationalists, Universalists, and Unitarians—roused fears among many Universalists that they would lose their separate identity, and so came to nothing. Renewed discussions between Unitarians and Universalists resulted in the organization in 1934 of the Free Church Fellowship as a federation which might also include participants from other denominations, but it received lukewarm support and never got off the ground. Persistent attempts of the Universalists to gain membership in the Federal Council of Churches indicated that the urge to maintain fruitful contact with liberals in several denominations was not dead, but when these efforts failed for the second time in 1946, it was clear that mainline Protestant leaders dismissed the Universalists as no more acceptable than the Unitarians.[60]

Though top-level negotiations for closer relations between Universalists and Unitarians had repeatedly sputtered and failed, significant cooperation was actually taking place elsewhere.[61] In 1933, under economic pressure, an arrangement was worked out whereby composition and printing of the *Christian Register* was taken over by the Universalist Publishing House; the *Register* and the *Leader* then included as many as eight pages of common material. Hymnbook commissions of the two denominations jointly compiled *Hymns of the Spirit* (1937). The Unitarian *Wayside Pulpit* and the *Universalist Community Pulpit* were combined as the *Wayside Community Pulpit*.

At the parish level, three federations of local churches in Florida were arranged in 1927; by 1945 there were at least twenty-one federated churches. Federated churches and dual fellowship of ministers made it relatively simple, psychologically at least, for ministers to cross over from one denomination to the other. The practice became frequent enough to require a policy statement in 1952 from the officials of the two denominations directly concerned to the effect that "no impediment" would be placed in the way of a Universalist minister seeking a Unitarian pulpit "on his own," and that he would continue to be recognized "as a primary Universalist minister, and is never urged to change."[62] Larger opportunities (and higher salaries) were tempting some Universalists to make the shift, and for a time, during active negotiations looking to merger, it seemed necessary to discourage the practice lest Universalist pulpits be drained of talented leadership. By 1955, 101 Universalist and 98 Unitarian ministers held dual fellowship.[63]

Despite differences in polity, the two denominations were becoming more alike in program and mode of administration, so communication between administrators in the two denominations seemed obvious and natural. In 1945, the Universalist Service Committee was organized, replacing an earlier War Relief Fund, and it worked closely with the Unitarian Service Committee in relief work on the European continent; it was not, however, separately incorporated.[64] The Universalists began to develop an equivalent of the Unitarian Church of the Larger Fellowship and to explore the possibility of fellowship units comparable to those the Unitarians had pioneered. In 1949–51, prodded by Dr. Cummins, the Universalists reorganized their headquarters structure along departmental lines as Dr. Samuel A. Eliot had done for the Unitarians earlier.[65]

The youth programs of the two denominations followed parallel lines, with recurrent occasions for cooperation. As far back as 1936, the AUA Commission of Appraisal had encouraged merger of the youth groups; after the war, American Unitarian Youth and the Universalist Youth Fellowship collaborated on a publication, if briefly, and in 1951 they met together in a conference that led in 1953 to merger, as Liberal Religious Youth.[66]

In such ways, direct personal interaction among Universalists and Unitarians was promoted at the working level. This interaction probably did more to pave the way for merger than had been accomplished over the years by top-level negotiations over blueprints for federation. The process of merger was actually well under way before a formal decision to merge could be considered with any chance of acceptance.

Meanwhile, a halfway measure called Federal Union had to be tried and its inadequacy shown. In 1949, the biennial conferences of the denominations authorized a Commission on Church Union "to develop a comprehensive plan for the federal union of all administrative and service agencies and all affiliated organizations above the level of the parish churches." In 1951, it recommended the development of a new administrative structure, to which the two denominations should transfer specified activities, at first publication, public relations, and education. When submitted to the churches, the proposal was approved by a generous margin. Joint biennial meetings in 1953 established the Council of Liberal Churches and designated education and public relations for common administration.[67]

Results were unsatisfactory on a number of counts. Transfer of functions to the new body proved to be unexpectedly difficult. Financial support from the parent denominations fell short of what had been promised. A third administrative structure added to the two already existing was burdensome, financially and otherwise. By 1955, the Joint Interim Commission on Federal Union reached the conclusion that the question of complete merger could no longer be avoided. Reporting to the biennial meetings of the two denominations held in Detroit, it proposed a merger commission, charged with conducting a plebiscite to determine the will of the churches.[68]

A Joint Merger Commission, authorized by both denominations, began work in the fall of 1956, chaired by the Reverend William B. Rice. It prepared a manual and a study guide on "Merger and Alternatives," and it conducted a plebiscite, which showed a clear preference for merger over other alternatives. A plan for merger, including proposed bylaws, was prepared for consideration by the two denominations at biennial meetings at Syracuse in the fall of 1959.[69] Meeting jointly and in separate sessions, the two denominations approved the plan with minor changes. Pros and cons of merger were vigorously discussed, but questions of polity were not central. Accepted in plebiscite by the churches of the two denominations, it was formally voted by their governing bodies in 1960, and merger was accomplished in 1961.[70]

THE STRUCTURE OF THE
UNITARIAN UNIVERSALIST ASSOCIATION

The Constitution and Bylaws of the new Unitarian Universalist Association, as worked out at Syracuse, drew more on Unitarian than on Universalist practice. Fundamental was the abandonment of the Universalist hierarchical structure of state conventions and General Assembly, "exercising jurisdiction" over "all clergymen, state conventions and parishes."[71] Except as its Board of Trustees passed judgment on the admission of churches to the Association, and its Fellowship Committee passed judgment on the admission of ministers to fellowship, the UUA was given no such judicial authority. It was to be, like the AUA, an organization in which the churches would associate to do together various practical tasks that no church could accomplish alone. Though not specified in the Constitution itself, these would obviously include such familiar activities as the organization of new churches, the credentialing of ministers, assistance in matching ministers with churches seeking leadership, the preparation of hymnbooks and educational materials, and the like.

The use of the word "Association" in the title, rather than the word "Church" so recently adopted by the Universalists, expressed a traditional understanding of congregational polity. That polity was specifically acknowledged by an affirmation of "the independence and autonomy of local churches, fellowships and associate members."[72] The one requirement for acceptance of a church into membership was a written statement that "it subscribes to the purposes and objectives of the Association," as spelled out in general and noncreedal terms in Article II, and that it "pledges itself to support the Association."[73]

While there was feeling in some quarters that Universalist state conventions should dissolve and turn their invested funds over to the UUA, there was no requirement that this be done. Some did so, but others survived, though no longer exercising an ecclesiastical jurisdiction. Similarly, no change was required in the status of Unitarian local conferences, which in any case had not accumulated invested funds or exercised disciplinary authority. How regional organizations might develop was left for future determination, so long as it was "based on the principle of local autonomy, consistent with the promotion of the welfare and interests of the Association as a whole and of its member churches and fellowships."[74]

Fellowshiping. Universalist practice had been to give to Fellowship Committees jurisdiction over both parishes and ministers. With respect to parishes, the Laws of Fellowship provided for disfellowshiping if a church settled "as a pastor a clergyman not in fellowship or who has been refused fellowship or who has been disfellowshiped."[75]

The Constitution of the UUA granted no such denominational control of a church's choice of its minister. Membership in the Association would not be jeopardized, no matter who was called. The only provisions for depriving a church of representation at the General Assembly were procedural, not disciplinary, designed simply to exclude defunct or dormant churches. To be represented by delegates, a church had to meet four requirements: an annual financial contribution to the UUA; "regular religious services"; a regularly constituted organization, with adequate membership records, elected officers, and annual meetings; and the submission of reports on statistics and activities. Responsibility of determining compliance rested with the Board of Trustees.[76]

With respect to ministers, Universalist practice had been for state conventions (or where none existed, the General Convention) both to authorize ordination and to grant fellowship. An "Ordination Vow of Faithfulness to the Universalist Ministry and to the Universalist Church of America" was required as part of the service of ordination. Fellowship once granted might be withdrawn for cause, such as becoming engrossed in secular business, or accepting a settlement in a parish not in fellowship, or for "unministerial conduct."

A minister might even be dropped "for the good of the service, without charges and trial," provided the state Fellowship Committee and the Central Fellowship Committee agreed unanimously. A disfellowshiped minister could no longer serve a Universalist church, even if he retained the confidence of the congregation; and the church itself was liable to be disfellowshiped if it retained him.[77]

Ordination by a church is a formal recognition of the candidate's inner call to ministry; fellowshiping is a credentialing procedure, giving assurance to the churches that a minister is deemed qualified to serve wherever called. Where the Universalists had merged these two functions and placed them in the control of denominational authorities,[78] the UUA Constitution explicitly divided them:

> The Association recognizes and affirms that member churches alone have the right to call and ordain their ministers. The Association alone shall have the right to grant Ministerial Fellowship with the Association.[79]

These provisions assure that a church that considers it best to call a minister who is not in fellowship loses none of its rights as a member of the Association, as was once the formal requirement with the Universalists, and it is entitled to all the services the Association offers. But it also means that no such minister automatically receives denominational standing by virtue of settlement in a Unitarian Universalist church, as is the case in certain other denominations of the congregational order. In this way, the right of the church to select its own leadership is protected, while its folly if it makes the wrong choice is limited to itself.

The Constitution made a clear distinction between the ministry as a calling and the ministry as a profession, reserving the ecclesiastical role for the churches, while giving administrative responsibility to the Association. It thus recognized a basic distinction between two statuses: that of being a *minister* and being *in ministerial fellowship.* Despite a tendency on the part of many of the clergy to conflate the two, and often to identify much more with the professional than with the ecclesiastical status, the distinction is important. One may be a minister without being in ministerial fellowship, or be in ministerial fellowship without any ministerial relationship to a covenanted religious community.

Meetings of the Association. Meetings of the Universalist Church of America and the American Unitarian Association had followed different schedules. The General Assembly of the UCA met biennially at various locations throughout the country. The business meetings of the AUA were held annually in Boston; in the fall of alternate years, however, "General Conference" meetings were held at various places outside the Commonwealth of Massachusetts. During discussions leading up to merger, joint biennial meetings of the two denominations were held—at Andover, Massachusetts, 1953; Detroit, Michigan, 1955; Atlantic City, New Jersey, 1957; and Syracuse, New York, 1959.

Universalists on the whole preferred biennial sessions for the new organization. Among Unitarians, there had been some feeling that three meetings every two years was too many, but that the traditional "May Meetings" were needed to take care of the formal business, to give opportunities for many related organizations to meet, and for people from the churches to gather and know each other. The new charter of incorporation imposed no restriction on the location of business meetings, as had been the case with the AUA. The bylaws of the UUA therefore provided for regular meetings to be held annually in April or May "at such time and place in the United States of America or in Canada as the Board of Trustees from time to time shall determine."[80]

Something of value was lost, however, when the biennial General Conference meetings of the AUA were discarded. These meetings had been structured to permit a detached review of the work and outlook of the denomination, without the immediate involvement in administrative matters such as concerned the annual meetings. The General Conference, rather than the annual meeting, elected Business, Program, and Nominating Committees. This may not have assured an independent perspective on the bureaucratic operations at headquarters. The central role of the Conference in the discussions leading to merger was nevertheless a vindication of its usefulness.

Officers and trustees and the boundary question. General charge of the affairs of their denominations had been given to the Board of Trustees of the UCA and the Board of Directors of the AUA. The two boards differed markedly in size. The UCA board comprised the president and ten trustees (together with the general superintendent, *ex officio,* without vote). The AUA board was composed of seven officers, including the moderator and president, and eighteen directors. The Universalist board was required to meet twice a year at least, but members could vote by mail. This suggests a somewhat lower level of activity than was the case for the Unitarians, who met at least three times a year. The new UUA Board of Trustees kept the Universalist name and the Unitarian size. It was made up of five officers and twenty other persons, but neither the president nor the treasurer was given a vote. Three regular meetings of the Board were prescribed between regular meetings of the General Assembly.[81]

A more important difference between the two denominations had been the defined relationship between the board and the chief executive officer. The general superintendent of the UCA was chosen biennially by the Board of Trustees. The president of the AUA was elected for a four-year term by the Annual Meeting, but he was nominated by the Board of Directors of which he was himself a member. He was also a member of all committees authorized by the bylaws, including the Nominating Committee. He was in a position to be involved in every aspect of headquarters administration, and for twenty years the role was defined by Frederick Eliot as one of active leadership. Eliot's views did not always prevail, but there was no one of comparable stature or influence among those who criticized or opposed him. He left behind the concept of a strong presidency, rather than that of an executive officer whose duty it was to carry out the policies of a strong board.[82]

The UUA bylaws suggest a desire to cut back the strong presidency of the Eliot years of the AUA. They specifically stated that the president was to be "subject to the direction and control of the Board of Trustees." He no longer would be a member of the Fellowship and Nominating Committees. As *ex officio* member of standing committees of the General Assembly and Board, he would not have a vote. He might be removed from office if three-quarters of the whole Board were of the opinion that he was incapacitated or that it would be "for the best interests of the Association." The role of the moderator was underlined: he or she would preside over meetings of the General Assembly, the Board of Trustees, and the Executive Committee, and would report for the Board of Trustees to regular meetings of the General Assembly.[83]

At the joint session of the two denominations at Syracuse in 1959, the question of a strong presidency came up briefly, but the body rejected an amendment to eliminate the provision making the president subject to the control of the Board.[84] The delegates were much more interested in the question of whether or how the denomination would acknowledge its Judeo-Christian heritage in the listing of Purposes and Objectives. Discussion of this issue has properly loomed large in general accounts of merger. But so far as polity is concerned, it was of little significance, since the wording was descriptive, not prescriptive. Both denominations had long since agreed that no formal mechanism should be erected to maintain their boundaries at any prescribed theological position, and that their identities should be established in the free flow of discussion. In matters of definition of boundaries, the issue of polity lies in the process by which the boundary is defined and maintained, not in the question of whether a particular point of view is included or excluded.

The UUA, 1961–1985

ORGANIZING THE MERGED DENOMINATION, 1961–1969

Between the Syracuse meeting of 1959 and the final accomplishment of merger in 1961, interim committees were at work planning for the organization and administration of the new denomination. Their reports—sometimes referred to as the "brown book"—were ready in time for the organizing meeting. They included recommendations with respect to the mode of organization, regional organization, and the ministry. In this same period, a commission on "The Church and Its Leadership," established by the AUA on the initiative of Dana Greeley, then president of the Association, was considering some of the same issues. Free from the obligation to make specific recommendations for action by the new General Assembly, its report could be more historical and analytical, and less organizational and administrative in focus.[1]

The conclusions and recommendations of both reports were consonant with a basic understanding of congregational polity. They affirmed the right of the churches to order their own affairs, while denominational organization provides resources enabling them to be more effective. The commission on "The Church and Its Leadership" in particular spelled out four rights to be reserved explicitly to the local church:

(1) the right of the church to admit members in accordance with its own definition of qualifications; (2) the right of the church to select its own leadership; (3) the right of the church to control its own property; and (4) the right of the church to enter freely and voluntarily into association with other churches.[2]

Agreement on adherence to congregational polity does not automatically solve all problems. Four areas of discussion and debate, with implications for polity, emerged in the years following merger: (1) the churches and the authority of the General Assembly; (2) the offices of president and moderator; (3) districting; (4) the concepts of "ministry" and "ministerial fellowship."

The Local Church and the Authority of the General Assembly. The Constitution of the UUA established the General Assembly as "the overall policy making body for carrying on the purposes and objectives of the Association" with authority to "direct and control its affairs." The General Assembly was to be composed of lay delegates from the churches, the number determined by the size of the church, together with their settled minister or ministers in fellowship with the Association including any minister emeritus. It is significant that, in contrast with earlier Universalist practice, a minister in fellowship with the Association would not be a voting member of the General Assembly unless settled in or the minister emeritus of a church.[3]

To become a member of the UUA, with the right to representation in the General Assembly, a church would indicate that it subscribes to the purposes and objectives of the Association and pledges to support it. A problem that arises in ecclesiastical bodies of this kind, however, is that churches sometimes maintain a legal corporate existence long after they have ceased being religious communities. Hence to prevent dormant churches from participating in the affairs of a living enterprise, the Constitution provided that only those churches are entitled to voting privileges in the General Assembly that conduct regular religious services, maintain a regularly established organization, furnish reports on church statistics and activities, and make a financial contribution. These were procedural requirements, intended to prevent dormant churches from playing the part of rotten boroughs. They were not designed to enable the Board of Trustees to discipline wayward or unruly churches.

Soon after merger, however, the General Assembly was presented with a proposed amendment to the Constitution that would have added a requirement of a very different kind. It would have prescribed the criteria to be used by the local church in admitting members to its covenant, subject to the denial of voting rights if a church failed to conform. This proposal was debated in terms of social policy, but the issue would have been the same had the proposal been to impose theological or creedal restrictions on the churches, accompanied by sanctions. The imposition on the churches of criteria for membership in the name of a liberal social philosophy presents the same problem as the imposition of a test phrased in theological language. In either case, an element of hierarchical authority is introduced into the polity.

The proposal was introduced in 1962 by a number of ministers from churches in the South, who felt that an explicit avowal of nondiscrimination inserted in the Constitution of the continental association would support them in their efforts to eliminate segregation locally. It provided that a church would be entitled to be represented by delegates only if in the preceding fiscal year it had "maintained a policy of admitting persons to membership without discrimination on account of race, color, or national origin."[4]

The proposal came up for decision in 1963 at the meeting in Chicago. Meanwhile, a considerable number of ministers and laypersons, who were wholly in sympathy with the intent of the amendment, questioned whether this particular proposal was the best way to achieve the intended goal. The

Association had never been given the right to set doctrinal standards for its member churches, and neither the Board of Trustees nor the General Assembly had been given the power to discipline or expel churches for doctrinal irregularity, or to intrude on the internal self-government of autonomous churches. The question was central to an understanding of the congregational way of the churches.

Furthermore, opponents of the proposal queried, what kind of ecclesiastical machinery would be necessary to implement it? The responsibility for determining whether the churches had complied would fall on the Board of Trustees. It would be charged with the duty of satisfying itself every year that every one of a thousand churches and fellowships was pursuing a policy of open membership. One way would be to require the churches to certify in writing each year that they had followed the specified policy. This might be described as the "loyalty oath" approach to the question. Alternatively, the Board might investigate systematically the practice of local churches. This would make the Board a sort of "un-Unitarian activities committee," charged with certifying whether the atmosphere was healthy and orthodox. How the Board could actually make such a determination would be a major problem, since exclusion from membership can be achieved by many subtle pressures concerning which one may be suspicious, but which never can be clearly proven.

Needless to say, procedures of this kind were not what the proponents of the amendment had in mind. They sought a resounding declaration of the denomination's stand on a crucial moral issue of the day, as a rallying point for forces making for righteousness. Because the matter was debated in Chicago at a time when civil rights dominated the headlines and the news from Birmingham was the grimmest, it seemed to many delegates impossible not to support any proposal in favor of desegregation and against discrimination. The proposal received the votes of a majority of the delegates, but failed to get the two-thirds required to amend the Constitution. The General Assembly then adopted almost unanimously a declaration of the mind of the denomination on the issue, and it established a Commission on Religion and Race "to promote the complete integration of Negroes and other minority persons into our congregations." The intent of the original sponsors was thereby advanced, without introducing the spectre of ecclesiastical courts and discipline, alien to the congregational way.[5]

The desire of many delegates to include an affirmation of "open membership" in the Constitution continued to be heard. Attention turned from the section dealing with membership (Article III, Section 4) to the Purposes and Principles (Article II). Proposed wording failed adoption in 1965, but passed in revised form in 1967. It declared the responsibility of both Association and churches "to promote the full participation of persons, without regard to race, color, sex, or national origin."[6]

Meanwhile the issue of open membership had become entangled in the question whether theological or ideological criteria for membership are legitimate. In the course of litigation in 1964 and 1965, involving a church in Providence, Rhode Island, counsel for one party asserted "that it is a tradition of the Unitarian Universalist religion that each member believe in a supernatural being or a God."[7] That assertion might have been descriptive a half-century earlier, but no longer.

The Constitution of the UUA had recognized diversity of theological belief by declaring that "individual freedom of belief" is "inherent in the Unitarian and Universalist heritages." Whether that should be interpreted to mean that churches might not adopt covenants or bonds of fellowship phrased in theological language suddenly became a matter of concern to some. A considerable semantic discussion ensued, which finally produced a general understanding that a church might adopt a statement of purpose, or a covenant, or a bond of union—or even a "creed"—without infringing on individual freedom of belief, so long as it was not used or intended as a "creedal test" for membership. A paragraph embodying that understanding was added to the Constitution in 1968.[8]

A different threat of intrusion by the Association into the self-government of the churches was a proposal in 1968 to require support of the UUA by "mandatory contributions." It would have provided that a church which failed to make "a financial contribution fixed in accordance with the By-Laws" would not only lose the right to send delegates to the General Assembly, but even worse would no longer be entitled "to receive the services of the Association or the Districts." The proposal was intended to address a serious financial problem then facing the Association; but the implications for polity were forcefully made in the discussion, and the proposal was overwhelmingly rejected when it came up for final action in 1969.[9]

President and moderator. The office of the president, as it had developed during Frederick Eliot's long administration of the AUA, became a matter of immediate concern at his death in February 1958. He had been a strong president; strong leaders elicit opposition and criticism. Some voices in the denomination asserted dictatorship; others argued more temperately that the demands of the position had become too much for one man. The need for reconsideration of the office was openly expressed; and the Board of Directors, in authorizing an election to fill the remaining three years of Eliot's term, looked upon the period as a time for study of the organization and functioning of headquarters. The nomination of Ernest Kuebler, an experienced administrator, to fill the vacancy, was consonant with this intention.[10]

The Board appointed a special committee of three to consider proposals for reorganization. Among the recommendations of the committee, which reported in October 1958, was a proposal to divide the functions of the president. He would be the religious leader of the denomination, elected by the

Annual Meeting; he would serve as chairman of the Board of Directors; and he would represent the denomination on public occasions and in fraternal relations with other denominations. A two-year term was suggested, to be filled by a distinguished minister, on partial or full-time leave from the parish. The chief executive officer would be an administrative director, appointed by the Board for an indefinite term, and subject to dismissal by it. The president, as a visible representative of the denomination, would thus fulfill many of the functions expected of the moderator when that office was established in 1937. The moderator was left to preside over the annual meeting, much as the presidents of the General Conference had done before 1925.[11]

A similar proposal was submitted as an amendment to the bylaws of the AUA at the annual meeting in May 1959. It would have established the position of Executive Director, to be "the chief executive of the Association acting on behalf of and under the direction of the Board of Directors or the Executive Committee."[12]

Little consideration was given to these proposals, since Dana Greeley had readily been persuaded to challenge Kuebler for the unexpired term and had been elected in May 1958. As a candidate, Greeley's avowed purpose was "to preserve the concept of a strong presidency," and once he was elected, the Board deferred to him. His concept of the presidency was doubtless shaped by the way it had developed under Frederick Eliot, and he was not disposed to be an appointee of the Board, let alone a part-time ceremonial head.[13]

The question of the presidency could not be avoided, however, when the Merger Commission drafted bylaws for consideration at Syracuse in 1959. The Unitarians were accustomed to a president elected by the delegates to the annual meeting; the Universalist general superintendent was appointed by the Board of Trustees, and the Universalists on the whole preferred that arrangement. The result of the Merger Commission's deliberations was a discordant combination of these alternatives. The president was to be elected by the General Assembly for a four-year term and was designated "the chief executive Officer of the Association." But he was to be "subject to the direction and control" of the Board of Trustees, which might remove him from office by a three-quarters vote if that action was considered to be "for the best interest of the Association." Though a member of the Board, the president was not given a vote, either there or on the Executive Committee.[14]

The Interim Study Committee on Mode of Organization understood these provisions to mean that the Board of Trustees would take leadership in the formation of policy, while the role of the president would be to implement it. Too often, the committee noted pointedly, past policy boards had been presented "with only those problems and policies which the executive chose to present to it, with the result that the dynamism possible in board leadership never materialized."

The moderator, as chairman of the board and of the Executive Committee, would necessarily play a significant role in the shaping of policy. The committee's understanding of the structure prescribed by the proposed constitution and bylaws is clear from the organizational chart included in the report. The General Assembly is properly at the top; below it is the Board of Trustees, chaired by the moderator; next below is the president.[15] After extended discussion, the Committee recommended a change in the bylaws to provide that the president be elected by the Board and serve at its pleasure. This proposal, however, was rejected by the delegates at the organizing meeting in May 1961.[16]

The first moderator of the UUA was Marshall E. Dimock, a professor of public administration who had had extensive and varied experience in government service. He had been on the Interim Study Committee on Mode of Organization, where he had been active in shaping the recommendations and drafting the report. As moderator he took seriously the bylaw provision that the president was to be "subject to the direction and control of the Board." He was given an office at 25 Beacon Street, where as chairman of the Board he began to consult with various members of the staff. Greeley, who took a decidedly different view of the role of the president, considered this to be an intrusion on his turf. It soon became clear that an elected full-time president, directly responsible for day-to-day administration, and evidently intending to be a stronger president than the bylaws had envisaged, had a more secure power base than a volunteer board meeting three times between annual sessions of the General Assembly, headed by an unpaid chairman. After three years, Dimock gave up and resigned before the expiration of his term, while the Board never developed as the democratic center of policy decisions that the Interim Committee had envisioned.[17]

It might seem at first glance that congregational polity was not at issue in the question of the relative authority of president and moderator. But many saw the issue as involving the question of democratic control of headquarters operations. In 1961, Greeley was opposed for election to the office of president by Dr. William B. Rice, who pointedly asked: "Should the president be a person committed to [Interim] Committee Two's concept of a truly democratic organization or should the trend be to greater centralization of authority?" Greeley, he intimated without naming him, would carry into the new association the patterns of the AUA, rather than be "prepared to do a new job in a new and creative situation."[18]

Greeley restated his view of the presidency in a symposium in *UUA Now* (as the denominational magazine was then called) in the fall of 1968; in contrast, a former district executive asserted: "The personal style of presidents Eliot and Greeley have, in short, created an image of the office which is rejected by a growing number of our leaders, both lay and professional." The result, he suggested, is that a directly elected president "with full time to devote to the building of political alliances . . . will be tempted to use his 'mandate' and his power to push his own programs, rather than responding fully to the sense of priorities reflected at other levels of the movement, such as the districts."[19] Issues of polity arise, not merely from formal constitutional provisions, but also by the way they are interpreted and implemented or ignored.

In 1961 and 1965 (as earlier in 1958), Greeley was elected by defeating rival candidates who stood for a more consensus-minded style of leadership. The very fact that these were contested elections had consequences for the role of president. The need to enlist support of a candidacy through active campaigning would henceforth give the successful candidate a validation of his (or her) leadership quite independent of the Board of Trustees. The 1961 bylaws provided that the president should be nominated by the Board, for formal election by the General Assembly. This was consonant with the expectation at that time that the president would be "subject to the direction and control of the Board." Nomination by petition was possible, but it clearly was assumed that that would not happen regularly, but only under special circumstances.[20]

Instead of being exceptional, nomination by petition quickly became usual. In 1968, a revised bylaw removed the Board completely from the nominating process, leaving nomination by petition as the only procedure. Required were petitions by the formal action of twenty-five societies, at least five in each of at least three different districts.[21] This action was taken apparently with little debate and certainly with little awareness of the likely consequences. It was incidental to other questions and issues of greater concern to the delegates: the election of trustees and controversial funding issues. But the consequences were significant and lasting.

Nomination by the Board had meant consideration by a body with a corporate responsibility for the health of the whole denomination, in a position to weigh the strengths and weaknesses of possible nominees against the requirements of the position and the perceived needs of the Association—and perhaps to use persuasion on an especially well-qualified but reluctant nominee.[22] Nomination by the sponsorship of twenty-five churches, with no sense of common identification for this particular purpose, meant in effect self-selected candidates, willing to go about to solicit the needed sponsorship by the requisite number of churches. It made contested elections almost inevitable, which in turn meant candidates willing to campaign actively over a period of months and spend considerable sums of money. This would enormously shrink the pool of talent from which presidential leadership would henceforth be drawn.

Speculation as to who would run to succeed Dana Greeley, since he himself was not eligible for election to a third term, began a year before the General Assembly in 1969. One candidate announced in September 1968, and in due course seven candidates had entered. Altogether, they spent more than $32,000.[23]

Districting. The Constitution of the UUA recognized the need for some sort of intermediate structure between the local churches and the continental administration, but it left the nature of such organization to future determination. The Universalist state conventions, with disciplinary authority, provided no helpful precedent. The Unitarians were accustomed to a patchwork of small local conferences in New England, larger ones elsewhere, and a variety of area meetings. Some rationalization had been attempted by the formation over time of a system of regional councils or conferences, which finally achieved full articulation, at least on paper, in the 1950s.[24] Some of these received support from the Annual Appeal;[25] all had part-time or full-time "Regional Directors."[26] Attempts over the years to maintain regional offices of the AUA itself had come and gone, but none remained at the close. Decentralization of headquarters operations was a policy rediscovered many times over, but never satisfactorily implemented.

The Interim Committee on regional organization tried

again. It recommended the establishment of six or seven "service centers" to expand the "specialized and organizational services" of headquarters administration "into the field and nearer to the churches." It also recommended as many as eighteen "Districts," comprising forty to seventy-five churches and fellowships. These would "encourage the development of lay participation and lay leadership" and "augment the 'face to face' relationships" that both Unitarian local conferences and Universalist state conventions had fostered.

Although plausible boundaries were suggested, churches would be free in their choice of districts; these would be associated churches, not the equivalent, as with Presbyterians or Episcopalians, of regional subdivisions prescribed by higher denominational authority. Districts would have governing boards elected by delegates from the churches. They should be staffed by "Executive Ministers," full time or part time, available for consultation on such matters as ministerial settlement, ordination, and installation; interchurch conferences; and district committees. Though separately organized to perform distinct functions, service centers and districts would necessarily cooperate in many ways; hence an advisory council for each service center was proposed, made up of representatives of the districts served.[27]

The proposal of the interim committee was a determined attempt to balance headquarters concerns and regional interests, but as of that date it was unrealistic in terms of financing. It was understood that organization of districts would have priority over the establishment of service centers. A "Guide for the Development of Districts" was promptly prepared, and the initial organization was substantially completed in less than three years.[28]

Criticism of the district structure quickly surfaced. In some quarters it was argued that the districts were too small and weak to stand in the way of the inevitable centralization of power, as the much larger Western Conference of the AUA had once done. Alternatively, others feared that districts would develop the same disregard for the denomination as a whole that had been a problem with Universalist state conventions. A report of the Commission on Appraisal in 1965 suggested that both tendencies had appeared: continental headquarters too often ignored and failed to inform the districts, while districts were tending to "develop into units operating separate and apart from the entire association."[29] The relationship between Dana Greeley as president of the UUA and the district executives was not always smooth; looking back later, Greeley acknowledged that while most district executives had cooperated with his administration, "the defined relationships were not what they should have been."[30]

One proposal was repeatedly made, until the General Assembly finally adopted it in 1968. It was to provide for representation of the districts on the Board of Trustees. The Board would then be made up of twenty-seven members, twenty chosen by the districts through procedures in which the churches participated. This would give regional interests direct involvement in headquarters policy and, it was hoped, might even improve communication between the regional and the continental structures.[31]

The ministry and ministerial fellowship. Prior to merger, the Universalists and the Unitarians had followed different practices with respect to fellowshiping. The Universalists had authorized fellowshiping both by state conventions and by the General Convention (later the UCA). The Unitarians had a central fellowship committee, which had originally been an instrument of the ecclesiastical National Conference, rather than the administrative AUA. At one time, there had been regional fellowship committees, but to assure uniformity a single committee was organized in 1924, just before the merger of the Conference with the AUA.[32] The new bylaws of the UUA established a single Fellowship Committee, appointed by the Board of Trustees as one of its standing committees and part of the administrative operation.

Subject to approval by the Board, the Fellowship Committee was authorized to adopt procedures to carry out its purposes. One of the interim committees drafted a set of rules, which the Board promptly approved. As often happens in such circumstances, the opportunity to start from scratch encouraged the rule-making mentality. What resulted was much more elaborate and detailed than anything either denomination had known. Ten pages of the "brown book" included both rules for the operations of the Fellowship Committee itself and detailed procedures for appeal to the Board of Trustees or the General Assembly.[33]

The rules made a distinction, which has lasted, between preliminary and final fellowship. A preliminary certificate might be granted to applicants who satisfied the committee with respect to such matters as "moral character, depth of religious concern, physical and emotional health, background in the history and purposes of the Unitarian Universalist Association, education, judgment, tact, moral earnestness and integrity."[34] This certificate would be subject to annual review. After three years, during which time the candidate would have to have been in active service in the ministry of the denomination, a final certificate might be issued.

The procedures for the granting of preliminary and final certificates were stated fairly briefly. Procedures for termination of fellowship, involving the possibility of appeal by an aggrieved minister, were much more elaborate and legalistic. The unexpressed assumption would seem to have been that termination in most cases would be based on charges of misconduct damaging to the reputation and career prospects of the minister. Appeal might be taken to the Board of Trustees, with a possibility of further appeal to the General Assembly. As first adopted, the appeal might as a last resort be heard on the floor of the General Assembly. On the initiative of the Unitarian Universalist Ministers Association, the by-laws of the UUA were amended in 1965 to provide for a General Assembly Board of Review instead of action by the delegates. Panels drawn from the membership of the board were authorized, whose determination would be final.[35]

No reference was made in these rules to specialized ministries, though it was becoming evident that that question could not be avoided. The authors of the report of the commission on "The Church and Its Leadership" had noted that nonparochial ministries would have to be recognized in some way. The concept of the ministerial role, they wrote, is complicated by "the specialization of our increasingly complex culture demands." Ministers in the chaplaincy—"military, hospital, school, prison"—represent the church in the community at large. "Theirs should be recognized as a genuine ministry despite the technical departure from strict congregationalism." Normally, the report argued, they should be ordained by the home church. The authors rejected the growing use of terms such as Minister of Music or Minister of Education as diluting the integrity of the ministry. "Such integrity is undermined if the title 'minister' is so widely and loosely used as to lose specific content." Professional standards for the ministry "should be increased rather than diminished."[36]

The first formal recognition of specialized ministries came with a revision of the rules of the Ministerial Fellowship Committee in 1969. A new section was added providing for the recognition as a "Specialized Minister" of a candidate who not only met the usual requirements for fellowship, including the Bachelor of Divinity degree, but also was accredited by a recognized agency in the field of specialization. A minister who intended to specialize in pastoral counseling, rather than undertake a traditional parish ministry, might present credentials in the field of clinical psychology. The practical consequence would be that he or she could be continued in full fellowship with the Association, even if not employed by one of the churches or by an agency of the Association—indeed, as had long been the case with chaplains, denominational officials, and divinity school teachers.[37] The category of specialized ministers as thus defined proved to be unworkable, however, and was abandoned in 1974.[38]

In addition to its proposed rules and procedures for fellowshiping, the "brown book" outlined procedures for ministerial settlement. They were fleshed out in two booklets prepared by the Department of the Ministry, one for churches seeking ministers, the other for ministers seeking new positions.[39] These cover in detail such matters as the appointment of a search committee by the church, notification to the field executive and consultation with him, preparation by the Department of the Ministry of a list of recommended candidates, and a candidating procedure by which only one candidate may be presented to the church for week-long introduction and decision. These booklets acknowledge specifically that "the selection and settlement of a minister is a responsibility that rests on the members of a church."[40] They describe the role of denominational executives as one of providing the information on available and plausible candidates that will enable the church to make the best possible decision.

The procedures were offered as suggestions based on much experience, rather than as rules authoritatively laid down. Yet the detail and specificity of the suggestions were greater than either denomination had previously known, and they seemed to carry greater authority.[41] It is a short step from rules as agreed-upon good ways of operating, to rules as the way things are supposed to be done, to rules as the way things have to be done—or else. The earlier practice of the two denominations fell pretty much in the first step; the new booklets represented the second. That the process was moving into the third was the fear of more than one observer.

In an essay entitled "Danger Signals for Liberals," David Parke asserted that, while churches might ignore the prescribed procedures in which the Department of the Ministry plays a pivotal role, individual ministers cannot "without jeopardizing their standing as Unitarian Universalist ministers, and therefore their professional careers." Its power of evaluation and recommendation is extraordinary, he asserted: "It is difficult for a minister who, for whatever reason, is negatively evaluated by the director of the Department to secure a new or superior pulpit."[42] Similarly, in an article submitted to the *Register-Leader*, Kenneth Patton protested that the Department of the Ministry was seeking "authoritarian" control of ministerial settlement. He complained of "inevitable" manipulation to influence pulpit committees for or against individual ministers, and "career management" by the Department.[43]

Such charges, it may be argued, were overdrawn, but they were a reminder of tendencies characteristic of all bureaucracies, even the most benevolent. The report of the Commission on "The Church and Its Leadership" warned of them in more general language:

Like all such human institutions it is to be expected that the Association will at times be tempted to adopt policies designed primarily to assure its own survival, and tempted also to assume that the churches' best interests are best served by the increase of its own authority and strength. Its officials will inevitably be led to pursue lines of policy that tend to continue them in office, or to adopt procedures whose real justification is administrative convenience. Having easy access to much information on which policy decisions must be based—including those directly affecting individual churches—they will, also, be tempted to conclude that it is their job to make these decisions themselves. Conformity, rigidity, fear of dissent, fear of change, these are typical institutional temptations, and it is not to single out our Association to suggest that it is subject to them. Our denomination needs its Association—how else can continental programs be maintained?—even if at times it acts "bureaucratically," and even though we may rightly argue that the bureaucratic way of life falls somewhat short of the kingdom of God.[44]

PERSISTENT PROBLEMS, 1969–1985

Dana Greeley's second term as president ended in 1969, and Robert N. West was elected his successor at the General Assembly in Boston in July. It was a time of deep unrest and controversy. The "black rebellion" in the denomination, as in the larger society, became confrontational, with the formation of the Black Caucus and the tactics of "non-negotiable demands."[45] At the same time, opposition to the Vietnam War was fueling hostility to established institutions on the part of many young people. The disorder and polarizing conflict at the General Assembly of 1969 was very much a part of the times.

Equally worrisome were long-term trends that threatened the health of the denomination. Membership, which had shown steady growth in the fifties and early sixties, was declining.[46] The UUA faced a major financial crisis: the Annual Fund had fallen short, income from investments was down, and it was reported that the projected budget of 1969 was $700,000 out of balance. For several years, annual deficits had been met by drawing on unrestricted capital funds; that resource was exhausted and there was a demand note for a bank loan of nearly $500,000. The 1968 Assembly had committed the denomination morally, if not legally, to grants of $250,000 a year for four years to the Black Affairs Council, which had been formed earlier that year.[47]

The Greeley administration had begun retrenchment, and the new administration underwent further cuts in headquarters staff and the funding of districts. But the problems were not narrowly administrative, and the proposed solutions had implications for polity. In the decade and a half that followed, issues of polity emerged in discussion of the following: (a) the General Assembly and the extent to which it was representative of the denomination as a whole; (b) the role of districts; (c) the changing nature of the ministry; (d) communication within the denomination; and, most basic of all, (e) the boundary question: a definition of the distinctive character and mission of Unitarian Universalist churches.

General Assembly. The constitution and bylaws adopted at the time of merger established the General Assembly, made up of delegates from the churches, as "the overall policy making body for carrying out the purposes and objectives of the Association." As a representative body, it was assumed to express the mind of the denomination. But the number of churches and delegates participating repeatedly fell far short of those entitled to be present. In the early 1970s, only about one-third of the churches sent delegates; in 1972 at Dallas, only 26.3 percent of the churches were represented.[48]

What kinds of delegates would be most likely to attend? Ministers had professional incentives for going: to renew contacts with colleagues, to seek support on matters of common concern, and sometimes to interview for better positions. Some of them prided themselves on going year after year without fail. But lay delegates would often be those who could afford to take time off and pay their way to a more or less distant city, not necessarily those best able to express the prevailing opinion of their churches. Compared to the ministers, a larger proportion would be first-time delegates, new to the work and ways of the Assembly. The choice of location for the meeting would affect the geographical distribution of delegates. Less affluent churches would often be unrepresented year after year.

The issue came into clearest focus with respect to General Resolutions, which deal with social issues of larger concern, rather than with denominational business. Some argued that "individual freedom of belief" is as much compromised when the Assembly passes resolutions on social issues as it would be by a declaration of theological dogma.[49] Others were concerned that delegates frequently had not taken seriously the need to become informed on the questions to be debated and the views of their home churches. There was the risk that hasty action on an emotionally charged issue might be taken by a transient majority of delegates.[50] The 1961 bylaws provided that any church, or by petition twenty-five legal members of a church, might submit a resolution to go on the agenda, leaving it to the Business Committee to sort out the proposals that could be "debated and dealt with adequately in the time available." A series of revisions of the bylaws attempted to cut down the number to a manageable size, to require that only resolutions presumed to have wide support should be considered, and that discussion in the churches should be part of preparation for General Assembly debate.[51]

In 1983 at Vancouver, the Assembly voted a complete overhaul of the procedure, to go into effect in 1986. It provided that each church might submit no more than one proposal in a given year to a new Committee on General Resolutions. A selection of these by the Committee is then referred to the churches to determine which three are considered of highest importance. These three are placed on the agenda of the Assembly, to determine whether they will be accepted for a year of study and possible reshaping by the churches. The Committee then prepares a final version to go to the General Assembly, where a two-thirds vote is required. This elaborate procedure was an attempt to increase the involvement of the churches, and to minimize the possibility of ill-considered action in a situation of temporary excitement.[52]

To make it possible for more churches to afford to send delegates, biennial sessions were repeatedly suggested. Such proposals were defeated year after year, even though there is every reason to believe that majority opinion throughout the denomination was strongly in favor. When the churches were polled in 1971, 209 of them responded in favor of biennials, while 34 were opposed. In meetings of the General Assembly, a majority was several times in favor, but the required two-thirds vote for revision of the bylaws was not attained; in 1973, the proposal lost by only six votes.[53]

District organization. How the district structure would have developed had there been no financial crisis in 1969 is a matter of speculation. The district organization had been created quite rapidly following merger, but how it would function was far from clear. While the UUA contributed to the salaries of district executives, the relationship between them and the Greeley administration was less than ideal. Some of the districts, Greeley later recalled, "never developed any real rapport with 25 Beacon Street, and many of them had little in common with each other."[54]

In 1969, under financial pressure, the new administration felt obliged to reduce the funding of districts by the Association. Contributions to the salaries of district executives were ended, and the available funds concentrated on seven "Interdistrict Representatives," each to work with an assigned group of districts. Their tasks were defined as "program oriented"—that is, they would not be involved in fund raising or ministerial settlement, but would be a means of making the resources of headquarters more directly available to churches and fellowships. They would serve some of the functions of the "service centers" proposed in the "brown book" at the time of merger, which had never been developed because districts had been given priority. A four-page supplement to the denominational magazine *UU World* acknowledged that the program was a response to a financial problem, but promoted it as having positive value in its own right.[55]

The program came in for strong criticism. Three Pacific Coast districts objected to it and tried to go it on their own. A resolution to terminate the program even before it was started was offered, though not acted on, at the 1970 Assembly. The following year, the Assembly voted that if further budget cuts were required, the Interdistrict Representatives should be given low priority. While the intent of the program was not to undercut the districts, some saw it as a movement toward centralization and the increase of the bureaucratic power of headquarters. A letter to the *UU World* complained: "this will in effect remove our intra-structure professionals from the lay direction by District Boards and will to all intents and purposes make them employees of the Continental, reporting to . . . 25 Beacon St." The grassroots membership, the letter continued, is not responsive "to the idea of supporting a remote, centralized, impersonal bureaucracy."[56]

The district organizations, to be sure, had barely begun to undertake significant activity on their own initiative with their own leadership prepared to give "lay direction by District Boards" to "intra-structure professionals." Not much had happened to overcome the parochialism of the local churches. Interest in district affairs was limited, and direct lateral relationships and communication among the churches were almost nonexistent. The face-to-face contacts essential to congregational polity did not extend beyond the local congregation. Appointment of Interdistrict Representatives was a response to a financial problem, but hardly a step toward a resolution of the persistent ecclesiastical problem of the relationship between the local churches and the extraparochial structure created to serve them. In any event, the Interdistrict program was discontinued after about a decade and a half and replaced by a district services program providing for joint support of district executives by the UUA and the districts.

The ministry. The most striking change in the ministry since 1961 has resulted from the feminist movement in society at large. One consequence has been the increase in the number and proportion of women ordained, fellowshiped, and serving in the parish ministry. Another result has been increased recognition and status for religious educators, predominantly women. A small step was taken in 1972, when a bylaw amendment gave status as delegates to the General Assembly to accredited directors of religious education regularly serving member societies.[57]

Local churches were quite free to ordain their directors of religious education if they chose, but the question remained whether they should be given recognition and status by the Fellowship Committee. In October 1974, the Board of Trustees appointed a Special Committee on Education and Certification for Professional Religious Leadership. Its report in 1977—commonly called the "Benson Report"—recommended recognition of two forms of ministry, parish ministry and ministry of education, and representation of religious educators on the Ministerial Fellowship Committee.[58] The report was widely discussed, at least among the ministers. Some argued that religious educators actually do minister to a large fraction of the congregations they serve, even though their ministry is more interactive and less public than that of the parish minister. Others expressed fear that the result would be a dilution of standards for the ministry; directors of religious education wishing the privileges and status of ministerial fellowship should meet the same standards as parish ministers. Admission to fellowship in the new category of religious educators was approved by the General Assembly in 1979.[59]

Two special kinds of parish ministries were meanwhile given sharper definition: "interim ministry" and "extension ministry."

"Interim ministry" is an enlarged equivalent of what was long called "stated supply." That term was used for the temporary supply of a vacant pulpit, at least by Unitarians, throughout the nineteenth and well into the twentieth century. Preaching was all that was required, with no pastoral responsibilities.[60] The role of stated supply changed as parish ministry became more complex, with counseling and administration increasingly expected, so "interim minister" replaced the more limited term.

In an earlier time, ministers had been called out of retirement to help when a church was temporarily without a minister, perhaps because its minister had died and a successor was yet to be chosen. More recently, a number of ministers have preferred, for one reason or another, not to make the commitment of a settled ministry. By 1979, the director of the Department of the Ministry could report that "interim ministry" had become a distinct specialty, and that a corps of seven ministers was available for assignment to temporary service. In due course, the Department of the Ministry established, with annual review, the formal categories of Accredited Interim Minister and Interim-Minister-in-Training. It may be noted that these categories are bureaucratic, not ecclesiological. The rationale soon developed that interim ministers offer special skills to deal with special situations, especially for those congregations "where there has been a long-tenured ministry or one characterized by dissension and/or low morale." It was urged further that "all churches in transition" should consider availing themselves of the expertise of an interim minister. But an interim minister who serves a sequence of one-year assignments, assisted in placement by the Department of the Ministry, does not—indeed is not expected to—develop the kind of identification with the churches he or she serves that is at the heart of congregationalism.[61]

"Extension ministry" is a modern version of what was once referred to as "home mission." In 1834, William Greenleaf Eliot, James Freeman Clarke, and Ephraim Peabody went west with the encouragement and support of the AUA to create new Unitarian churches. Today, an extension minister will be supported by the denomination in a church for a limited period of time, after which he or she may be regularly called to that pulpit or move on to another post. The concern has been expressed that the assignment of an extension minister involves none of the candidating procedures prescribed for a regular settlement, and he or she is in effect there by bureaucratic assignment, accepted by the church because it has no real choice: "as this process has now become an alternative route to permanent ministerial settlement, it represents not just a serious compromise but a violation of essential traditions of the free church."[62]

It may be argued that bureaucratic assignment of extension ministers presents at most a marginal threat to the congregational principle that churches have the right to choose their own leadership without coercion, explicit or implied. The effect on the ministers is more problematic. Both interim ministers and extension ministers are dependent on denominational authority in a way that settled ministers— successful ministers, at least—are not.

Communication. The state of communication within the denomination was a problem that the West administration addressed promptly in 1969. The denominational journal, resulting from the combination following merger of the *Unitarian Register* and the *Universalist Leader,* had had three editors in eight years and its name had been changed five times. No consistent understanding had developed as to its character and function. The coverage of news of the denomination was erratic. At the end, in 1968, it became *UUA Now,* a slick paper magazine with many pictures, featuring big topic issues, such as "Youth and Education" or "The Arts in Worship." It reported General Assembly meetings, but relegated ongoing news events to an occasional "Newsletter" supplement, appearing between the regular issues. In addition, headquarters was sending regular mailings, called "Packets," to the ministers and lay heads of each church. This was one-way communication of promotional materials and notices of coming events.[63]

An undercurrent of discontent with the situation was apparent. In December 1963, Kenneth Patton complained that the editor of the *Register-Leader* refused to open the pages to "criticisms of the policy and program of the administration." In 1965, the Commission on Appraisal reported massive indifference to denominational affairs on the part of the membership at large and called for new methods to "break through the communications barrier." In 1967, the Committee on Goals stressed the need to improve communication "in the broadest sense of that term," and a study committee was appointed "to review the two-fold problems of publications and communications." Four of the candidates for the presidency in 1969 mentioned the problem in their campaign statements.[64]

In his campaign, West proposed "a balanced, good newspaper going regularly into the homes of all members of our congregations" and a reduction of "the flood of mimeographed material mailed from headquarters, material designed to convey information that is not reaching most of our individual members." Shortly after his election, distribution of the packets ceased, and a tabloid newspaper replaced the slick paper magazine version of *UUA Now*.[65]

Beginning with January 1970, the *Unitarian Universalist World* began to go twice a month (except in the summer) to all Unitarian Universalists recorded as giving financial support to their local churches. The outreach of the denominational journal was thereby widened to a degree hardly even imagined previously. The paper gave coverage to doings throughout the denomination more systematically than had been the case ever since the *Unitarian Register* and the *Universalist Leader* ceased being independent publications. Decisions at Board meetings were regularly reported; the annual budget was given a two-page spread in large type; a full page was allowed for letters, and criticism of policy was frequently expressed; organizations like the Service Committee, Beacon Press, the Women's Federation, and Liberal Religious Youth were given an occasional full page or more to promote their endeavors; ordinations, installations, lists of vacant pulpits, and obituaries were regularly included. A resolution passed by the 1974 General Assembly encouraged the editor "to seek and report criticisms, alternative opinions, and background information concerning current UUA matters."[66] Not every Unitarian Universalist may have been all that interested in denominational affairs, and the newsprint format was not flashy like the full-page picture spreads of *UUA Now*. But the paper had a clear purpose, which it accomplished without frills: to draw all Unitarian Universalists into a vital communications network, essential to provide understanding and support of common endeavors.

"Principles and Purposes": The boundary question. There are varieties of religious experience, and no religious community can encompass them all. So the different denominations occupy different parts of the vineyard, and by their varieties of doctrine, ways of worship, and polity, their churches may meet differing needs.

Many churches and denominations define their chosen territory by creedal statements—though formal doctrine actually may not be the most significant factor in their cohesion as religious communities. To maintain their identity, some churches use creedal formulations as tests for admission or as a basis for discipline. Religious liberals do not. But that does not exempt them from the necessity to define in some other way what it is they stand for, and what might encourage others to join them. While liberals are allergic to anything that is identified as a creed, they have no hesitation in formulating "principles and purposes" on theological matters or passing "general resolutions" on social issues. These are boundary-defining statements, which may be somewhat fuzzier for that purpose than the historic creeds of Christendom, but which perform the same function. The importance that Unitarian Universalists attach to such definition of boundaries was seen in the intensity of debate in the Syracuse meeting (1959) over the definition of the relationship of the new denomination to "the Judeo-Christian heritage." Its importance was equally demonstrated in the extended discussion leading up to the adoption in 1985 of a revised statement of the "Principles and Purposes" of the denomination.

One difference between the boundary-defining process of the Unitarian Universalists and that of many other denominations is that no consensus statement or formulation of principles and purposes has ever achieved the standing of a sacred test that may not be revised or replaced. The Winchester Profession at times approached that status among Universalists. In any event, the adoption of formal statements of principles has been only one element in the definition of boundaries, and usually not the most important one.

A second difference—perhaps the essential one—is that it is left to the individual to decide whether he or she belongs within the covenant of a particular local religious community, and power is not assigned to ecclesiastical authority to decide whether the applicant is to be allowed in. Similarly in "a voluntary association of autonomous, self-governing local churches and fellowships," it is left to each church to "freely choose to pursue common goals" with others like-minded.

The definition of the boundary is a result, not of hierarchical control of wayward churches, but of living together, and communicating to one another our deepest and most thoughtful insights as to human experience and the mystery that surrounds it.

Postscript

The structure and operation of the denominational machinery have always been objects of criticism and subjects of debate; but in the decade from 1985 to 1995 a number of issues with implications for polity have been raised with such urgency that major reports with specific recommendations have been offered for consideration. Five such issues may be identified as of continuing concern: (1) the presidency of the UUA and the relationship between the president and the moderator; (2) the General Assembly, both its representative character and its position in the midst of a convention week of assorted activities; (3) the nature of the ministry, particularly the problem of validation of nonparochial ministries; (4) the relationship between ordination and fellowshiping; and (5) communication within the denomination.

The presidency of the UUA. In 1990, responding to a recommendation of the General Assembly, which in turn was the result of initiative by the Commission on Appraisal, the Board established a Commission on Governance. The central charge to the commission was "to review the structure and roles and process of selection of the president, the moderator, and the Board of Trustees."[1]

The five members of the commission reported to the General Assembly in 1993. The major recommendation was to combine the public roles of the moderator and president into a single elected office of president; to create the position of Executive Director as the chief executive officer of the Association, appointed by and accountable to the Board of Trustees; and to create a new standing committee of the General Assembly to serve as Presidential Nominating Committee. These proposals reflect a "central conclusion" of the commission "that Board of Trustees functioning needs to be strengthened." The Board, it argued, "must not allow a strong leader to pre-empt its role in setting policy for the Association."[2]

This proposal was not new. It went back at least as far as a recommendation of a special committee of the AUA in 1958, following the death of Frederick Eliot. It addressed the problem of friction between the president and the moderator, which was apparent during the administrations of both Dana Greeley (1961-69) and Eugene Pickett (1979–85) and which was seen to have been structural to a significant degree. It also addressed the problem of campaigns for the presidency, which had become long, expensive, and increasingly politicized, so as to deter well-qualified candidates from being willing to participate. It recognized a difference between the requirements for administrative leadership and spiritual leadership, and it argued that "there is nothing inherent in UU principles, theology, or polity that requires these leadership functions to be wrapped up in one office."[3]

The proposals were rejected by the General Assembly in 1994, as its central recommendation had been earlier, in 1976. But the work of the commission had revealed widespread dissatisfaction with the status quo. Since the concerns that had led to the appointment of the commission remained unresolved, its key recommendation, though not accepted in 1994, will doubtless reappear.

The General Assembly. In its report, the Commission on Governance acknowledged that a review of the role of the General Assembly had not been part of its charge. It nevertheless noted that it had encountered concern in various quarters "that General Assemblies are becoming meaningless in determining the policies and direction of the Association." More particularly:

> Some have expressed concern about how representative the General Assembly can be. Usually there are a relatively small number of people in a congregation interested in denominational involvement. Efforts to influence denominational elections or policies often come from special interest groups organized around status or a single issue. There is usually more widespread interest in Association business in years when presidential elections are being held. Some have pointed out that the programmatic focus of the GA's has become more important than the Association's business. Some have suggested that this commission recommend resurrection of biennial General Assemblies, or perhaps programmatic GA's alternating with ones devoted to business.[4]

These various kinds of dissatisfaction remain to be focused and addressed.

Nonparochial ministries. In 1991, the General Assembly gave final approval to an amendment to the bylaws recognizing "community ministry" as a category distinct from parish ministry and ministry of religious education, within the jurisdiction of the Ministerial Fellowship Committee. The recent acknowledgment of ministers of religious education had led to the question whether nonparochial ministries should likewise be formally recognized. Ordained ministers of religious education, to be sure, represent no departure from the basic principle of congregational polity that ministers are chosen by those to whom they minister and whom they will continue to serve. It is more of a problem to ordain persons who have no parish base and never expect to serve in a parish. Yet it has long been accepted that ministers who serve as chaplains, or denominational officials, or teachers in theological seminaries, or "ministers-at-large" or some modern equivalent do not lose their standing as "in ministerial fellowship" and continue to be regarded as "ministers."

In response to the increase in the number and variety of such ministries, the Society of the Larger Ministry was formed in 1986. It identified 135 ministers—15 percent of Unitarian Universalist ministers in fellowship—doing ministry outside the parish. The formal recognition of "community ministry" soon followed. The problem of how to validate nonparochial ministries had long been latent; now it became insistent. Reporting in 1992, the Commission on Appraisal noted that much of its time and energy had been devoted "to exploring ways in which these community ministries can best relate to the Association and its constituent congregations," both on the practical and on the theoretical levels. It offered for consideration several ways by which a community ministry might be related to a congregation or a group of congregations, but gave no answer to the problem. "An ongoing discussion should be held," it concluded, "regarding the best way or ways for ordaining community ministers consistent with the congregational polity."[5]

Fellowshiping and settlement. Our practice of congregational polity is predicated on a relationship of mutual benefit and obligation between churches and denomination. The churches rely on denominational headquarters for services they cannot easily provide for themselves; the denominational administration is dependent on financial support from the churches. In the crucial matter of ministerial leadership, our polity is predicated on a balance between churches and denomination: each church "has the exclusive right to call and ordain its own minister or ministers," but the Association "has the exclusive right to admit ministers to ministerial fellowship with the Association."

Seen as a power relationship, however, this balance is far from equal. The imbalance is most obvious in matters of ministerial settlement. The Department of the Ministry is an ongoing bureaucracy, which needs established policies and procedures to operate effectively; and so we have a *Settlement Handbook* thirty-nine pages in length. But churches are involved in settlement at intervals, not continuously; their search committees are not permanent or full-time officers, and they are each time new to the task. For them, the practical effect of the *Handbook* is prescriptive rather than advisory.[6]

Quite apart from what may be the attitude and behavior of denominational staff, such a detailed codification produces a pressure to conform. The pressure is especially heavy on candidates for settlement, whose professional careers depend greatly on the extent to which they are seen as cooperative by those who are in a position to recommend them.[7] The pressure to conform is explicit in the "Code of Professional Practice" of the Unitarian Universalist Ministers Association, which requires this commitment: "I will inform myself of the established candidating procedures of the UUA and I will strictly observe them."[8]

The resulting problems are not of the kind to be solved by tinkering with administrative machinery, let alone by railing at particular bureaucrats. They are inherent in the polity we have chosen to adopt. The Commission on "The Church and Its Leadership" pointed to them a generation ago:

> Whenever a church is led to suppose that unless it cooperates with officials, limited funds may be channelled elsewhere, its numbers realize than even in an association of free churches, power exists, and can be used. Whenever a minister gets the impression, rightly or wrongly, that his professional advancement depends on subordinating his honest conventions to the presumed preferences of those who participate in the process of settlement, he wonders whether the discipline of hierarchical churches is really as different from his own as he had supposed. Such anxieties may

be based on phantoms, and often are, but they are real, nonetheless, and have repeatedly found expression in our periodicals.[9]

A problem of this kind is never solved once and for all time. It is, as the Commission concluded, "a problem that must be faced without evasion"—not just once, but continuously.

Communication. The problem of adequate communication within the denomination is a perennial one, going back at least as far as the takeover by the AUA of the previously independent *Christian Register*. Most recently the Commission on Governance has declared:

> A contributing factor to apathy about the business processes and decisions of our Association is the absence of timely information. When the *UU World* changed in 1986 to a bimonthly magazine format with a new name (*The World*), whatever role it had served as a timely source of information about issues before the Association was diminished.

The Commission acknowledged that this matter fell outside the scope of its charge, but concluded:

> a minimum requirement of effective governance is information about the issues facing the association. We lack consistency and quality in the source of such information. This is an area . . . which deserves further study by both the staff and the Board.[10]

The loss of a widely distributed common instrument for the dissemination of information has resulted in a severely segmented communications network. Special interest groups have their own newsletters, which do not circulate beyond their constituencies. The ministers have their UUMA newsletter and *First Days Record,* but the laity in their churches are not in the loop and have little idea what the professional concerns and difficulties of their ministers may be. The UU Christians have *Good News;* the Pagans have *Pagan NUUS;* the humanists sponsor *Religious Humanism;* the Women's Federation distributes *Communication;* the Conservative Forum publishes *Sigma;* and so on.

Such publications serve a useful purpose, but in the absence of a common publication to which such organizations might contribute, from time to time, in order to make themselves known, the segmented communications network points to increasing fragmentation of the denomination and doubtless contributes to it as well.

One result of the segmentation of the communications network is that lateral communication is difficult, and a common response to issues that may affect all the churches is inhibited. The General Assembly is an insufficient instrument for such response because—quite apart from questions of its representative character—many significant policy issues are decided elsewhere, at the administrative level. Our bureaucracy can best serve us if comment on its activity can be widespread, not limited to formal channels or constricted by an inadequate communications network. There is more danger of subversion of congregational polity from the encroachment of bureaucratic hierarchy than from any tendency toward ecclesiastical hierarchy.

Finally, the segmentation of the communications network and the lack of a widely distributed instrument for lateral communication inhibit the development of a sense of the larger religious community of which we are a part. That larger religious community includes the UUA, but also the Service Committee and other "Associated Member Organizations." It encompasses "Independent Affiliated Organizations" and theological schools. It includes all the churches and fellowships. It reaches out in some measure to religious liberals in other parts of the world.

It is altogether too easy to mistake the denominational machinery, with its administrative policies and procedures, for the denomination itself. The Unitarian Universalist Association is not the denomination, but an instrument created to serve it. The UUA is entitled to support; it is to the larger religious community that loyalty is owed.

Notes

1. The eight sets of queries that follow were used to structure a critique of present-day practices in the denomination in Conrad Wright, *A Doctrine of the Church for Liberals*, Boston: Unitarian Universalist Ministers Association, 1983; reprinted in Conrad Wright, *Walking Together* (Boston, 1989), pp. 1–24.

CONGREGATIONALISM PRIOR TO THE UNITARIAN CONTROVERSY

1. Perry Miller and Thomas H. Johnson, eds., *The Puritans* (New York, 1938), p. 197.

2. Williston Walker, *The Creeds and Platforms of Congregationalism* (New York, 1893; reprinted Boston, 1960), pp. 194–237.

3. *Ibid.*, p. 203.

4. *Ibid.*, p. 209.

5. *Ibid.*, pp. 207, 208.

6. *Ibid.*, p. 223.

7. *Ibid.*, p. 205.

8. *Ibid.*, p. 210.

9. The reference here is to the Renaissance logic of Peter Ramus, which analyzed propositions by the use of dichotomies, divid-

ing and subdividing until the smallest units have been determined. A convenient discussion of the Puritan use of the Ramean logic may be found in Perry Miller, *The New England Mind* (New York, 1939), chap. 5, though considerable scholarly work has been done on Ramus since Miller's pioneering study.

10. Walker, *Creeds and Platforms,* p. 211.

11. On the ministry in the seventeenth century, see David D. Hall, *The Faithful Shepherd* (Chapel Hill, North Carolina, 1972). For the early eighteenth century, see J. William T. Youngs, Jr., *God's Messengers* (Baltimore, 1976); and for continuation into the nineteenth century, see Donald M. Scott, *From Office to Profession* (Philadelphia, 1978).

12. Walker, *Creeds and Platforms,* p. 212.

13. Harold F. Worthley, "The Colonial Diaconate: An Example of the Allocation and Exercise of Authority in the Particular Churches of New England," *Proceedings of the Unitarian Historical Society,* Vol. 12, Pt. 2 (1959): 27–52.

14. Walker, *Creeds and Platforms,* pp. 216, 217.

15. The term "autonomy" as applying to the independent character of the particular church is modern, not seventeenth-century, usage.

16. Lorman Ratner, in Irwin H. Polishook, ed., *Roger Williams, John Cotton, and Religious Freedom* (Englewood Cliffs, New Jersey, 1967), p. iii.

17. Walker, *Creeds and Platforms,* p. 236.

18. Edmund S. Morgan, *Roger Williams: The Church and the State* (New York, 1967), p. 63.

19. Walker, *Creeds and Platforms,* pp. 205–206.

20. The scholarly literature on the Half-Way Covenant and its consequences is considerable. The most recent major study is Robert G. Pope, *The Half-Way Covenant* (Princeton, New Jersey, 1969).

21. S. K. Lothrop, *A History of the Church in Brattle Street, Boston* (Boston, 1851), p. 22.

22. Quoted from Winthrop's Journal in Harold F. Worthley, "The Massachusetts Convention of Congregational Ministers," *Proceedings of the Unitarian Historical Society,* Vol. 12, Pt. 1 (1958): 49.

23. Cotton Mather, *Ratio Disciplinae Fratrum Nov-Anglorum: A Faithful Account of the Discipline Professed and Practised in the Churches of New England* (Boston, 1726), pp. 176–177.

24. Walker, *Creeds and Platforms,* p. 506.

25. One result was that the liberalism in doctrine that emerged in the eighteenth century and that led in due course to Unitarianism found no rootage in the churches of the Standing Order in Connecticut. For Unitarians, the tradition of congregational polity stems directly from the Cambridge Platform, its localism reinforced by a deliberate rejection of the presbyterianizing tendencies that developed in Connecticut.

26. Williston Walker, *A History of the Congregational Churches in the United States* (New York, 1894), p. 232.

27. The terms "town," "parish," "precinct," and "society" are functionally equivalent. When the growth of population in a town dictated the provision of public worship (and the gathering of a new church) in some distant part of it, the town was divided by act of the General Court for ecclesiastical purposes, the older part usually called the "First Parish," the newer part called a "precinct"—as, for example, Menotomy Precinct, part of Cambridge, set off in 1732. This was often the first step in the process by which a town was divided for civil purposes as well. (Menotomy Precinct became the town of West Cambridge in 1807, renamed Arlington in 1867.) Both parishes and precincts were territorial units with the same power of taxation of all inhabitants (except recognized minorities, such as Quakers) for the support of public worship as had originally been exercised by the town. The term "society" was used for the body, incorporated or unincorporated, that performed the same function on behalf of a church where, as in Boston, there was no

territorial jurisdiction. Probably in the case of the old Boston churches, societies acted as quasi-corporations long before the legal system provided for formal incorporation. In the case of dissenting groups after the Great Awakening, the line between an unincorporated religious society and a church might be a fuzzy one. But the term "society" has no theological significance, as though a "society" were theologically more liberal than a "church," or as though "society" was being used in preference to "church" because it represents a less orthodox understanding of religion. In 1780, Article III of the Declaration of Rights of the Constitution of the Commonwealth of Massachusetts refers to "towns, parishes, precincts, and other bodies politic, or religious societies," as equivalent terms in securing to them the right to select their own "public teachers."

28. It is not uncommon today to find references to an "establishment" of the Congregational Church in colonial Massachusetts, New Hampshire, and Connecticut. But what was "established" was the institution of public worship, not the congregational churches, let alone the "Congregational Church." Dissenters from the prevailing worship, such as the Baptists, accused it of being an establishment of religion, but the supporters of the Standing Order rejected the accusation, since for them an establishment of religion meant something comparable to the favored position of the Church of England in the Mother Country and in Virginia. Since the differences between the two situations were philosophically as well as practically different, it is best to avoid the term "establishment" for New England. "Standing Order" is more specific and does not carry with it a host of misleading connotations.

29. *Province Laws*, chap. 46, session of 1692/3. See also Susan M. Reed, *Church and State in Massachusetts, 1691–1740* (Urbana, Illinois, 1914).

30. David Craig Harlan has argued that recent historiography has exaggerated the tendency toward professionalization, and in particular that ministerial associations were irregularly organized, did not include all ministers, and avoided exercising authority. Their role was much more social than specifically

ecclesiastical. But the difference of opinion would seem to be a matter of degree. Ministerial associations in the eighteenth century no doubt fell far short of being truly professional associations. The tendency was in that direction, nonetheless. See David Craig Harlan, "New England Congregationalism and Ministerial Professionalism in the Eighteenth Century," *Bulletin of the Congregational Library*, Vol. 34, No. 2 (Winter 1983): 4–18; Vol. 34, No. 3 (Spring/Summer 1983): 4–17.

31. C. C. Goen, *Revivalism and Separatism in New England, 1740–1800: Strict Congregationalists and Separate Baptists in the Great Awakening* (New Haven, Connecticut, 1962).

32. In Massachusetts, three have survived: Malden, Saugus, and Stoughton.

33. Information on Universalist practices is much harder to come by than for Unitarianism and its antecedents in the same period. Scholars have been less interested in Universalism than in Unitarianism; in any case, the informal and short-lived character of many Universalist churches means that records are often hard to find and may never have been adequately kept. Some guidance is given in Russell E. Miller, *The Larger Hope* (Boston, 1979), and in Richard Eddy, *Universalism in America*, 2 vols. (Boston, 1884, 1886).

34. Eddy, *Universalism in America*, Vol. 1, pp. 174–195.

35. *Ibid.*, pp. 175–178; Richard Eddy, *Universalism in Gloucester, Massachusetts* (Gloucester, 1892), pp. 154–156.

36. John D. Cushing, "Notes on Disestablishment in Massachusetts, 1780–1833," *William and Mary Quarterly*, 3rd ser., 26 (1969): 169–190.

37. Eddy, *Universalism in America*, Vol. 1, pp. 207–208.

38. *Ibid.*, Vol. 1, pp. 294–301. See also Elmo A. Robinson, "The Universalist General Convention: From Nascence to Conjunction," *Journal of the Universalist Historical Society* 8 (1969–70): 44–52.

39. See, for example, Conrad Wright, "The Dedham Case Revisited," *Proceedings of the Massachusetts Historical Society* 100

(1988): 15–39; reprinted in Conrad Wright, *The Unitarian Controversy* (Boston, 1994), pp. 111–135.

40. For a discussion of the "spiritualization" of the office of deacon, see Harold F. Worthley, "Colonial Diaconate."

41. Cf. Charles H. Lippy, "The Massachusetts Constitution: Religious Establishment or Civil Religion?" *Journal of Church and State* 20 (1978): 533–549; also Conrad Wright, "Piety, Morality, and the Commonwealth," *Crane Review* 9 (1967): 90–106; reprinted in Wright, *Unitarian Controversy*, pp. 17–35.

42. Conrad Wright, "Institutional Reconstruction in the Unitarian Controversy," in Conrad Edick Wright, ed., *American Unitarianism, 1805–1865* (Boston, 1989), pp. 3–29; reprinted in Wright, *Unitarian Controversy*, pp. 83–170.

43. Bellows to J. F. Clarke, March 13, 1865, Bellows Papers, Massachusetts Historical Society.

DENOMINATIONALISM: ASSOCIATIONS AND CONVENTIONS

1. The gradual divergence between Arminians and Calvinists from 1740 to 1805 is traced in Conrad Wright, *The Beginnings of Unitarianism in America* (Boston, 1955).

2. A conspicuous instance was the controversy in Dorchester, 1810–1812. See Conrad Wright, "Institutional Reconstruction in the Unitarian Controversy," in Conrad Edick Wright, ed., *American Unitarianism, 1805–1865* (Boston, 1989), pp. 1–29; reprinted in Conrad Wright, *The Unitarian Controversy* (Boston, 1994), pp. 83–110.

3. Conrad Wright, "The Dedham Case Revisited," *Proceedings of the Massachusetts Historical Society* 100 (1988): 15–39; reprinted in Wright, *Unitarian Controversy*, pp. 111–135.

4. For an account of the attempt, ultimately unsuccessful, of a minister to sustain the role of "public teacher" in the face of sectarian divisions, see John Wood Sweet, "The Liberal Dilemma and the Demise of the Town Church: Ezra Ripley's Pastorate in Concord, 1778–1841," *Proceedings of the Massachusetts Historical Society* 104 (1992): 73–109.

5. William G. McLoughlin, *New England Dissent, 1630–1833: The Baptists and the Separation of Church and State*, 2 vols. (Cambridge, Massachusetts, 1971), chaps. 32–36, 54–63. An older and less reliable treatment is Jacob C. Meyer, *Church and State in Massachusetts from 1740 to 1833* (Cleveland, 1930).

6. Russell E. Miller, *The Larger Hope: The First Century of the Universalist Church in America, 1770–1870* (Boston, 1979), pp. 63–67.

7. Cyrus A. Bartol, *Church and Congregation: A Plea for Their Unity* (Boston, 1858); Sylvester Judd, *The Church: In a Series of Discourses* (Boston, 1854). Bartol was a Transcendentalist of sorts; Judd described himself as "an old-fashioned Unitarian." Their agreement on this matter is therefore the more significant. Judd was sympathetically reviewed by Edward Everett Hale, who argued that the distinction between church and congregation was a survival from earlier times that no longer accorded with Unitarian theology. E. E. Hale, "Judd's Discourses on the Church," *Christian Examiner* 56 (1854): 428–445.

8. In 1868, the Reverend E. H. Sears sent a questionnaire to ministers of the South Middlesex Conference inquiring as to the practice in their congregations. In most cases there was a distinct church, but only one-tenth to no more than one-third of the members of the parish or society had joined the church. The replies indicate a concern on the part of the ministers to make the communion service more significant—itself suggestive of the declining importance of the church as such. See the responses to questionnaires, bMS 121/2, Andover-Harvard Theological Library, Harvard Divinity School.

9. All Souls in New York is an example of the "church" now become vestigial. Walter D. Kring, *Liberals Among the Orthodox* (Boston, 1974), pp. 88–89, 91.

10. The fullest account of the organization of the AUA is George W. Cooke, *Unitarianism in America* (Boston, 1902), pp. 124–138.

11. For a fuller discussion of the organization and operation of the voluntary societies, and the process by which they were eventually absorbed by the ecclesiastical structures of the denominations, see Conrad Wright, "The Growth of Denominational Bureaucracies: A Neglected Aspect of American Church History," *Harvard Theological Review* 77 (1984): 177–194.

12. Conrad Wright, *Unitarian Universalist Denominational Structure: An Historical Survey.* Unitarian Universalist Advance Paper no. 36, 1986; reprinted in Conrad Wright, *Walking Together* (Boston, 1989), pp. 73–95.

13. When an ecclesiastical council met in 1841 to try to resolve a dispute between the Reverend John Pierpont and certain of the proprietors of the Hollis Street Church, this procedure was already obsolescent in Unitarian circles. When the proprietors declined to accept the council's vindication of Pierpont, and the members of the council in turn were subjected to what they felt to be an unfair attack by the Reverend Theodore Parker, such councils had clearly become obsolete.

14. Comparable to the AUA, and similar in structure though narrower in scope, was the Sunday School Society. It began in 1827 as an organization of Sunday school teachers in the Boston churches, but soon included others who were interested in its work, on the basis of annual subscriptions or life memberships. It was reorganized in 1854 as a general denominational body. In 1866, it was proposed to merge the Society into the AUA, but its friends demurred. The Society was incorporated in 1885. It was dissolved at the time of merger with the Universalists, but its major activities had long since been taken over by the AUA. See Cooke, *Unitarianism in America,* chap. 12; also Robert Dale Richardson, *125 Years of Unitarian Sunday Schools* (Boston, 1952).

15. Wright, *Walking Together,* pp. 82–85.

16. Henry W. Bellows, *The Suspense of Faith* (New York, 1859), pp. 5, 10, 38; reprinted in Sydney E. Ahlstrom and Jonathan S. Carey, *An American Reformation* (Middletown, Connecticut, 1985), pp. 373–374, 376, 393.

17. Conrad Wright, "Henry W. Bellows and the Organization of the National Conference," *Proceedings of the Unitarian Historical Society,* Vol. 15, Pt. 2 (1965): 17–46; reprinted in Conrad Wright, *The Liberal Christians* (Boston, 1970), pp. 81–109.

18. The discussion of Universalist polity in this section relies heavily on Miller, *Larger Hope,* Vol. 1, chaps. 5, 7. See also Elmo Arnold Robinson, "The Universalist General Convention from Nascence to Conjugation," *Journal of the Universalist Historical Society* 8 (1969–1970): 44–93.

19. Miller, *Larger Hope,* pp. 44–48; Richard Eddy, *Universalism in America* (Boston, 1891, 1894), Vol. 2, pp. 48–56.

20. Eddy, *Universalism in America,* Vol. 2, p. 5.

21. Miller, *Larger Hope,* p. 83.

22. A "Plan of Church Government" adopted in Philadelphia in 1790 provided that each church had the power to ordain in accordance with its own judgment as to the qualifications of the candidate, and it declared that "All the general acts of the convention which relate to the interest of particular churches, shall be issued only by way of advice or recommendation." Eddy, *Universalism in America,* Vol. 1, pp. 299, 301.

23. Miller, *Larger Hope,* p. 97.

24. *Ibid.,* p. 138.

25. Among the Universalists, discipline was a recurrent concern in the sessions of the General Convention, which sought to create an ecclesiastical structure competent to deal with it. The Unitarians felt no such need for a centralized authority with disciplinary power until after the Civil War. Such centralization as developed was bureaucratic rather than ecclesiastical. The contrast between the two denominations is instructive. Why was discipline so much more of a problem for the Universalists? The answer is probably to be found in sociological factors. They were more widely scattered; they were not part of a decision-making elite; their ministers were less well educated; their system of associations and conventions was so loose-jointed that there was not even a central compilation of Universalist

churches and ministers. Ill-equipped and unstable men could altogether too easily get a hearing in a small church, and then move from one association to another, leaving a trail of damage behind.

The Unitarians, on the other hand, were more closely knit. Their strength was more localized in eastern Massachusetts, where they occupied positions of influence and authority in the community and so were very visible. Harvard College trained many of their lay leaders, and the Harvard Divinity School many of their ministers. Common educational experiences, often reinforced by family connections, produced a network of informal relationships. Through the AUA, a listing, even if unofficial, was available of churches and ministers generally recognized as Unitarian, and of ministers seeking a settlement; and the secretary of the Association was in a position to know a good deal about the successes and failures of his colleagues. Discipline could be maintained by the Unitarians, therefore, through social pressure, rather than judicial proceedings.

In any event, Universalists came to think of denominational structures as existing for ecclesiastical control, not—as with the Unitarians—organizations to provide services to the churches. But the ethos of local Universalist churches was congregational and democratic, so tension existed between the institutional structure and the ethos of the denomination—a tension that was never resolved even down to the time of merger with the Unitarians in 1961.

For a discussion of disciplinary proceedings, especially when members of a congregation had a grievance against their minister, see *United States General Convention of Universalists, Minutes of the Session of 1860*, pp. 26–33. The need for a registry of churches and ministers was forcibly stated in the "Report of the Committee on the State of the Church," *Minutes of the United States Convention of Universalists, for 1859* (New York, 1859), pp. 24–25.

26. Miller, *Larger Hope*, pp. 144–146.

27. *Proceedings of the Maine Convention of Universalists . . . (1853)* (Augusta, 1853), pp. 18–19.

28. *Proceedings of the United States Convention of Universalists . . . (1858)* (Boston, 1858), p. 16.

29. *Minutes of the United States Convention of Universalists, for 1859* (New York, 1859), p. 20.

30. *Minutes of the United States Convention of Universalists, for 1860* (Boston, 1860), p. 26.

31. For a description of the "pure" congregationalism that was rejected, see *Minutes* (1860), pp. 37–39.

32. *Minutes* (1860), pp. 10 ff.

33. *Ibid.,* pp. 8–9.

34. *Ibid.,* p. 40.

35. *Ibid.,* p. 8; *Minutes* (1861), p. 27.

36. *Minutes* (1863), pp. 10–30.

37. *Minutes* (1865), pp. 13–14. Elbridge Gerry Brooks became Secretary of the convention and General Agent in 1867. He had long been an advocate of more effective organization. See Elbridge Streeter Brooks, *The Life-Work of Elbridge Gerry Brooks* (Boston, 1881), pp. 164–171.

38. *Minutes* (1870), p. 61.

39. *Minutes* (1865), p. 13.

40. *Proceedings of the Maine Convention of Universalists . . . 1850* (Augusta, 1850).

41. Miller, *Larger Hope,* pp. 152–153.

42. James Freeman Clarke made a point of this when explaining the "social principle" of the Church of the Disciples. James Freeman Clarke, *The Church of the Disciples in Boston* (Boston, 1846), p. 20.

43. Only one-fifth of the subscribers intended to join the new congregation. The greater number were leading members of other churches who felt an obligation to promote liberal Christianity by facilitating the development of a new religious soci-

ety. Among them were Samuel Parkman, Andrews Norton, George Ticknor, Nathan Appleton, Amos and Abbot Lawrence, Dr. James Jackson, Alexander Parris (the architect of the new building), Solomon Willard, John A. Lowell, George Shattuck. See Lewis G. Pray, *Historical Sketch of the Twelfth Congregational Society in Boston* (Boston, 1863), pp. 106–108.

44. *Ibid.*, chap. 3.

45. *Ibid.*, p. 26.

46. *Ibid.*, chap. 4. The Twelfth Congregational Society soon became one of the largest and most prosperous of the Unitarian denomination in the city. It is sad to record, however, that it failed to solve the problem of recruitment of newer members as the founders aged and their children moved on to careers in other places. The West End encountered demographic change, and new families moving in were frequently evangelical Protestants or Roman Catholics. By the 1850s, the Society was having difficulty meeting its annual expenses. Barrett retired in 1858 at the age of sixty-three after more than thirty-five years of service. A successor was chosen, but after a year he decided the situation could not be salvaged. The congregation disbanded at the end of 1861, the property was sold, and the Society was dissolved in 1863. The meetinghouse was acquired by the Catholics and still stands as St. Joseph's Church.

47. William Channing Gannett, *Ezra Stiles Gannett* (Boston, 1875), pp. 81, 82.

48. John Ware, *Memoir of the Life of Henry Ware, Jr.* (Boston, 1846), pp. 158–159.

49. Clarke, *Church of the Disciples*, pp. 18, 19.

50. *Ibid.*, pp. 21, 22, 6.

51. *Ibid.*, pp. 24, 26, 27, 28. Because Clarke was a Transcendentalist, the principles embodied in the Church of the Disciples have sometimes been cited as an example of Transcendentalist church reform. Thus William R. Hutchison, *The Transcendentalist Ministers* (New Haven, 1959), p. 143. But the impetus was demographic more than Transcendental, and its roots were

antecedent to the rise of Transcendentalism. Octavius Brooks Frothingham asserted that these novelties were not popular, and "in fact they were against all its habits and especially repugnant to" Unitarians of his father's kind. Octavius Brooks Frothingham, *Boston Unitarianism, 1820–1850* (New York, 1890), p. 61.

52. *Theodore Parker's Experience as a Minister* (Boston, 1859), p. 167.

53. Joseph Tuckerman, *A Sermon Preached on Sunday Evening, Nov. 2, 1834, at the Ordination of Charles F. Barnard and Frederick T. Gray, as Ministers at Large in Boston* (Boston, 1834), p. 6.

54. "Appendix" to William E. Channing, *The Ministry for the Poor* (Boston, 1835), p. 45.

55. W. E. Channing, "The Charge," in Tuckerman, *Ordination of Barnard and Gray*, p. 39.

56. Alvan Lamson, "The Validity of Congregational Ordination," Dudleian Lecture, 1834, *Christian Examiner* 17 (1834): 189–190.

57. Leonard Woods, *History of the Andover Theological Seminary* (Boston, 1885), pp. 257–260.

58. Williston Walker, *The Creeds and Platforms of Congregationalism* (New York, 1893; reprinted Boston, 1960), pp. 230–231.

59. Wright, *Beginnings of Unitarianism*, pp. 67–75.

60. Ezra Stiles Gannett, "Mr. Parker and His Views," *Christian Examiner* 38 (1845): 268, 272. The refusal of more conservative Boston ministers to exchange with Parker should not be construed as indicating that they were more intolerant than he, or less generous and inclusive in their sympathies. Parker protested their way of drawing boundaries, but he had his own, and no one was more intolerant than he in condemning with vituperation and sarcasm the popular theology of election, predestination, and original sin.

ASSOCIATION PROLIFERATION AND BUREAUCRATIC DEVELOPMENT

1. Henry W. Bellows, *The Suspense of Faith* (New York, 1859), pp. 38, 35, 45. This address is included in Sydney E. Ahlstrom and Jonathan S. Carey, eds. *An American Reformation* (Middletown, Connecticut, 1985), pp. 371–397.

2. Octavius Brooks Frothingham, *The Unitarian Convention and the Times* (New York, 1865), pp. 3, 6. This tract was a reprint from *Friends of Progress*, 1 (1864–1865): 225–230.

3. Ralph Waldo Emerson, "Self Reliance," *Essays*, 1st ser.

4. Edmund C. Stedman, *Octavius Brooks Frothingham and the New Faith* (New York, 1876), pp. 48, 15, 43–44.

5. Other free churches that did not survive the departure or death of their minister were T. W. Higginson's in Worcester, Massachusetts; F. E. Abbot's in Dover, New Hampshire, and Toledo, Ohio; and Samuel Johnson's in Lynn, Massachusetts.

6. Francis Ellingwood Abbot, "The Two Confederacies," *Christian Register* (June 24, 1865).

7. William J. Potter, *The Free Religious Association: Its Twenty-Five Years and Their Meaning* (Boston, 1892), p. 12; Sydney E. Ahlstrom, "Francis Ellingwood Abbot and the Free Religious Association," *Proceedings of the Unitarian Historical Society,* Vol. 17, Pt. 2 (1973–1975): 1–21.

8. While the name of Henry W. Bellows immediately comes to mind, he was not alone. See, for example, Charles Lowe, "Denominational Organization," *Monthly Journal of the American Unitarian Association* 10 (1869): 97–112.

9. *Report of the Second Meeting of the National Conference* (Boston, 1866), pp. 9–11.

10. *Report of the Third Meeting of the National Conference* (Boston, 1868), pp. 65–69; *Report of the Fourth Meeting of the National Conference* (Boston, 1870), pp. 92, 82. When the National Conference made its recommendation, four conferences or the equivalent were already in existence. The New Hampshire Unitarian Association (1863) and the Maine Conference

of Unitarian Churches (1864) had been organized as "a help and auxiliary" to the AUA; they fitted into the new territorial scheme. Both the Western Unitarian Conference (1852) and the Unitarian Association of the State of New York had been invited from the beginning to send delegates to the National Conference, and the Western Conference was duly represented. But smaller local conferences were organized within those regions as well. By 1874, there were seventeen conferences in all, independent of but reporting to the National Conference.

11. *Report of the Fourth Meeting,* p. 89.

12. Thomas E. Graham, "The Bishop of the West: 1880–1884," *Proceedings of the Unitarian Universalist Historical Society,* Vol. 21, Pt. 2 (1989): 49–70.

13. *Report of the Fourth Meeting,* p. 60.

14. The failure of local conferences to assume responsibility for missionary activity occasioned recurrent comment. Brooke Herford argued in 1884 that the work of planting churches would have to be distributed and localized if it was to prosper, that it was becoming "too vast" for the AUA to handle. *(Report of the Eleventh Meeting of the National Conference* [New York, 1884], pp. 73–76.) That same year, Jenkin Lloyd Jones wrote a report to the National Conference critical of the local conferences and urging support of a fully articulated system of state conferences, legally incorporated, controlling their own funds, electing administrative secretaries, and sponsoring missionary activity. The experience of the Universalists with a comparable structure suggests that it is just as well his scheme was not adopted. *(Report of the Eleventh Meeting,* pp. 40–46.) As late as 1901, the Rev. R. C. Loring was urging that state conferences assume major responsibilities in the fellowshiping of ministers, the promotion of missionary work, and advising new churches as to how to increase their membership and strengthen their organization. *Christian Register* 80 (Aug. 8, 1901): 890–891.

15. In 1865, the best answer the *Monthly Journal* could give to the question, "how shall I enter the ministry," was to secure a

letter of introduction from some minister with whom the candidate was well acquainted. *Monthly Journal of the AUA* 6 (1865): 288.

16. *Monthly Journal* 4 (1863): 558. The difficulties and disappointments of candidating were described in "The Journal of a Candidate," *Monthly Journal* 5 (1864): 507–514, 557–564; 6 (1865): 84–91, 125–133, 187–194.

17. *Monthly Journal* 4 (1863): 521, 524, 557.

18. The earliest record book of the Ministerial Union, covering the years 1864 to 1888, is in the Andover-Harvard Theological Library, Harvard Divinity School.

19. "Record Book, 1864–1888," pp. 4, 40.

20. *Ibid.*, p. 129.

21. *Ibid.*, p. 112.

22. The name of the Ministerial Union was changed in 1922 to: Unitarian Ministerial Union. In 1947 it became the Unitarian Ministers Association, now the Unitarian Universalist Ministers Association.

23. "Record Book, 1864–1888," p. 135.

24. *Report of the Seventh Meeting of the National Conference* (Salem, Massachusetts, 1876), pp. 79–84, 178.

25. In 1893, the Bureau was reorganized as a five-man committee of the Ministerial Union, with its own Executive Secretary. For an explanation of the workings of the new committee, see D. M. Wilson, "Candidating," *Christian Register* 76 (March 25, 1897). A brief response was published in the issue of April 22, 1897, p. 243.

26. Later titles were Committee on Vacant Pastorates and Ministerial Settlements, and Committee on Supply of Pulpits.

27. "Record Book, 1864–1888," pp. 121–122, 215–220, 234, 237–240. The Trinitarian Congregational churches continued to give ministerial associations the authority to review the qualifications of would-be ministers. See Henry Martin Dexter, *A*

Hand-Book of Congregationalism (Boston, 1880), pp. 123–124: "it has long been the regular Congregational practice for students intending to enter our ministry to present themselves for examination as to culture and character to some Association of ministers, whose certificate of approval becomes thereafter sufficient commendation to the churches." Ministerial Associations likewise were "custodians of each others' professional character." Should a member "lapse into irregularity of belief or looseness of life, while it cannot try or depose him, [the Association] can say that it no longer esteems his professional character regular, his presence desirable, or his membership agreeable, and can turn him out." Since the published list of Congregational ministers included only those in good standing in some ministerial Association, "some approximation at least is made toward a list weeded of pretenders and reprobates. . . ." The development of a Committee on Fellowship by the Unitarians, as a credentialing authority, meant a significant difference between the two denominations in the practice of congregational polity.

28. *Report of the Fourth Meeting,* p. 136.

29. *Report of the Fifth Meeting of the National Conference* (Salem, Massachusetts, 1873), pp. 89–92.

30. *Report of the Eighth Meeting of the National Conference* (Salem, Massachusetts, 1878), pp. 146, 149; *Year-Book of the Unitarian Congregational Churches for 1880* (Boston, 1879), p. 42; Augustus Woodbury, "Unitarian Fellowship," *Official Report of the Proceedings of the Fourteenth Meeting of the National Conference* (Boston, 1891), pp. 74–78. In 1889, the Conference authorized the Council of the Conference instead of the Conference itself to name the members of the Fellowship Committee. *(Thirteenth Meeting,* 1889, p. 14.) This change was roundly criticized by Woodbury in his report in 1891.

31. *Report of the Fourteenth Meeting,* p. 75; *Official Report of the Proceedings of the Seventeenth Meeting of the National Conference* (Boston, 1897), p. 21; *Official Report of the Proceedings of the Eighteenth Meeting of the National Conference* (Boston, 1899), p. 25.

32. *Christian Register* 66 (May 5, 1887): 274.

33. *Report of the Ninth Meeting of the National Conference* (Boston, 1881), p. 130.

34. *Report of the Ninth Meeting,* p. 154; *Official Report of the Proceedings of the Tenth Meeting of the National Conference* (New York, 1882), pp. 16–24. For a summary and discussion of the majority and minority reports submitted in 1882, see Francis A. Christie, "Past Experience with Unitarian Organization," *Quarterly Bulletin of the Meadville Theological School,* Vol. 27, No. 3 (April 1923): 20–24.

35. Howard N. Brown, "The Proposed Amendments," *Fifty-eighth Anniversary of the American Unitarian Association with the Annual Report of the Board of Directors* (Boston, 1883), p. 20.

36. *Fifty-ninth Anniversary of the American Unitarian Association* (Boston, 1884), p. 9. A proposal in 1894 to abolish voting life memberships was referred to committee and rejected the following year. *Sixty-ninth Anniversary of the American Unitarian Association with the Annual Report of the Board of Directors* (Boston, 1894), p. 5; *Seventieth Anniversary of the American Unitarian Association, with the Annual Report of the Board of Directors* (Boston, 1895), pp. 6–7.

37. *Christian Register* 68 (Nov. 6, 1884): 710.

38. Details of the history of the Sunday School Society may be found in George Willis Cooke, *Unitarianism in America* (Boston, 1902), pp. 262–281, and Robert Dale Richardson, *125 Years of Unitarian Sunday Schools* (Boston, 1952). The manuscript records of the Society are at the Andover-Harvard Library.

39. Emily A. Fifield, *History of the Alliance* (n.p., 1915), pp. 6, 9, 24, 25.

40. *Ibid.,* pp. 145, 147.

41. J. T. Sunderland, "The Supply of Ministers: Is It Declining, and, If So, Why?" *Official Report of the Thirteenth Meeting of the National Conference* (Boston, 1889), p. 77.

42. T. R. Slicer, "The Young People's Guilds," *Official Report of the Fourteenth Meeting of the National Conference* (Boston, 1891), p. 61. A whole evening session of the Conference was devoted to "Our Young People." Slicer's paper was followed by one from Jenkin Lloyd Jones, defending the "Thought Side of Religion." He yielded to no one, he said, "in admiration of the beauty of devotion, the joy of worship, and the grace of reverence." But: "The heart is a much overworked organ of piety" (p. 62).

43. Vote of the union committee as reported in the *Christian Register* 74 (November 2, 1895): 772.

44. Constitution and By-Laws of the Young People's Religious Union, in the manuscript records of the society, Vol. 1896–1907, Andover-Harvard Library, bMS 462/1. See also "Young People's Religious Union," *Christian Register* 76 (March 4, 1897): 137.

45. For indications of an awareness of the importance of this development in local church life, see Joseph H. Crooker, "The Intellectual Work of the Church," and Edward Everett Hale, "The Charitable Work of the Church," *Official Report of the Proceedings of the Twelfth Meeting of the National Conference* (New York, 1886), pp. 118–125; also Thomas R. Slicer, "Building the Church," *Report of the Thirteenth Meeting*, p. 111, and Julian C. Jaynes, "A Working Church," *Report of the Thirteenth Meeting*, pp. 112–117.

46. Mrs. L. J. K. Gifford, "The Church as Distinct from the Parish," *Religious Magazine and Monthly Review* 46 (1871): 61, 64.

47. Just as the distinction between church and congregation was obscure, so too the distinction between church and parish became less plausible. Unitarian churches outside New England had seldom reproduced the dual organization. In Massachusetts, where the system was embedded in the legal structure, the General Court in 1887 authorized churches to incorporate, and the parishes or religious societies associated with them to convey to the new bodies their real and personal property, subject to the same uses and trusts (Chapter 404 of

the Acts of 1887). Probably in many instances the church atrophied and the parish in effect became the viable religious community. The church-parish dualism survives to this day in some Massachusetts churches.

48. Edmund H. Sears, "Church Organization," *Monthly Religious Magazine* 40 (1869): 87. The original responses to the questionnaire are in the Sears Papers, Andover-Harvard Library.

49. Sears, "Church Organization," pp. 90, 92, 93, 98, 102.

50. *Ibid.*, pp. 94, 102.

51. Henry D. Sedgwick, "The Layman's Demand on the Ministry," *Report of the Ninth Meeting*, pp. 81–117.

52. S. G. Bulfinch, "A Changing Ministry, or the Brevity of the Pastoral Relation in These Days," *Monthly Religious Magazine* 40 (1868): 165–181.

53. *Christian Register* 76 (June 3, 1897): 341.

54. See chapter 4 in Conrad Wright, ed., *A Stream of Light* (Boston, 1875), pp. 62–94.

55. Conrad Wright, *The Liberal Christians* (Boston, 1970), p. 96.

56. The "Report on Revision of the Constitution," followed by the "Laws for Securing a Uniform Organization of the Universalist Church" and recommended constitutions and bylaws for state conventions and parishes, was printed in *Minutes of the General Convention of Universalists . . . Centennial Session* (New York, 1871), pp. 53–95.

57. Russell E. Miller, *The Larger Hope: The Second Century* (Boston, 1985), pp. 68–77; Mary F. Bogie, "The Minneapolis Radical Lectures and the Excommunication of the Reverend Herman Bisbee," *Journal of the Universalist Historical Society* 7 (1967/68): 3–69.

58. *Minutes of the Universalist General Convention: Annual Session . . . 1873* (New York, 1873), pp. 42–54.

59. Miller, *Larger Hope*, pp. 78–93.

60. Ida M. Folsom, ed., *A Brief History of the Work of Universalist Women, 1869 to 1955* (Boston, 1955).

61. *Minutes of the Universalist General Convention . . . New York, 1874* (New York, 1874), p. 17.

62. Alan Seaburg, "Missionary to Scotland: Caroline Augusta Soule," *Transactions of the Unitarian Historical Society* (British) 14 (1967–70): 28–41.

63. *Minutes of the Universalist General Convention . . . Philadelphia, Pennsylvania, 1871* (New York, 1871), p. 25.

64. *Descriptive Catalogue of the Universalist Publishing House, Boston, Mass. with a Short History of the House and an Outline of Its Plan of Organization,* 2nd ed. (Boston, 1883).

65. *Minutes of the General Convention of Universalists . . . Baltimore, Maryland, 1867* (New York, 1867), p. 16.

66. *Minutes of the Universalist General Convention . . . Chicago, Illinois, 1877* (New York, 1877), p. 20.

67. [American Unitarian Association], *Annual Report 1899* (Boston, 1899), p. 46.

68. Thus Samuel A. Eliot in *Annual Report,* 1899, p. 22: "I do not urge a compromise which rests upon the sandy foundation of merely verbal agreements, nor do I advocate any organic union of these distinct Christian bodies. Each has its own work to do, each has its honorable tradition to preserve; but I hold that it ought to be possible for these two organizations to work side by side with heartier good will and with mutual helpfulness."

69. For a general survey of relationships between the two denominations, with full recognition of both theological and sociological factors, see Miller, *Larger Hope,* chapter 28.

PROFESSIONALIZED ADMINISTRATION

1. Other denominations experienced similar pressure toward bureaucratic organization in the same years. For the Presbyterian case, see Louis Weeks, "The Incorporation of American Reli-

gion: The Case of the Presbyterians," *Religion and American Culture* 1 (1991): 101–118.

2. [American Unitarian Association], *Sixty-ninth Anniversary . . . with the Annual Report of the Board of Directors* (Boston, 1894), p. 61.

3. Renamed in 1904 the Society for Ministerial Relief.

4. *Christian Register* 73 (1894): 825.

5. *Christian Register* 75 (1896): 198, 273.

6. [AUA], *Annual Report*, 1896, pp. 10–11.

7. Arthur Cushman McGiffert Jr., *Pilot of a Liberal Faith: Samuel Atkins Eliot, 1862–1950* (Boston, 1986), p. 68. One indication of the drift toward centralization was Eliot's suggestion in 1899 that churches deed their real property to the AUA, "reserving the right of occupancy so long as they shall continue to be living Unitarian churches." The suggestion was generally disregarded, though the Association did undertake to receive and invest funds established for the benefit of local churches and parishes. [AUA], *Annual Report*, 1899, pp. 14, 15.

8. [AUA], *Annual Report*, 1900, p. 18.

9. [AUA], *Annual Report*, 1900, p. 17. The problems the appointment of the publication agent was designed to address were explained by Eliot in the *Christian Register* 80 (1901): 676–677. An extensive account of the operations of the Publications Department by Charles Livingston Stebbins, the first agent, is in *Christian Register* 81 (1902): 219–223.

10. [Edward Darling], "The Livingston Stebbins Period—First Use of the Beacon Imprint," *The Beacon*, Vol. 2, No. 1 (January 1965).

11. [AUA], *Annual Report*, 1904, p. 17.

12. *Ibid.*, pp. 19–20.

13. [AUA], *Annual Report*, 1901, p. 15.

14. Robert Dale Richardson, *125 Years of Unitarian Sunday Schools* (Boston, 1952), pp. 26–27.

15. *Christian Register* 90 (1911): 636–637. Criticisms voiced in meetings of the Ministerial Union resulted in a session in January 1912 in which Eliot defended his administration. His responses to a series of pointed questions were published in the *Register* and reprinted as a pamphlet. See *Christian Register* 91 (1912): 124–125, 148–149, 172–173, 196–197.

16. *Christian Register* 91 (1912): 525, 527. Eliot received 697 votes; 67 were cast for Dr. Samuel M. Crothers, who was not a candidate and had specifically requested that his name not be used. Under the circumstances, the vote for Crothers suggests a significant amount of discontent with tendencies of the Eliot administration.

17. *Official Report of the Proceedings of the Twenty-first Meeting of the National Conference* (Boston, 1906), p. 68.

18. *Ibid.*, pp. 69–70. Batchelor's comments are the more significant because he himself had been the secretary of the AUA for almost three years, just prior to Eliot's accession to power.

19. [National Conference], *Official Report*, 1897, p. 21; *Official Report*, 1903, p. 37; *Official Report*, 1909, pp. 33–34.

20. [AUA], *Report of the Committee to Collect and Codify the Covenants and Statements of Faith in Use in Unitarian Churches* (Boston, 1901), p. 6.

21. *Ibid.*, pp. 6–10. The Ames covenant was: "In the love of truth and the spirit of Jesus Christ, we unite for the worship of God and the service of man." Ames was minister of the Spring Garden Church (Philadelphia) from 1880 to 1888.

22. *Ibid.*, pp. 10–18.

23. *Ibid.*, pp. 15–18, 24–25.

24. *Ibid.*, pp. 27–28.

25. [AUA], *Handbook for Unitarian Congregational Churches* ([Boston], 1901). It is worth noting that Eliot frequently used the

adjectives "Unitarian Congregational," instead of simply "Unitarian," as a reminder that the Unitarians had as clear a historic claim to the congregational tradition as did the Trinitarian Congregationalists who called themselves simply "Congregational." He was not alone in this; the *General Catalogue* of the Harvard Divinity School, listing all former students, followed the same practice.

26. [AUA], *The Organization of Parishes and Churches of the Unitarian Congregational Order, and Their Methods of Work* (Boston, [1886]).

27. *Handbook*, p. 6.

28. *Ibid.*, p. 22.

29. *Ibid.*, pp. 29, 35, 36.

30. *Ibid.*, pp. 10, 12.

31. *Ibid.*, p. 29.

32. *Ibid.*, pp. 30–32.

33. *Ibid.*, p. 13.

34. *Christian Register* 80 (1901): 508.

35. *Handbook*, pp. 38, 41, 43.

36. One response found in certain denominations was the development of "institutional churches," so-called, which engaged in a whole range of educational work, especially for newly arrived immigrants, in addition to the usual preaching services, Sunday school, and prayer meetings. Thus the Berkeley Temple (Congregational) in Boston sponsored classes in sewing, painting, stenography, dressmaking, elocution, penmanship, etc. (Cf. Edmund K. Alden, "The Berkeley Temple of Today," *Christian Union*, January 9, 1892, p. 78.) Jenkin Lloyd Jones's Abraham Lincoln Center in Chicago represents this movement, as does the "Every Day Church" (the Shawmut Universalist Society) in Boston. But Unitarians generally preferred to support settlement houses, or adult education enterprises like the Prospect Union in Cambridge, of which Francis Greenwood Peabody

was one of the founders. (Cf. Zelda Lions and Gordon W. Allport, "Seventy-Five Years of Continuing Education: The Prospect Union Association," *Cambridge Historical Society Proceedings* 40 [1964–1966]: 139–158.) The Unitarian approach to immigrants was through the Department of New Americans of the AUA and the publication of tracts in German, Italian, and other languages.

37. Louis C. Cornish, "Parish Workers," *Christian Register* 91 (1912): 107–109.

38. [AUA], *Annual Report*, 1906, pp. 20–21.

39. The School for Social Workers was an initiative of the new Department of Social Ethics at Harvard, of which Francis Greenwood Peabody was one of the leading spirits. See Samuel Eliot Morison, *The Development of Harvard University Since the Inauguration of President Eliot* (Cambridge, 1930), p. 225.

40. [AUA], *Annual Report*, 1907, pp. 48–49.

41. Eliot reiterated his argument for the capitalization of bequests and the need of a substantial endowment as late as 1912 in the *Christian Register* 91 (1912): 196–197.

42. [AUA], *Annual Report*, 1912, pp. 93–94.

43. Cf. [AUA], *Annual Report*, 1910, p. 13: "those who best understand the Congregational ideals must repudiate the interpretation of Congregationalism which makes it equivalent to an isolated independency." See also Samuel A. Eliot, "As to Its Organization and Administration," [National Conference], *Official Report of the . . . Twenty-third Meeting*, 1909, pp. 210–217.

44. *Manual of the Universalist General Convention* (New York, 1900), p. 46.

45. *Ibid.*, pp. 12–13.

46. Robert Cummins, "The Superintendency of the Universalist Church of America," *Annual Journal of the Universalist Historical Society* 3 (1962): 14–16; Willard C. Selleck, "The General Superintendency," *Christian Leader* 120 (November 29,

1938): 1439–1440; *Christian Leader* 67 (1897): 2; *Universalist Leader* NS 1 (October 29, 1898): 12.

47. *Christian Leader* 67 (October 28, 1897): 11; Cummins, "Superintendency," pp. 17–19.

48. *Universalist Leader* NS 1 (February 5, 1898): 3; NS 1 (June 4, 1898): 18; NS 1 (October 28, 1898): 18.

49. *Minutes of the Universalist General Convention . . . 1899* (Providence, Rhode Island, 1899), pp. 35, 101, 103. See also Cummins, "Superintendency," pp. 27–31. Cummins states that in 1901, Atwood travelled 85,910 miles. This was a cumulative figure, covering three years.

50. *Universalist Leader* NS 3 (February 17, 1900) 206: NS 4 (September 21, 1901): 1197.

51. Russell E. Miller, *The Larger Hope* (Boston, 1979, 1985), Vol. 2, pp. 235–240.

52. *Ibid.,* pp. 341–360.

53. David Hicks MacPherson, "Trends in Universalist Churches in Massachusetts in the First Half of the Twentieth Century" (S.T.B. thesis, Crane Theological School, 1952), esp. pp. 29–61; Richard M. Woodman, "An Evaluation of Data Relevant to the Decreasing Number of Churches in the New York State Convention of Universalists, 1900–1954" (B.D. thesis, St. Lawrence Theological School, 1954). Abridgements of these theses were published in the *Annual Journal of the Universalist Historical Society,* Vol. 6 (1966), but for important details, the original theses are essential.

54. Ida M. Folsom, ed., *A Brief History of the Work of Universalist Women, 1869 to 1953* (Boston, 1955), and Miller, *Larger Hope,* pp. 379–386, 174–213.

55. [AUA], *Annual Report,* 1908, p. 74; *Annual Report,* 1909, p. 81; *Annual Report,* 1910, pp. 86–87.

56. [AUA], *Annual Report,* 1913, pp. 30–39, 104.

57. [AUA], *Annual Report,* 1914, pp. 115–142; *Annual Report,* 1915,

p. 110. The Commission recommended an elaborate procedure for nominations (1914, pp. 130–138), but the annual meeting of 1915 adopted a much simpler revision.

58. [AUA], *Annual Report*, 1914, pp. 124–126. The Commission's suggestion was that when aid is given, a debt be created "which must be repaid to the Association with interest at such time as the council of the 'General Conference' shall rule, upon application of either party that such church is not properly within the Unitarian denomination."

59. *Christian Register* 66 (May 5, 1887): 274.

60. *Christian Register* 97 (April 25, 1918): 406.

61. [AUA], *Annual Reports*, 1936, pp. 74–75. See also *Christian Register* 115 (May 28, 1936): 367, 371–372.

62. *Christian Register* 99 (March 4, 1920): 232–234.

63. The initial suggestion may well have been a letter to the *Register* 98 (September 4, 1919): 845, by the Reverend Robert S. Loring of Newton Centre. See also *Christian Register* 98 (September 18, 25, October 2, 1919): 893, 917, 932, 938; 99 (March 25, 1920): 302. The energizing leader was Ernest G. Adams: 99 (November 4, 1920): 1073–1074.

64. [General Conference], *Official Report . . . of the Twenty-ninth Meeting* (1921), pp. 54, 26. A key figure in this initiative was the Reverend Frederick R. Griffin of Philadelphia, Chair of the Council of the General Conference, who reported for it to the Detroit meeting and was named to head the Commission.

65. "Report of the Commission on Polity," *Official Report . . . of the Thirtieth Meeting* (1923), pp. 29–48.

66. There were still seven voting life members listed in the UUA Directory for 1994.

67. [General Conference], *Official Report* (1923), p. 36.

68. *Ibid.*, p. 47.

69. Dr. Albert C. Dieffenbach in the *Christian Register* 104 (1925): 1077.

70. I. M. Atwood, "The Organization of the Universalist Church," *Christian Leader* NS 11 (1908): 939–942.

71. [Universalist General Convention], *Forty-second Annual Report of the Board of Trustees* (1907), pp. 5, 8; *Forty-fourth Annual Report* (1909), pp. 11, 15.

72. *Forty-fourth Annual Report* (1909), pp. 14, 91, 92; *Forty-sixth Annual Report* (1911), p. 42. Sunday schools throughout the denomination were losing ground: in 1913 it was reported that "our Sunday School enrollment has fallen 36.6 per cent in twenty years" (1913, p. 95). Despite an admonition from the Board of Trustees that the Commission on Sunday Schools was the proper instrument for improvement, a National Sunday School Association was formed in 1913 with a full array of officers and a complete set of bylaws. This was just the time when the Unitarians were transferring the work and salaried staff of the long-established Unitarian Sunday School Society to the new Department of Religious Education in the AUA.

73. *Forty-fourth Annual Report* (1909), p. 18; *Forty-sixth Annual Report* (1911), p. 17; *Forty-eighth Annual Report* (1913), pp. 9–10; *Fiftieth Annual Report* (1915), p. 32.

74. [Frederick A. Bisbee], "A Crisis at Springfield," *Universalist Leader* NS 14 (1911): 1222–1223. See also Frederick W. Perkins, "'The Crisis' and the Way Out," *Universalist Leader* NS 14 (1911): 1292–1293, in which the executive duties of such an office are more explicitly indicated.

75. [Universalist General Convention], *Forty-sixth Annual Report* (1911), pp. 12–13; *Forth-eighth Annual Report* (1913), pp. 67, 69.

76. "Report of the President, *Fifty-second Annual Report* (1917), pp. 3–11.

77. "Report of the President," *Fifty-fourth Annual Report* (1919), pp. 5–13. By way of contrast, the Unitarians from an early date had rented office space, and in 1886 occupied 25 Beacon Street, built especially for them.

78. *Universalist Yearbook for 1926*, pp. 9–10, 36–37; *Universalist*

Yearbook for 1928, p. 11. Such coordination as was possible came through the development of a Council of Executives of the several auxiliary bodies. It began in 1936 as a conference of representatives of the Sunday School Association, the YPCU, the Women's National Missionary Association, and the General Convention. Monthly meetings of the executives based at 16 Beacon Street followed. A "united organization and program for the Universalist Church" was the objective, but it was recognized that "no established or proven pattern existed to unify the work of the denomination," as so "many steps must be taken before we are ready to consider the one of changing our denominational machinery." It would seem that the Council was more a recognition of a problem than a solution to it. *Christian Leader* 120 (July 9, 1938): 866–887.

79. Miller, *The Larger Hope*, Vol. 2, p. 53.

80. The question of a change of name was raised at the 1937 convention. (*Universalist Biennial Reports and Directory, 1937–1938*, pp. 7, 18.) Two years later, the Board of Trustees reported that it "planned to give further study to this question." (*Universalist Directory, 1939–1940*, p. 29.) At the 1941 convention, in response to a report from a special committee, the Convention voted to authorize the Trustees to request from the New York legislature a revised charter of incorporation. ("Minutes" of the 1941 convention, bound with the *Report of the Biennial Session*, 1943, p. ix.) The legislature complied with the request on February 13, 1942. (*Report of the Biennial Session*, 1943, p. 35.)

81. John Haynes Holmes, *New Churches for Old* (New York, 1922). In the *Christian Register* 98 (1919): 875–886, 898–900, Holmes described imaginatively what church life would be like in 1960, when 75 percent of the population of a town would belong to its community church. Among other consequences would be the abolition of the distinction between church and state. Of a number of critiques, one of the best was by Minot Simons, then minister in Cleveland. (*Christian Register* 98 [1919]: 948.) The vote of Holmes's church on May 10, 1920, to affirm its status as a Unitarian church, despite the change in its name, was noted in the *Register* on June 3, 1920.

82. Henry Wilder Foote, *The Minister and His Parish: A Discussion of Problems in Church Administration* (New York, 1923).

83. *Ibid.*, pp. 38, 40–41.

84. *Ibid.*, p. 93.

85. *Ibid.*, pp. 14, 114, 29.

86. *Ibid.*, pp. 157, 159, 163.

87. *Ibid.*, pp. 31, 171–173.

88. *Ibid.*, pp. 14–17.

89. Foote noted that sometimes ministers advertised for churches in the denominational press. I have not seen any instance of this in the *Christian Register,* so he must have had examples from other denominations in mind.

90. Foote, *Minister and His Parish,* p. 8.

91. For example, in the Cambridge church in 1934, three announced candidates preached on successive Sundays. One of them wore spats, the sermon of the second was a mosaic of quotations, the third (Leslie Pennington) was called.

92. Dana Greeley was called by the Arlington Street Church (Boston) in March 1935; only then did Dr. Samuel A. Eliot announce that he would retire on September first. Raymond Bragg was called to the Minneapolis church as the "probable successor" to Dr. John H. Dietrich, who was ready to stay as long as needed before retirement, until the new man had won the "admiration and affection and loyalty" of the congregation. See "A New Method of Succession in Minneapolis," *Christian Register* 114 (1935): 232.

93. For surveys of the relationship between Unitarians and Universalists, see especially Miller, *Larger Hope,* Vol. 2, chaps. 28, 30; also Charles Vickery, "A Century of Attempted Rapprochment Between the Universalist Church of America and the American Unitarian Association" (S.T.B. thesis, Tufts College School of Religion, 1945).

94. *Manual of the Universalist General Convention* (New York, 1916), p. 40.

95. *Fifty-second Annual Report* (1917), p. 37; *Universalist Year Book for 1928*, p. 11.

96. Miller, *Larger Hope*, Vol. 2, chap. 29.

97. *Universalist Year Book for 1930*, pp. 266–278.

PARALLEL ROUTES TO MERGER

1. "Frederick May Eliot, 1889–1958," a memorial address by Wallace W. Robbins, in Alfred P. Stiernotte, ed., *Frederick May Eliot: An Anthology* (Boston, 1959), p. xxi. See also Carol Ruth Morris, "Frederick May Eliot, President of the American Unitarian Association (1937–1958)," Ph.D. Diss., Boston University, 1970.

2. [AUA], *Annual Report*, 1929, p. 14; *Annual Report*, 1931, p. 11.

3. *Unitarians Face a New Age: The Report of the Commission of Appraisal to the American Unitarian Association* (Boston, 1936). The recommendations with respect to organization are on pages 20–26 and 333–336. Detailed analysis of "Organizational Evolution and Problems" by the staff of the commission are found on pages 233–304. The report as a whole is a major historical document, which at the same time contains much of continuing relevance.

4. *Ibid.*, p. 247. The "distinctive values of the Conference" were ecclesiastical, specifically congregational and democratic. It was organized, as the Commission on Polity stated in 1925, "that there might be more democratic conference and discussion than prevailed in the Association." The value system of the AUA, on the other hand was bureaucratic, inescapably hierarchical to some degree. For a discussion of the problem of merging ecclesiastical and bureaucratic structures with different value systems, see "Unitarian Universalist Denominational Structure," in Conrad Wright, *Walking Together* (Boston, 1988), pp. 73–95. The Universalists had one version of the problem, which they never solved because their ecclesiastical structure

stood in the way of creating an effective administration. The Unitarians had the opposite version of the problem, in which the bureaucratic structure tended to overwhelm the ecclesiastical.

5. *Unitarians Face a New Age*, pp. 20, 21.

6. [AUA], *Annual Report*, 1936, p. 74.

7. [AUA], *Year Book*, 1938, p. 15. The revised bylaws were also printed in the *Christian Register* 116 (1937): 371–373.

8. [AUA], *Year Book*, 1938, p. 16.

9. *Ibid.*

10. *Unitarians Face a New Age*, pp. 263–265.

11. *Ibid.*, pp. 267, 269.

12. *Ibid.*, pp. 333–334.

13. [AUA], *Annual Report*, 1938, p. 28; *Christian Register* 117 (1938): 737–738. Further progress toward regional responsibility was reported in *Christian Register* 120 (1941): 105–106, 118.

14. Charles E. Snyder, "The Leaven Is Working: A Report on Unitarian Regionalism," *Christian Register* 122 (1943): 51–52, 54.

15. *Unitarians Face a New Age*, pp. 22, 295–304.

16. *Ibid.*, p. 22. Dr. Cornish protested that the Commission had not consulted with his administration in preparing its findings, and that the incompleteness of the investigation had led to inaccuracies. See "An Open Letter to the Chairman of the Appraisal Commission," *Christian Register* 115 (1936): 64–65; Dr. Eliot's response (an insert tipped into the *Register* after it had gone to press); and a letter in support of Cornish two weeks later, p. 95.

17. [AUA], *Annual Report*, 1938, pp. 13–14; [AUA], *Address of the President to the Annual Meeting of the American Unitarian Association*, May 22, 1941, pp. 7–10.

18. *Address of the President*, p. 6.

19. *Ibid.*, p. 12.

20. *Unitarians Face a New Age*, p. 85.

21. George H. Ellis, "The Christian Register," *Christian Register* 96 (1917): 1226; "Incidents in the History of the Register," 100 (1921): 390–392.

22. *Unitarian Face in a New Age*, p. 85.

23. *Christian Register* 118 (1939): 635, 672–673, 706–707.

24. *Christian Register* 120 (1941): 101.

25. *Ibid.*, p. 124.

26. *Ibid.*, p. 163. Jones declared that approval of his editorship was suddenly withdrawn when he published an article by Forest K. Davis entitled "The Trend Toward Disintegration" in the issue of November 15, 1940. (*Christian Register* 119 [1940]: 435–436.) See "The Editor to His Readers," *Christian Register* 120 (1941): 163–164.

27. *Christian Register* 120 (1941): 133–135, 152–155, 171–177. Central to Pennington's criticism was the assertion that the decision had been made by the Board without taking the people into its confidence. He could see no distinction between the *Register* as it was now contemplated and "a 'house organ' of promotion under the control of the administration of the AUA." He also commented on the "well known" fact that there had been friction over the Davis piece. "It is hard for one on the outside to believe that the present action is wholly unrelated to that friction" (p. 153).

28. *Christian Leader* 121 (1939): 560–571, 793–794, 819–820.

29. *Ibid.*, pp. 857–859, 958–959.

30. *Ibid.*, pp. 1050–1055. For comment on the proposals, see pp. 1079–1080, 1134–1135, 1143, 1218–1220.

31. *Ibid.*, pp. 1050–1051.

32. Edna P. Bruner, "General Field Work," *Christian Leader* 123 (1941): 156–157.

33. Reports of the Board of Trustees, the General Field Worker, and the General Superintendent were too long for publication in the *Leader*, but were made available in mimeographed form (copy in UCA Archives, Andover-Harvard Theological Library, Harvard Divinity School). Cummins was particularly aroused by an address to the Illinois Universalist Convention by Frank D. Adams, "The Fatal Policy of Centralization," published in the *Christian Leader* 123 (1941): 555. Among other things, Adams described the accomplishments of the Cummins administration as "futile gropings . . . in which the only clear note has been a demand for money," as increasing centralization "with its steady and insistent sapping of local and state resources," as being swayed by "the current world-wide movement toward regimentation and government by decree from Berlin, Moscow, or Boston." Cummins's rebuke of what he termed "slanderous charges" by a former president of the Convention was the talk of the Convention and was duly reported by the Boston daily papers.

34. *Christian Register* 123 (1944): 162–163, 433–436; Carol R. Morris, "Frederick May Eliot," pp. 262–276.

35. Morris, "Frederick May Eliot," p. 200; *Christian Register* 123 (1944): 361–362; 128 (September 1949): 34.

36. The Post Office Mission dated from 1884; it was still going strong in some branch Alliances fifty years later. For the beginnings and early years, see Emily A. Fifield, *History of the Alliance* (n.p., 1915), pp. 16–18, 79–82, 97, 133–134.

37. In the summer of 1946, Call devoted much time to analyzing the reasons for the disappearance of 254 churches since 1900. His report indicated that unwise choice of location for church extension was a major factor. The Association had provided subsidies for many churches that had never become self-supporting and had dissolved. Instead of simply responding to initiatives from the field, often in locations where there was little realistic hope of success, he advocated a deliberate policy of concentrating resources where there was assurance that new churches could survive and become self-supporting. He developed criteria for the selection of such locations. Elsewhere lay

centers should be encouraged with guidance from headquarters but not financial subsidy. See Lon Ray Call, "A Research on Church Extension and Maintenance Since 1900: A Progress Report" (mimeographed, 36 pp., 1946). See also Laile E. Bartlett, *Bright Galaxy: Ten Years of Unitarian Fellowships* (Boston, 1960), chap. 4, and Rosemary Thompson, "Origins of the Fellowship Movement," *Christian Register* 136 (April 1957): 8–9.

38. Bartlett, *Bright Galaxy*, p. 45.

39. *Ibid.*, p. 193.

40. Lon Ray Call, Letter to the Editor, *Christian Register* 129 (February 1950): 10. See also his report to May Meetings, 1948, "Extending Unitarianism . . . ," printed as a broadside by the Division of Publications, which warned: "Do not give way to the enthusiasm of 20 or 30 or 40 or even 50 people and encourage them to form a church."

41. *Unitarian Yearbook . . . and Annual Report for 1950–51* (Boston, 1951), p. 14.

42. Carl R. Scovel, Arlington Street, Boston, 1957; Webster L. Kitchell, All Souls, New York, 1957; Virgil E. Murdock, Westford, Massachusetts, 1958.

43. Alan Deale, Hubbardston, Massachusetts, 1953; Paul Hayes, San Francisco, 1956; Bruce T. Wyman, Whitman, Massachusetts, 1958; Walter S. Mitchell, Niagara Falls, New York, 1960; Kenneth R. Mochel, Rochester, New York, 1960.

44. Walter S. Mitchell, Niagara Falls, New York, 1960. It may be noted that the report of the Commission on Appraisal, entitled *Our Professional Ministry: Structure, Support and Renewal* (1992), states: "the ordaining body should preferably be the congregation from which the ordinand has received and accepted the first call" (p. 36).

45. Carl R. Scovel, Arlington Street, 1957; David B. Loomis, Arlington Street, 1958; Richard G. Kimball, Fitchburg, Massachusetts, 1959.

46. Ernest W. Kuebler, Kings Chapel, Boston, 1938.

47. Sophia L. Fahs, Montgomery County (Bethesda), Maryland, 1959.

48. The "Fritchman Case" of 1946–1947 involved much more than the *Christian Register,* though that is all that is considered here. For other aspects of it—accusations that Fritchman was a member of a communist cell, his appearance before the House Unamerican Affairs Committee, his influence on the young people in American Unitarian Youth (AUY)—see Stephen H. Fritchman, *Heretic: A Partisan Autobiography* (Boston, 1977), chap. 11. For personal testimony by one of those who, from personal experience in AUY, became suspicious of Fritchman's association with left wing youth movements, see Robert Jones in *UU World* 17 (February 15, 1986): 15.

49. Fritchman, *Heretic,* p. 65.

50. Morris, "Frederick May Eliot," p. 300.

51. Thus Homer Jack's memorandum entitled: "Threat of American Communists to the Liberal Church and Other Institutions," cited in Morris, "Frederick May Eliot," p. 299. For the charge that communist sympathizers on the Service Committee were biased in favor of Communists in dispensing aid to refugees, see Ghanda DiFiglia, *Roots and Visions: The First Fifty Years of the Unitarian Universalist Service Committee* (n.p., 1990), pp. 49–52.

52. Detailed documentation of the actions of the Board and Fritchman's responses, based on Board records, is in Morris, "Frederick May Eliot," pp. 287–322. A statement by Dr. Eliot on behalf of the Board was printed in the *Christian Register* 125 (1946): 455.

53. Morris, "Frederick May Eliot," p. 313.

54. *Ibid.,* p. 308.

55. *Ibid.,* p. 313.

56. The text of the unpublished editorial is printed in full in Fritchman, *Heretic,* pp. 90–92.

57. Morris, "Frederick May Eliot," p. 319.

58. *Ibid.*, pp. 312–321; Eliot's oral summary of the circumstances of Fritchman's dismissal, addressed to the annual meeting, is on pp. 318–320. Written statements by Eliot and Judge Lawrence G. Brooks appear in the *Register* 126 (1947): 248–249. Fritchman's remarks to the annual meeting were printed in the same issue (June 1947), pp. 255, 271.

59. Morris, "Frederick May Eliot," pp. 330–331; DiFiglia, *Roots and Visions*, pp. 52–53.

60. The account by Russell Miller of relations between Unitarians and Universalists from 1870 to merger is by far the fullest and most adequate available. See Miller, *The Larger Hope* (Boston, 1985), Vol. 2, chaps. 28–31, 33.

61. *Ibid.*, pp. 605–607.

62. *Christian Register* 132 (January 1953): 28.

63. *Directory of Universalist Churches and Ministers: 1955–1956*, pp. 76–93, 96–99.

64. DiFiglia, *Roots and Branches*, pp. 41 ff.

65. *Christian Leader* 131 (1949): 343, 396–397; 133 (1951): 288–289, 292. The departmental structure was written into the bylaws in 1951; see the revision of 1953 in *Christian Leader* 135 (1953): 145–156.

66. Wayne B. Arnason, *Follow the Gleam* (Boston, 1980), pp. 113–121.

67. Miller, *Larger Hope*, Vol. 2, pp. 649–652. For key documents in the history of the Council, see *Christian Register* 128 (November 1949): 10; 129 (January 1950): 28–30; 130 (May 1951): 28; 130 (September 1951): 32–33; 132 (May 1953): 26–27; 132 (September 1953): 36.

68. The text of the report is in *Christian Register* 134 (October 1955): 20–21.

69. As presented to the 1959 biennial sessions, the plan was printed (with a blue cover) as *A Proposed Plan to Consolidate the American Unitarian Association and the Universalist Church*

of America. The approved text was printed (with a green cover): *The Plan to Consolidate the American Unitarian Association and the Universalist Church of America.*

70. Approval by plebiscite required 60 percent participation of the churches, and 75 percent in favor of those participating, in each denomination. Steps in the merger process may be traced in the *Unitarian Register*—the name was changed from *Christian Register* in May 1957—and the *Universalist Leader;* see especially *Unitarian Register* 136 (December 1957): 16; 137 (April 1958): 6; 137 (December 1958): 5, 27; and for a detailed account of the Syracuse meeting, 138 (December 1959): 19–24. See also Miller, *Larger Hope,* Vol. 2, pp. 655–663.

71. UCA Bylaws, Art. III, Sec. 1.

72. UUA Constitution, Art. II, Sec. 3.

73. UUA Constitution, Art. III, Sec. 3.

74. UUA Constitution, Art. V, Sec. 1.

75. UCA Laws of Fellowship, Art. II, Sec. 1.

76. UUA Constitution, Art. III, Sec. 4.

77. UCA Laws of Fellowship, Art. VII, Sec. 2.

78. UCA Laws of Fellowship, Art. IV, Sec. 1.

79. UUA Constitution, Art. VI, Sec. 1.

80. UUA By-Laws, Art. I, Sec. 2.

81. UUA By-Laws, Art. VII, Sec. 1; AUA By-Laws, Art. V, Sec. 1; UUA By-Laws, Art. III, Sec.1.

82. UCA By-Laws, Art. VII, Sec. 2; AUA By-Laws, Art. VII, Sec. 2; UUA By-Laws, Art. V, Sec. 4.

83. UUA By-Laws, Art. IV, Sec. 2; Art. VII, Sec. 2; Art. IV, Sec. 1.

84. *Unitarian Register* 138 (December 1959): 22. An amendment to eliminate the provision for removal of the president "for the best interests of the Association" was likewise rejected.

THE UUA

1. The two reports were: *The Organization and Administration of the Unitarian Universalist Association: The Report of the Coordinating Committee on Consolidation* (Boston, 1961), sometimes referred to as "the brown book"; and "The Church and Its Leadership," in *The Free Church in a Changing World* (Boston, 1963), pp. 1–20. The Commission on the Church and Its Leadership was one of six commissions appointed at that time, the others being charged with issues of theology, education, the arts, ethics, and world religion.

2. *Free Church,* p. 12.

3. Art. V, Sect. 1.

4. The position of proponents of the amendment is stated in Arthur Graham and Robert West, "Rebel Yell from the New South," *Register-Leader* Vol. 145, No. 3 (May 1963): 7.

5. The amendment was defeated by a vote of 436 to 379, and on reconsideration by a vote of 459 to 383. A summary of the debate may be found in the *Register-Leader,* Vol. 145, No. 3 (Midsummer 1963): 11–12. The January, March, and April 1963 issues contain comment, pro and con. After the vote, Kenneth K. Marshall, one of those most active in opposition, wrote to me: "This was the most heavy-hearted 'victory' I had ever been a part of"; while Dana Greeley referred to the proceedings as "a long and vigorous, and to many persons disheartening debate." For some, the disheartening aspect was that a proposal they strongly favored was defeated. For some, it was the expression in debate and in the corridors outside of vindictiveness and bitterness. For some it was the realization that the denomination was saved from a serious blunder by the technicality that a two-thirds vote and not a simple majority is required to amend the Constitution. For some, finally, the disheartening aspect was the realization that the implications for congregational polity were thrust aside by many as a false issue. Irving Murray wrote me that he was "shocked" by the widespread misunderstanding of the issues. Well he might have been, when one of our most prominent ministers made the extraordinary

assertion that among us "Congregational polity permits the Association to set theological, liturgical, educational, and financial conditions upon membership, voting, and fellowshipping." For these reflections, I rely on an unpublished sermon, preached by me in Cambridge on July 7, 1963, entitled: "Whom Shall We Segregate?"

6. The text of the proposal is in the minutes of the 1968 General Assembly, printed in the *Directory* for 1969, p. 43. The shift from Article III to Article II eliminated the problem of polity. For comment, see *UUA Now*, Autumn I (1968): 4; Autumn II (1968): 5; December (1968): 29; March 5, 1969: 4; April 28, 1969: 4–5.

7. The church was the Church of the Mediator (Universalist), of which the Reverend Albert Q. Perry was the minister. An earlier minister, Dr. Henry H. Schooley, had attempted to strengthen the church by admitting new members, some of whom "were nominally members of other religious denominations." The church divided into two factions, one more theologically conservative than the other. Members of one group instituted court proceedings, seeking to prevent the spending of capital funds for current expenses and the admission of new members who did not believe "in the traditions and tenets of the Universalist religion." See *Register-Leader*, Vol. 147, No. 5 (May 1965): 26; Vol. 147, No. 8 (October 1965): 21.

8. At the General Assembly in 1965, the initial impulse was to add the word "theology" to the resolution on open membership already under discussion dealing with race, color, sex, or national origin. It was soon pointed out that a person's "theology" is a matter of choice, while the other qualifications are "things people are born with." Theology was therefore separated from the other criteria. The original resolution became an amendment to the Constitution (Article II, Section 4) approved in 1967. The question of theology was referred to a special Committee on Congregational Polity and Membership Practices, which reported in 1966 and 1967. Final action approving a new Article II, Section 5 was taken in 1968. See the General Assembly minutes printed in the *Directory* for 1966 (p. 66); for 1967

(p. 62); for 1968 (pp. 33 and 34); and 1969 (p. 43). Note that there is an error in the text as printed in the *Directory* for 1968: the amendment at the bottom of page 33 and the one at the top of page 34 should be transposed. For comment on the issue, see *Register-Leader*, Vol. 147, No. 7 (Midsummer 1965); Vol. 147, No. 9 (November 1965): 14; Vol. 148, No. 3 (March 1966): 10–11; Vol. 148, No. 7 (Midsummer 1966): 15.

9. The text of the proposed amendment is in the minutes of the 1968 meeting, in the 1969 *Directory*, pages 43–44. The "overwhelming" rejection is recorded in the minutes of the 1969 meeting, in the 1970 *Directory*. For comment on the proposal, see Harry H. Hoehler, "On Mandatory Contributions," *Journal of the Liberal Ministry*, Vol. 8, No. 3 (Fall 1968): 51–59; *UUA Now*, Vol. 150, No. 8 (Autumn I, 1968): 4; No. 9 (Autumn II, 1968): 15; No. 10 (Winter I, 1968): 29; No. 11 (Winter II, 1969): 4; No. 12 (Spring 1969): 4–5.

10. Joseph Barth, "Contests for the Presidency: AUA 1958—UUA 1961," *Proceedings of the Unitarian Historical Society*, Vol. 15, Pt. 1 (1964): 52–59, 62.

11. Dale DeWitt was one of the regional directors whose advice was sought at the time of Frederick Eliot's death, and he was one of the members of the special committee on reorganization. He summarized the report and explained its rationale in Dale DeWitt, "Participation and Democracy," *Unity* 144 (1959): 139–145. See also Dale DeWitt, "The Presidency of the Association," *Unity* 148 (1962): 20–25. How these issues looked to Dana Greeley and his supporters may be seen in Barth, "Contests for the Presidency," pp. 26–47.

12. *Unitarian Register*, Vol. 139, No. 5 (May 1960): 29.

13. Dana McLean Greeley, *25 Beacon Street and Other Recollections* (Boston, 1971), pp. 46–48; Barth, "Contests for the Presidency," pp. 30–31.

14. UUA Constitution, Article IV; By-Laws, Art. IV; *UUA Directory* (1961–1962), pp. 26, 30.

15. *Organization and Administration*, pp. 41, 47, 45.

16. *Ibid.,* p. 50; *Unitarian Register,* Vol. 140, No. 7 (Midsummer 1961): 11.

17. Greeley, *25 Beacon Street,* pp. 62–63.

18. *Unitarian Register,* Vol. 140, No. 4 (April 1961): 23.

19. "The UUA Presidency: A Study in Concepts," *UUA Now,* Vol. 150, No. 5 (Autumn II): 26–28. The former district executive was Dwight Brown.

20. *UUA Directory,* 1961–1962, p. 39.

21. *UUA Directory,* 1969, p. 44.

22. The persuasion needed to convince Frederick Eliot to accept the nomination of the AUA Board in 1937 is detailed in Carol R. Morris, "The Election of Frederick May Eliot to the Presidency of AUA," *Proceedings of the Unitarian Historical Society,* Vol. 17, Pt. 1 (1970–1972): 1–45.

23. The campaign expenses of the seven candidates were:

Carleton M. Fisher	$1,614.00
John Ogden Fisher	1,500.00
Aron S. Gilmartin	5,697.05
J. Harold Hadley	5,747.00
Philip M. Larson, Jr.	2,284.70
Deane Starr	6,999.02
Robert N. West	8,512.00
	$32,353.77

See *UUA Now* (December 8, 1969), p. 4.

24. The listing of conferences, councils, and area meetings takes up more than ten pages in the *Unitarian Year Book;* see pages 43–53 of the *Year Book* for 1957/58.

25. The Annual Appeal was an umbrella organization, incorporated separately from the AUA, through which the churches supported eighteen organizations including the AUA, the Women's Alliance, the Laymen's League, etc.

26. The regional directors were not functionaries of the AUA and were on occasion independently active in denominational poli-

tics. According to Dana Greeley, the regional directors "almost to a man" opposed his election in 1958, "almost unanimously" opposed merger, and "most of them, quietly or otherwise," supported Bill Rice for the presidency in 1961. Greeley's uneasy relationship with at least some of them carried over to the district executives after the merger; some of them had earlier been regional directors of the AUA. Greeley, *25 Beacon Street*, p. 95.

27. *Organization and Administration* (the "brown book"), pp. 36–38.

28. The results of the districting process were summarized, with maps, in Marie H. Walling, "Districting—'So I Can Understand It,'" *Unitarian Universalist Register-Leader* 146 (February 1964): 36–38.

29. *Register-Leader* 147 (Midsummer 1965): 18.

30. Greeley, *25 Beacon Street*, p. 96. While Greeley supported the concept of district organization and wanted headquarters and district executives to work together, he evidently had continuing concern lest they become too free-wheeling. See also an interview with Greeley in *UUA Now*, Newsletter (July 5, 1969) pp. 7, 8.

31. UUA *Directory* for 1969, p. 44; *UUA Now*, Newsletter Issue, August 10, 1968, p. 1. For discussion leading up to adoption, by Dale DeWitt, Arthur Graham, Deane Starr, and others, see *Register-Leader*, Vol. 148 (January 1966): 6; (March 1966): 14; (April 1966): 19; *Register-Leader*, Vol. 149 (October 1967): 6; *Register-Leader*, Vol. 150 (May 1968): 32, 33.

32. Dan Huntington Fenn, "The Fellowship Committee," in *Unitarians Face a New Age* (Boston, 1936), p. 130.

33. *Organization and Administration*, pp. 97–107.

34. *Ibid.*, p. 98.

35. See minutes of the 1965 General Assembly, *Directory* (1966), pp. 66–68, 96–98, also *Register-Leader*, Vol. 147, No. 7 (Midsummer 1965): 21.

36. *Free Church,* pp. 16–17. An egregious example of the tendency to dilute the concept of ministry was the action in 1967 of the Arlington Street Church (Boston) to install its lay moderator as "Minister of the Congregation." The office was described as "a ceremonial office which honors a layman who has made outstanding contributions to his church." The action was promptly condemned by the officers of the Unitarian Universalist Ministers Association as "a possible infringement on the role of professional clergymen." *Register-Leader,* Vol. 149, No. 7 (Midsummer 1967): 29. But Jo and Laile Bartlett thought it was a good idea! Josiah R. and Laile E. Bartlett, *Moment of Truth* (Berkeley, California, 1968), p. 128.

37. Ministerial Fellowship Committee, *Rules* (1969), pp. 3–6.

38. *UU World,* May 1, 1974, p. 2.

39. The booklets were *Recommended Procedures for Churches Seeking a Minister* and *Procedures for Ministers Seeking New Settlement,* both dated January 1962.

40. *Procedures for Churches,* p. 3.

41. Compare the codified procedures with Henry Wilder Foote's discussion in *The Minister and His Parish* (New York, 1923), supra, pp. 141–142.

42. David B. Parke, "Danger Signs for Liberals," *Journal of the Liberal Ministry* 1 (1961): 62–63.

43. Patton submitted the article to the *Register-Leader,* but Victor Bovee, the editor, rejected it. His reasons, given in a long editorial, are suggestive of the bureaucratic instinct for self-preservation. The problem, if it exists, he wrote, is "a professional problem for ministers rather than one of especial interest for laymen." The complaints should be called to the attention of the Department of the Ministry "on the assumption they would be seriously considered." Other ministers might be involved, but public criticism of the Department of the Ministry would not be printed in the *Register-Leader.* Patton replied that an earlier article of his critical of the administration had also been refused, and Bovee had turned down articles by others

voicing criticism "because he did not think it was yet time to criticize the new set-up." Despite protests by Bovee, Patton insisted that the magazine was "simply a 'house organ'" and the "public relations agency of the administration." *Unitarian Universalist Register-Leader,* Vol. 145, No. 8 (October 1963), p. 3; Vol. 145, No. 10 (December 1963), p. 13.

44. *Free Church,* p. 10.

45. For divergent views of the "Black Rebellion," see Daniel G. Higgins, "The Unitarian Universalist Association and the Color Line" (D. Min. diss., Meadville/Lombard Theological School, 1977), and Victor H. Carpenter, *The Black Empowerment Controversy and the Unitarian Universalist Association, 1967–1970* (Boston, 1983). The Commission on Appraisal reported on the same events in *Empowerment: One Denomination's Quest for Social Justice, 1967–1982* (Boston, 1984). Comment on the Commission Report and Carpenter's book by Harry Hoehler, Donald Harrington, Glover Barnes, and others is in *UU World,* Vol. 15, No. 3 (March 15, 1984).

46. As recorded in the *UUA Directory,* adult membership fell from 177,431 in 1968 to 154,751 in 1972 and to 149,610 in 1975. Church school enrollment showed an even faster drop, from 104,876 in 1968 to 55,897 in 1972. In part, this was because of a deliberate effort on the part of the West administration to secure more accurate figures, in view of flagrant instances of overstating the number of adult members in the reports from the churches. This was a time when many mainline churches were likewise losing members to a significant degree.

47. *UU World,* March 1, 1970.

48. The turbulent 1969 meeting in Boston, when Bob West won the contested election as president and the funding of the Black Affairs Council aroused controversy, was nevertheless attended by delegates from no more than 50.3 percent of the churches. For the next seven years, participation was low, ranging from 26.3 to 34.7 percent. Only toward the end of the decade did the figure climb above 40 percent. (More recently, in 1992, it was 48.3 percent.)

Churches Represented at General Assembly, 1969–1978

1969	Boston	541	of	1,076	50.3 percent
1970	Seattle	359		1,038	34.6
1971	Washington	356		1,025	34.7
1972	Dallas	268		1,019	26.3
1973	Toronto	343		1,011	33.9
1974	New York	337		1,007	33.5
1975	Minneapolis	325		1,004	32.4
1976	Claremont	275		1,001	27.5
1977	Ithaca	409		1,000	40.9
1978	Boston	421		991	42.5

Source: UUA Directories.

49. Paul H. Beattie, "Can the Church Reform Society," in Irving R. Murray, ed., *Highroad to Advance* (Pacific Grove, California, 1976), p. 68.

50. Irving R. Murray, "Social Action in UU Societies," in Murray, *Highroad to Advance,* pp. 79–80.

51. *UUA Directory,* 1961–1962, p. 41. In 1967, a parish poll to determine which proposed resolutions commanded the widest interest was instituted. By 1974, the number required for submission of a resolution had risen to 15 churches, or 250 legal members, no more than ten from any one church. *UUA Directory,* 1961–1962, p. 41; 1968, pp. 34–35; 1974, p. 201.

52. *UUA Directory,* 1984, pp. 306, 309–312.

53. The financial burden on the churches to send delegates every year was not the only argument for biennials. Interruption of headquarters operations was another, as many staff members had to be away from their duties for as long as a week. The suggestion was sometimes made that costs might be reduced (and decision-making improved) if the size of the General Assembly were cut down, but such proposals were never seriously

considered. (See Paul H. Beattie, *The UUA Still in Crisis,*
sermon preached March 9, 1969, Indianapolis, Indiana.) It goes
almost without saying that a number of those at General Assembly are those who especially like to go to conventions, so
there will always be a considerable number present who do not
want to give up their annual jubilee, regardless of the number
of those who, by their absence, are silently voting otherwise.

54. Greeley, *25 Beacon Street,* p. 94.

55. *UU World,* May 15, 1971, Supplement.

56. *UU World,* May 15, 1970, p. 11; July 1, 1970, p. 5; July 15, 1971,
    p. 12.

57. *UUA Directory,* 1973, p. 199. The proposal had failed of ap-
    proval by the required two-thirds vote the previous year. *UUA
    Directory,* 1972, p. 251.

58. *UU World,* May 15, 1977, p. 1.

59. *Kairos,* No. 11 (Spring 1978), pp. 8–9; *UU World,* May 1, 1979,
    pp. 6–7.

60. Thus Emerson in East Lexington, 1835–1838.

61. *UU World,* August 15, 1979, p. 3; *Settlement Handbook for
    Congregations and Professional Religious Leaders,* January 1984,
    Appendix, p. 54.

62. Earl K. Holt, "Congregational Ordination and the Call to Min-
    istry," sermon at the ordination of Cynthia Johnson, June 9,
    1991. See also Josiah R. Bartlett, "Are We Unwittingly Hanging
    Our System of Settling Ministers?" Memo for the UUA Com-
    mission on Appraisal, April 1988.

63. Beginning in May 1961, the title was *The Unitarian Register
    and the Universalist Leader,* the volume number being a con-
    tinuation of the *Leader.* For a year, beginning with May 1964,
    the editor experimented with calling it simply *The Leader.* The
    experiment was not well received, and in May 1965, it became
    The Register Leader of the Unitarian Universalist Association.
    That lasted until the appearance of *UUA Now* in the summer
    of 1968. The editors were: Victor Bovee, through Midsummer

1964; Edward Darling, Acting Editor through February 1965; Joseph N. Ulman, Jr., March 1965, until he became a victim of financial retrenchment in February 1968; Edward Darling to the end of *UUA Now* in 1969.

64. *Register-Leader*, Vol. 165, No. 10 (December 1963), p. 13; Vol. 147, No. 7 (Midsummer 1965), p. 19; *Report of the Committee on Goals* (1967), p. 12; *Register-Leader*, Vol. 149 (April 1967), p. 25.

65. *UUA Now*, Vol. 150, No. 11 (June 19, 1969), p. 15.

66. *UUA Directory*, 1975, p. 168.

POSTSCRIPT

1. *The Final Report of the Commission on Governance of the Unitarian Universalist Association*, April 24, 1993, p. 8.

2. *Ibid.*, p. 13.

3. *Ibid.*, p. 73.

4. *Ibid.*, pp. 48–49.

5. *Ibid.*, p. 38. Some larger implications of community ministry, as well as implications for congregational polity, are discussed in [Starr King Community Ministry Project], *Community Ministry: An Opportunity for Renewal and Change*, Berkeley, California, 1995. Included is a history of the society for the Larger Ministry. See also Daniel D. Hotchkiss, "Defining Community Ministry," a paper prepared August 1995 for the Department of the Ministry of the UUA.

6. The tendency of bureaucracies to multiply rules and regulations is shown in the development of the *Settlement Handbook*. The "brown book" (1961) included five pages on procedures for ministerial settlement (pp. 108–112). Leon Fay restated them in a 16-page pamphlet, *Procedures for Ministers Seeking a New Settlement*, distributed by the Department of the Ministry in 1962. (A complementary booklet was prepared at the same time for churches seeking a new minister.) In 1975, this had become *Ministerial Settlement: A Manual for Congrega-*

tions and Ministers, 23 pages of smaller type. This in turn became the *Settlement Handbook* (1984): 90 pages of text plus 71 of Appendix, for sale for $21.00. Mercifully, this was cut back to 39 pages in 1995.

7. This pressure is felt very strongly by seminary students seeking fellowship. Criticism of the Ministerial Fellowship Committee has been widespread and sometimes bitter, and so was addressed by the Commission on Appraisal in 1992. The criticism has been directed more at the processes of the Fellowship Committee than at the scope of its mandate. See the Commission on Appraisal, *Our Professional Ministry* (1992), and for examples of criticism: *Critical Mass,* Vol. 1, No. 1 (1986): 14–19; Vol. 1, No. 2: 18–21; *First Days Record* (September 1992): 28–30; (April 1993): 33–34.

8. *Guidelines for the Unitarian Universalist Ministry* (September 1994), p. 14. Back in the days before merger, the Unitarian Ministers Association prepared a statement of professional standards; it was a mimcographed pamphlet, 6 pages, each half–size typewriter paper. In May 1968, *Guidelines* of the UUMA was 6 full–size mimeographed pages, with appended memoranda on continuing education and sabbatical leave. In 1979, the *Guidelines* were thoroughly revised, appearing as a loose-leaf booklet, 44 pages, "Price: $2.00 per copy (two copy minimum order)." By 1994, it had become 47 pages plus index, 8.5" by 11" format, $4.00. For the history of the May 1979 revision, see Rudolph Nemser, "We Are Not Alone: the Origin of the UUMA Guidelines," *Kairos,* No. 15 (Summer 1979), p. 6.

9. *The Free Church in a Changing World* (Boston, 193), p. 10. Elliot Dunlap Smith was the member of the Commission chiefly responsible for the wording of this paragraph of its report.

10. *Commission on Governance, Report,* pp. 50-51.

Topical Index

The Role of the Minister
—the parochial relationship: 11, 18-19, 26-27, 164-165
—the pastoral relationship: 9-11, 24, 85-86, 113-114, 139-142
—the professional relationship: 20, 74-75, 218-219, 258
—ministry of religious education and community ministry:
    200-201, 209-210
—interim ministry and extension ministry: 201-203
—discipline of ministers: 45-46, 223-224, 230-231

Non–parochial Ministry
—church of the larger Fellowship: 160-161
—"specialized ministries" and community ministry: 192-193,
    209-210

Ordination and Fellowshiping
—Unitarian practice: 75-78, 111, 140-142, 257
—Universalist practice: 143-144
—since merger: 173-175, 210-212

Ecclesiastical Organization
—ecclesiastical councils: 16-17, 35-36, 77-78, 222
—Universalist associations and conventions: 24-26, 44-50, 89-92
—Unitarian Autumnal Conventions: 42
—Unitarian National Conference: 43-44, 67-71, 78-79, 125-129
—Unitarian local conferences: 71-73, 228, 229
—fellowship committees: 75-78, 191-192
—authority of the General Assembly: 180-194
—UUA districts: 189-191, 199-200
—the general Assembly: 197-198, 208-209, 259-261

Administrative Organization
—organization of the AUA in 1825: 40-42
—AUA ministerial supply and settlement: 73-75
—Universalist administration: 95-98, 119-122, 130-135, 242-243

About the Author

As professor of American church history at the Harvard Divinity School, **Conrad Wright** introduced the history of the denomination to many of those now active in the Unitarian Universalist ministry. His books and articles, most recently *The Unitarian Controversy* (1994), have significantly revised scholarly understanding of Unitarian history, and his essay "A Doctrine of the Church for Liberals," published in *Walking Together* (1989), is widely recognized as the essential starting point for discussion of polity in the denomination. Other books by Conrad Wright include *A Stream of Light* (revised 1995) and *Three Prophets of Religious Liberalism: Channing, Emerson, Parker* (1986).